Prophet's Prey

Prophet's Prey

*My Seven-Year Investigation into Warren Jeffs
and the Fundamentalist Church of
Latter-Day Saints*

Sam Brower

BLOOMSBURY
New York   Berlin   London   Sydney

Published by Bloomsbury USA, New York

All papers used by Bloomsbury USA are natural, recyclable products made
from wood grown in well-managed forests. The manufacturing processes
conform to the environmental regulations of the country of origin.

LIBRARY OF CONGRESS CATALOGING-IN-PUBLICATION DATA HAS BEEN APPLIED FOR.

ISBN: 978-1-60819-275-5

First U.S. edition 2011

1 3 5 7 9 10 8 6 4 2

Typeset by Westchester Book Group
Printed in the U.S.A. by Quad / Graphics, Fairfield, Pennsylvania

This book is dedicated to
Rita
for her encouragement and criticism,
but most of all for all those moments of eternal perspective,
joy, and meaning.

. . . but others there are, who, of necessity and by force, are driven to write history, because they are concerned in the facts, and so cannot excuse themselves from committing them to writing, for the advantage of posterity; nay, there are not a few who are induced to draw their historical facts out of darkness into light, and to produce them for the benefit of the public, on account of the great importance of the facts themselves with which they have been concerned.

—*Josephus*

Contents

Preface

Warren Jeffs is a tall, bony man with a bulging Adam's apple and a frightening sense of his own perfection in the eyes of God. The self-proclaimed prophet of the Fundamentalist Church of Jesus Christ of Latter-Day Saints (FLDS), now fifty-five years old, has taken more than seventy women and girls as wives—one of whom was just a few weeks past her twelfth birthday when he commanded her to lie on a ceremonial bed in the sanctum of his massive Texas temple and brutally raped her. He demands absolute, unquestioning obedience from his ten thousand followers. He has sodomized children as young as five years old (including his own nephew, who wrote a book about it). He and the FLDS are currently being investigated for defrauding the government of millions of dollars. He has destroyed untold hundreds of lives.

Jeffs conducted his reign of terror with impunity for three decades thanks to a pervasive, Mafia-like code of silence that he systematically instilled in the congregation. Then, in the winter of 2004, a private investigator named Sam Brower began looking into the FLDS Church. Shocked by what he uncovered, Brower concluded that Warren Jeffs needed to be put behind bars posthaste. Thanks in large part to Brower's courageous efforts, in May 2006 Jeffs was placed on the FBI's "Ten Most Wanted List," was arrested three months later, and on September 25, 2007, was convicted of two counts of rape as an accomplice. His conviction has since been reversed on a technicality, but presently Jeffs is incarcerated at Big Lake, Texas, awaiting trial on felony child abuse charges.

For the better part of five years I watched with awe (and occasionally provided assistance) as Brower relentlessly tracked Jeffs down, earned the trust of the prophet's victims, and provided state and federal law enforcement agencies with crucial evidence. A remarkable man on many levels, Sam Brower is the real deal. Readers are apt to find his firsthand account of bringing Warren Jeffs to justice both extremely disturbing and absolutely riveting.

Jon Krakauer

2011

CHAPTER 1

Prey

November 30, 2010

The prisoner's hands were cuffed to a belly chain that was cinched tight around his scrawny waist and secured by a padlock. The shackles on his ankles hobbled his stride to a shuffle as two large men, each gripping one of his arms, escorted him across the tarmac of Salt Lake International Airport toward an unmarked plane. Clad in green-and-white prison stripes stenciled conspicuously with the letters UDC, for Utah Department of Corrections, the man in custody appeared emaciated, frail, and disheveled. His guards wore Stetson hats, spit-shined cowboy boots, and freshly creased slacks; one of them had the distinctive badge of the Texas Rangers pinned to his chest.

Snow was still banked along the side of the taxiway from a recent blizzard and the air had a wintry bite. Noticing that the prisoner was shivering, Ranger Nick Hanna offered him a gray sweatshirt. As they proceeded toward the airplane, the man in cuffs bent over and tried to adjust his Coke-bottle glasses, which had slipped down his nose. Ranger Hanna patiently helped him secure them, eliciting a meek "thank you." Hanna was struck by the man's unassuming voice. He had expected something much more commanding.

An observer unfamiliar with the inmate's identity would have found it hard to believe that this was Warren Steed Jeffs, the notorious leader and self-proclaimed prophet of the Fundamentalist Church of Jesus Christ of Latter-Day Saints (FLDS), the largest polygamous religious organization in North America. Hanna was under orders from Texas governor Rick Perry to pick up Jeffs in Salt Lake City and transport him to the state of Texas, to stand trial on charges of sexual assault of a child, aggravated sexual assault of a child under the age of fourteen, and bigamy—serious charges in any state but which carry a life sentence in Texas. It was a place Jeffs had been desperately trying to avoid.

I am a private detective. For the past seven years, cases involving the FLDS Church and its pedophile prophet have consumed most of my waking hours. I live just outside of Cedar City, Utah, a stunning high-desert community of some thirty thousand residents. Just beyond town, densely forested mountains, capped with snow for much of the year, rise ten thousand feet above sea level, overlooking a vast arid wilderness dotted with lonely buttes and red rock canyons. Even today, southern Utah remains a rugged landscape, and some regard it to be the middle of nowhere. But I find it to be quite accommodating, having moved here from Southern California as a young man, when I made the deliberate decision to raise my family in a smaller, safer environment. Cedar City is an awfully long way from the bright lights of New York or Los Angeles, both literally and metaphorically. But for me, it felt like the right place to be.

As Ranger Hanna led Jeffs up the steps into the plane, he may have been wondering the same thing I did upon seeing Warren Jeffs in person for the first time: What is it about this man that would allow him to so completely dominate the lives of thousands of people? He didn't have the appearance of a maniacal prophet, didn't sound like one either. His droning voice and gangly appearance were more likely to bring to mind a nerdy middle-school science teacher than an all-powerful tyrant. Usually Brylcreemed into an immaculate pompadour, his black hair had been haphazardly chopped by a prison barber, giving him the look of a ridiculous comic-book character. For weeks he had been force-fed through a tube threaded through his nose and into his stomach, owing to his refusal to eat prison food. The lack of nutrition made him look pasty and alarmingly gaunt. Not one of his personal traits could be considered remotely charismatic. He is, nevertheless, a man who exudes an almost mystical power over his more than ten thousand FLDS followers, most of whom would do literally anything he commanded of them.

An extremist offshoot of the traditional Church of Jesus Christ of Latter-day Saints—commonly known as the Mormon (LDS) Church—the FLDS was founded when its forebears broke away from the mainstream Mormons more than a hundred years ago, after the latter officially renounced the practice of polygamy. Warren Jeffs's followers, who still regard so-called plural marriage to be "the most holy and important doctrine ever revealed to man on earth," consider themselves to be the only true Latter-Day Saints. They are zealous believers for whom absolutely nothing is more important than obedience to their religious tenets and priesthood leaders.

In response to the many charges of child abuse that have been leveled against him in recent years by both civil and criminal courts in Utah and Arizona, Warren Jeffs defiantly announced to his followers that he would "answer them nothing." Instead, in 2003 he went on the run, cowering in a network of safe houses he had set up throughout the country, trying to blend in with the world beyond the parochial confines of his church—a world he claimed to despise.

As a private investigator, I always have cases cycling through my files, working through them fairly quickly, taking them as they come and then moving on. Never could I have anticipated back in 2004, when I volunteered to help a family struggling to extricate themselves from the FLDS (I agreed to take on the case for a fee of one dollar, and had to lend them that dollar), that I was about to step into a curious and dangerous alternate universe hidden in plain sight, just a little more than an hour from my home. I couldn't believe that such a brutal cult could exist, virtually unnoticed, in the United States in the twenty-first century.

Through my efforts to help this one struggling FLDS family, I was unwittingly drawn into a desperate battle to bring Warren Jeffs to justice that has lasted, thus far, for more than seven years. Over the course of those years, I discovered many of Warren Jeffs's most closely held secrets. Because I was a private investigator and had extensive knowledge of the FLDS culture and its leadership, I was asked by state and federal law enforcement agencies, shortly after Warren Jeffs went on the lam and was placed on the FBI's Ten Most Wanted list, to help try to find him and put him behind bars.

By taking on that initial FLDS case in 2004, I had unintentionally become the "polygamy expert," an expression bestowed on me by people unfamiliar with the main focus of my investigations. In reality, I had become the expert on a paranoid theocracy, run by a madman whose lust for power and compulsion to prey on children were his signature traits. Although polygamy is illegal in all fifty states and more often than not leads to abuse in one form or another, it was not the focus of my investigation. That focus was child abuse, and my job had taken on a dual purpose: investigating civil grievances on behalf of my clients, and alerting a complacent bureaucracy to the sickening and illegal activities that had been taking place under all of our noses for so many years.

One of my greatest challenges has been to locate and identify Jeffs's extensive network of hideouts, and determine who owns these properties. Despite an unsophisticated first impression conveyed by the nineteenth-century attire favored by the church's faithful, FLDS accountants have become extremely adept at hiding assets through money laundering. Jeffs's lieutenants are experts at establishing shell corporations to shelter property, equipment, and cash from the prying eyes of government auditors and corporate lenders. Lending institutions have been duped into financing loans worth millions of dollars, which the FLDS then allows to go into default, to the benefit of the church. Tracking down covert FLDS businesses is tedious work, but it has paid big dividends, including cracking bogus corporate facades established to secretly finance the Yearning for Zion Ranch, the massive religious stronghold constructed by Warren Jeffs in West Texas as a place for his most devout followers to safely ride out the coming apocalypse.

My dogged investigations into illegal FLDS affairs have led Jeffs and his followers to view me as a major irritant. While other law enforcement officers and private investigators who have attempted to penetrate the cult's formidable defenses have over time left the case, it has become increasingly clear to Warren Jeffs and the FLDS that I am not going away.

On the afternoon that Jeffs arrived in Texas, under tight security, to stand trial, I was resting at home in Utah, recovering from recent open-heart surgery to correct the same kind of ailment that one month later would kill diplomat Richard Holbrooke. It turned out to be an exceedingly complex, eight-hour operation that I barely survived, and I couldn't help but think that had Warren Jeffs known about it, he would surely have taken credit for my near demise. Over the years I have been the subject of many of his "prayer circles," in which he would call upon God's "whirlwind judgments" to wipe me from the face of the earth for interfering in the activities of the "Lord's faithful servants" and the "affairs of His church." I am hated by Jeffs, the police who act as his personal militia, and most of the church's membership. The more I lifted the veil of secrecy shrouding Jeffs and his cult, the more I came to fear that there was nothing that he was not capable of. My family wisely insisted that I take careful security precautions before going into surgery. Nobody but family and close friends was told that I was even sick, and I was admitted to the hospital in St. George, Utah, under an alias. Much to what I am sure would be Jeffs's chagrin had he been aware of it, I would go on to make a full and complete recovery.

At times I felt a little silly over the precautions taken over my care in the hospital, but in the end I'm grateful that good sense prevailed in making sure that the FLDS did not have access to me while I was in a vulnerable state. About a week before the operation, I had visited the surgeon at his office in the hospital. As I crossed the parking lot and got into my car after the appointment, I was on the phone with my colleague Gary Engels—the only other investigator who was actively gathering evidence of criminal activity within the FLDS organization. Finishing the call, I glanced up at the passenger window and saw a camera pressed up against the glass. I flew out of the car, shouting a few choice expletives at the heavyset person snapping photos of me in the privacy of my own vehicle. I became even more infuriated at what I saw. The man lurking behind the camera was none other than Willie Jessop—better known in southern Utah as "Willie the Thug"—the loudmouth FLDS spokesman, bodyguard, and church enforcer. Outraged, I ordered him to get his hands off my car and step back or I would notify the police. As he backed away from my vehicle, he asked what I was doing in the hospital parking lot.

"Oh, didn't I tell you?" I said.

Willie got a screwy look on his face. "No, you didn't," he said.

"I guess I must have thought it was none of your damn business, then," I replied.

I went on to let him know that this wasn't Short Creek (the hometown of the FLDS church and thousands of its members on the Utah-Arizona border, and in my estimation the most lawless town in America), it was the real world where people could come and go without having to ask permission of their church leaders. Again I warned him away from my car, and I whipped out my own camera and took photos of him as he lumbered away and climbed into a truck on the other side of the parking lot. My phone was still in my hand and Gary had heard the entire exchange.

The incident helped to remind me of the necessity of taking precautions to protect myself from any actions the FLDS might provoke. I had always considered an organized attack against me by FLDS goons unlikely, because such a move would draw attention to the cowardly men at the top of the organization who ordered the assault. I doubt Warren or his capos would want to face the legal consequences for such a crime. I am concerned, however, that some lone FLDS zealot might decide to take matters into his own hands. And the fact is, nothing would please Warren Jeffs and the FLDS hierarchy more than to see me dead. But I wasn't the only one making Jeffs's list of most hated enemies. There were many more whose demise he has prayed for: those who had found the courage to expose the crimes taking place within his secret society, as well as entire sections of the United States which he deemed wicked enough to call down the judgments of God.

Warren loved to travel the country under the pretext that God had commanded him to witness the gross wickedness of the world. He would ride with bodyguards and a favored wife or two in a small convoy, cursing and condemning the entire United States along the way. Six months before Hurricane Katrina slammed into the Louisiana coast, God had sent Warren to New Orleans to report on the depravity on display at Mardi Gras, and to deliver the city over to the Lord for his great destruction. After taking in some of the parades in the French Quarter and as many strip joints as he could cram into his two days on the town, the sanctimonious prophet raised his right arm to the square—as if swearing an oath in court—and prayed for the destruction of the entire city and its occupants.

When Katrina later hit the Louisiana coast, Jeffs was quick to take credit for being the conduit that had brought death and destruction to thousands of people in the aftermath of the hurricane.

It wasn't so much Warren's grandstanding that bothered me, but that his followers believe every word that "proceeds forth from the mouth of the Lord's anointed," no matter how ludicrous. In the FLDS culture, Warren Jeffs is the anointed, and that kind of blind obedience, especially in an outlaw organization, can be a very dangerous thing.

Most Americans only became aware of the FLDS in April 2008, when someone identifying herself as a teenage girl called authorities to say she was being sexually abused at the FLDS's 1,700-acre compound called the Yearning for Zion Ranch, located in West Texas outside the small town of Eldorado. Texas authorities obtained a search warrant and served the ranch but were unable to find the girl in question. What they found instead was shocking evidence of child abuse on a massive scale that had been kept hidden behind the strictly enforced FLDS code of silence. Believing they had no other choice, the authorities made the unprecedented and difficult decision to remove more than 460 children from the religious compound and make them wards of the state. Images of cops taking crying children from their distraught mothers were broadcast to riveted television audiences around the world.

Those video clips portrayed only a tiny fraction of the real story. For instance, neither cameras nor reporters had been present to deliver the shocking blow-by-blow when innocent preteen girls were led by the hands of their mothers and fathers to a massive temple complex at the ranch and placed into a ritualistic sexual union with the prophet Warren Jeffs himself, each girl just another in his series of underage concubines. Nor were the cameras there when other young girls were handed over by Jeffs to one of his many cohorts to buy their loyalty and silence. Many in the press, diverted by the images of distraught mothers, entirely missed the larger outrages perpetrated by the FLDS, the abuse of little girls born and bred to satisfy the church priesthood's seemingly insatiable appetite for underage brides.

The occurrence in Texas actually had its roots in the secluded FLDS town known as Short Creek, located in an isolated area along the Utah border known as the Arizona Strip. The church, under the direction of the prophet, owns and runs Short Creek and the lives of almost everyone in it from cradle to grave. Young girls are taken to the altar without even an elementary understanding of sex education or marital relationships with their new "husband." Established families are arbitrarily broken up at the prophet's bidding: the man of the house kicked out of town, his children assigned another father, and the mothers ordered to take up intimate relations with other men. Unwanted young boys are literally discarded like trash along the highway in order to reduce competition for young brides.

In Short Creek, "education" is mostly a means of indoctrinating children with religious dogma, and the FLDS enforces its dictates by controlling all town services, including the police force, which pays no heed whatsoever to "the laws of man" if those laws conflict with what the police consider to be the laws of God or religious edicts imposed by the self-proclaimed prophet. Religious zealots and bullies sort out dissenters and chase away strangers on a more unofficial and occasionally violent basis.

Perhaps the most chilling example of how the prophet uses FLDS beliefs to control the community is found in the doctrine of "blood atonement." Introduced by Brigham Young in the 1850s but since disavowed by the mainstream Mormon church, this doctrine says that some sins are so heinous that there can be no redemption for those who commit them—not even redemption from Christ himself. The only way to obtain forgiveness for such a sin is for the transgressor to die, thereby spilling his own blood in atonement. Rulon Jeffs and his son Warren used the threat of this archaic rite for revenge and extortion against their own people. Who would disobey, when the prophet might declare that a disobedient act was forgivable only by death?

And the influence of that prophet is large. While Short Creek is their base, FLDS leaders have thousands of followers in secret hideaways and safe houses that stretch from Canada to Mexico, all of whom consider it an honor to help the leaders hide from the law and carry out their prophetic commandments, legal or not. The YFZ Ranch in Texas is just one of scores of "places of refuge" ranging in size from town houses to huge compounds consisting of thousands of acres.

Much has happened since the early days of my involvement, and my understanding of the culture has evolved considerably. My files now bulge with cases involving the FLDS and its practices, including rape, sodomy, extortion, child abuse, tax fraud, forced underage marriages, suicides, and kidnappings. It is, at its core, a very large, well-organized, and elaborately funded criminal enterprise. I found that hundreds of children make up a central part of the FLDS work force for projects from routine residential carpentry to fulfilling sophisticated U.S. government contracts, in clear violation of labor laws.

As I gathered evidence and interviewed witnesses throughout the years, I was always looking for the biggest piece of the puzzle, the "smoking gun" that seemed to be just beyond my grasp. Even when Warren Jeffs made the FBI's Ten Most Wanted list and was finally arrested on a lonely stretch of I-15 in Nevada, I still felt there was more to be discovered. Maintaining accurate records is encouraged in Mormonism, and I knew Jeffs had a compulsion for keeping an exhaustive accounting of his activities. In his case, it was also a matter of saving mementos of his reign as supreme leader, a trait he shared with despots throughout history. I knew that compulsion was his Achilles heel and increasingly I was feeling a compulsion of my own to find the trophies that he was driven to preserve to prove his greatness to posterity.

As it turned out, the smoking gun, along with frightening insights into the innermost thoughts, activities, and crimes of the prophet of doom, was there in Texas. Police discovered a cache of material, carefully hidden in a sealed, secret vault beneath the temple grounds, that consisted of Warren Jeffs's daily journals, the "Private Priesthood Record of President Warren Jeffs." The information they contained was beyond anything that any investigator could have ever imagined or hoped for. There were volumes of documents, marriage records, computer disks and hard drives, audio recordings and flash drives, along with thousands of pages dictated by the self-absorbed prophet detailing his most deeply held beliefs, mad impulses, dreams, feelings, fears, and aspirations, often right down to the minute.

The find was conclusive and graphic, validating conclusions I had come to over the course of my own investigation and shedding light on many unanswered questions. What made this man tick? Who was Warren Jeffs, what was his magic, and what were his sins? Events and practices that had been assumed or guessed at could now be woven into a tapestry of facts dating back years. The darkest secrets and crimes within the FLDS were laid bare, exposing the "who, what, when, where, why, and how" of Warren Jeffs and his Fundamentalist Church of Jesus Christ of Latter-Day Saints.

At 11:00 A.M. on December 1, 2010, Jeffs was escorted by Ranger Hanna and a host of law enforcement personnel into a side entrance of the Fifty-first District Court in San Angelo for his initial court appearance in Texas. He was still wearing the gray sweatshirt, but his stripes had been exchanged for bright orange jail pants.

Judge Barbara Walther made Jeffs aware of his rights under the law and then asked him if he had an attorney, to which he replied, "I need more time." The judge then gave him a 120-day schedule in which she made it clear she intended to have all three charges against him tried and sentenced. Taken aback at the timetable, Jeffs refused to sign a document acknowledging that he had been made aware of the court's schedule. It appeared that he was again falling back on his "answer them nothing" approach to the criminal justice system.

Still recovering from surgery and unable to witness the initial hearing, I felt an overwhelming sense of relief that Jeffs had finally made it to a Texas courtroom. For more than four years, he had been bounced around among jails and prisons in four states, and he had been convicted by a jury of his peers in Utah in 2007 for being an accomplice to rape; but in 2010, the Utah Supreme Court remanded his case back to the trial court based on a technicality, so that officially, Jeffs no longer had a conviction on his record. Although there are still ancillary charges pending against him back in Utah and the Feds still have fugitive charges waiting in the wings, the indictments in Texas are by far the most serious. He is accused of being the actual perpetrator who sexually assaulted preteen girls, not just an accomplice to rape as he was in Utah. Based on previous trials of FLDS members, it is likely that DNA evidence will be presented, as will admissions in Jeffs's own words taken from his journal that will come into play as the magnitude of his crimes unfold in a Texas courtroom.

I began my work on the FLDS cases, ferreting out the facts and evidence of Warren Jeffs's atrocities, barely a year after he named himself prophet and seized control of the church, its assets, and its thousands of followers. I have spoken to hundreds of victims and witnesses who allege crimes and abuses at Jeffs's hands. Some of those victims were clients, some just wanted someone to listen to them, and some became my friends. I have combed and read through and listened to thousands of hours of sermons and documents, including nearly nine thousand pages of Jeffs's "Priesthood Record," and I believe I have come to know the culture better than anyone not born into the group—and in some respects, perhaps even better than many who were. I know about the rampant child abuse that evolved into such an important part of the FLDS culture and caste system, and I know that the group will go to the greatest of lengths to protect their church leaders from having to answer for their crimes.

On December 5, 2010, the Sunday after Warren took up residence at his new home in the Reagan County Jail in Big Lake, Texas, I was perched atop one of the red rock bluffs overlooking Short Creek, my camera focused on the sprawling FLDS meeting house about a mile away in the distance below me. Judging by the number of vehicles packed into the parking lots and side streets adjacent to the building, the entire town seemed to be packed into its four thousand seats. The streets were empty, and in the three hours I spent looking down from my vantage point, I saw only a handful of vehicles moving through town. I found the silence eerie and a bit unnerving, almost like the calm before the storm.

I would later find out that Warren had been placing calls to the meeting house on Sundays from the jail's pay phone; he had actually been patched into the sound system and was delivering sermons. This allowed him to maintain control over his flock from the Texas jail. Lately though, those sermons were taking on a more ominous tone. Back in his element at the pulpit, Warren's voice took on the hypnotic tenor so familiar to his followers, as he revealed an event of impending doom. "Very, very soon," the prophet intoned, ". . . two meteors will strike the earth"—resulting in a firestorm in which the wicked would be destroyed and the righteous would be lifted up and spared God's "whirlwind judgments." He prophesied that the lost ten tribes of Israel would once again be reunited as foretold, and God would deliver His Prophet from prison and punish all those who had persecuted His chosen people.

As absurd as it sounds, thousands of people believe those bizarre predictions with every ounce of their soul, simply because Jeffs says it is so. I've come to the conclusion that the only chance to eliminate child abuse within the FLDS is if the church membership can be awakened to the fact that the man they call Prophet is a criminal and a fraud. But because they have been subjected to generations of mind control and subservience, I no longer believe that they have the ability to come to that conclusion independently. Realistically, the best that can be hoped for is that Jeffs will be held accountable for his crimes by spending the remainder of his life in a Texas prison. Perhaps with some time and distance between Warren and his dutiful followers, the latter will begin to develop the ability to think for themselves and make decisions on their own, without having to first seek counsel from their religious leaders.

For the time being, Warren Jeffs is awaiting trial in a Texas prison. I still find it astounding that, although he has been incarcerated in various locations in Utah, Arizona, Nevada, and Texas for the past four years, he has no conviction for any crime on his record. So for many reasons I will most definitely be in Texas to observe Warren's trial, and I hope that thousands of his followers and hundreds in the news media will be there to witness it as well. As one of my colleagues in Texas who is close to the case succinctly put it, *It's time that it all comes out.*

CHAPTER 2

Ross

It began for me on a winter morning in the middle of January 2004, as I skimmed through the newspaper before heading to my office. An overnight storm had crashed through the area. The air in Cedar City would be clean and refreshing. Then a picture on the front page caught my eye, and I paused to read the story while munching a doughnut and sipping a can of V8 juice.

Everyone in our area was aware of the ongoing saga of the FLDS down in Short Creek and of its strange leader, the self-proclaimed prophet Warren Jeffs. News coverage of the secretive Jeffs and his flock was usually sparse, but it had taken on a magnetic, soap-opera flavor after the prophet carried out an internal political bloodletting on January 10 by banishing twenty-one men from the sect in one swoop, and reassigning all of their wives and children to other men. The shake-up caused anxious authorities in surrounding areas to offer assistance to the Short Creek police in case there was a riot. Jeffs sniffed at such attention by the law and the media because he considered the actions he took with his large and obedient congregation to be a private matter—what he called "setting the people in order."

Now he apparently was at it again, wreaking havoc on yet another family, but this time with a surprising result. The front-page photo was of a man by the name of Ross Chatwin, who was holding high a copy of *The Rise and Fall of the Third Reich*, William L. Shirer's account of Nazi Germany. I had read that book when I was a kid and had been fascinated at how an entire nation had lost its collective mind and followed a madman like Hitler into utter destruction. Chatwin was claiming the same despotic phenomenon was occurring in Short Creek with Jeffs, who in turn was charging that Chatwin had been booted out of the church because he was a "master deceiver." This time, the expelled member of the obedient flock had said "No! I'm not going," after being commanded to leave his home, family, and community. It was an act of defiance that just didn't happen within obedient FLDS culture.

That was when my curiosity got the best of me. Short Creek was only a little more than an hour southwest of my home. I decided to drive down and see if I could meet this unusual man who was standing up against the prophet, seer, and "revelator" of this strange religion.

Short Creek is actually two towns, in two different states, although they operate in most ways as a singular entity. On one side of the border, it is Colorado City, Arizona, while literally on the other side of Uzona Street, it is Hildale, Utah. Local residents just call the community "the Crick." No one bothered me when I rolled into town, something I would soon discover was unusual, and I found the address of the Chatwins simply by walking into the town clerk's office and asking. The receptionist apparently was so shocked at fielding a question from a tall stranger wearing sunglasses and cowboy boots that she just blurted out the directions to 245 North Willow. Within a few minutes, I was sitting in my car before a clutter of lumber and drywall at a small home that was still a work in progress. My impulsive decision was bothering me: Was I doing the right thing by intruding unannounced on a besieged family in a time of crisis? I was almost ready to turn around and leave when a man stepped outside, the guy in the picture. His sudden, friendly greeting caught me off balance.

"Hey! How you doin'?" he called out. He was of medium build with a round, pleasant face and neat brown hair. The discount store sneakers, slacks, and long-sleeved shirt buttoned at the wrist and collar stamped him as FLDS. Almost everyone around Short Creek, more than ten thousand souls, belongs to or has been discarded by that one church, the only one in town. Everyone else in the world is referred to as a gentile, and gentiles, who seldom convert to rigid fundamentalist beliefs, are not welcome in their insular community. The children of Short Creek are taught to fear them and their world.

I gave a wave, smiled, and eased open the door of my four-wheel-drive, climbing out with care to show that I had nothing to hide and was no threat. I am quiet by nature, but a pretty big guy, and my size and appearance can be a helpful psychological deterrent to potential problems. I stand close to six-four in my boots, weigh about 225 pounds, and appear even bigger in the cold months when I wear a cowboy hat and a heavy jacket over bulky winter clothes. I have a mustache, and at times, chin hair; my eyes have a natural squint from working long hours beneath the harsh Western sky. "I'm looking for Ross Chatwin," I said.

"Well, that's me," the man replied, his gentle voice betraying not even a quiver of nervousness. Chatwin had been openly disgraced, excommunicated from his church, and deprived of his livelihood, and he was under direct orders from the prophet to leave his home, his wife, and his children. He was shunned by local businesses, had been abandoned by life-long friends, and was being watched by the town marshals. In his own mind, he had done nothing wrong: Everyone, especially God, was still his friend. Few in Short Creek agreed.

"Mr. Chatwin, my name is Sam Brower and I'm a private investigator. I think I might be able to help you."

It was a pretty vague reason for a big guy he had never seen before to suddenly appear in his driveway. Chatwin had been expecting some other visitors: thugs from the "God Squad," the church-controlled local law and possibly a few unofficial enforcers who might be coming by to make him leave town.

He gave me a welcoming nod. "Well, then. Come on in."

So I did, and by crossing that threshold, I set a new course for my life.

While construction of the house was under way, the Chatwin family was living in the unfinished basement, a chilly place with ribs of bare studs exposed against the gray cement walls. Once downstairs, Ross introduced me to his wife, Lori, a soft-spoken woman wearing a light blue blouse and a long skirt, with her wavy hair pulled back and braided. Their five energetic children tumbled about. Ross was eager to talk, even to a sympathetic stranger, and he opened up as soon as we settled around an old plastic laminate kitchen table. He was thirty-five years old, and had only about an eighth-grade education, which was not unusual in Short Creek.

I would eventually discover that most boys were pulled out of school at about that age to work on construction sites, but even while in the classroom, their private-school curriculum was more focused on the history of the FLDS and an individual member's duties to the church and its leaders than it was on reading, writing, or arithmetic. The townsfolk had turned openly hostile toward the Chatwins, and Ross was selling used cars and working as a mechanic whenever he could rustle up work to support his family. The couple had been married for about twelve years and had remained monogamous—an unfortunate distinction in this fertile homeland of polygamy.

I understood that almost everyone in the town was a zealous participant in what they politely called "plural marriages." Even as FLDS members smoothly lie to outsiders that there is no polygamy, multiple marriages are the norm, and there has always been a steady trafficking in underage girls bound for the altar. Ross Chatwin was not a polygamist, but he wanted to be one.

That, I found, was the real reason he was in trouble.

Until recently, things had been looking up for the Chatwins, as evidenced by their having been blessed with this unfinished home. The church owns all the property in Short Creek through its financial operation, the United Effort Plan Trust (UEP). One of Ross's brothers, as a reward for his faithfulness, originally had been given the little piece of land on which to build a house. When the brother turned against the church and left town, the church leaders reassigned the property to Ross. Prior to that, Ross and Lori had been living with their kids in something that was little more than a dugout house with a roof.

Delighted with their new lodgings, the Chatwins figured the time had come to bring a new addition into their family—a young girl who would be another bride for Ross and a *sister wife* to Lori. That, however, was not their decision to make. Only the prophet had the authority to decide who married whom, so by pursuing the matter on their own, they were treading on dangerous turf and teetering on the brink of heresy.

The forty-eight-year-old prophet, at the pinnacle of the FLDS hierarchy, could and did marry at will; and he had a large harem of his own at that time, estimated at about fifty "ladies," a number that was growing fast. But for someone like Ross, near the bottom of the church pecking order, that option just did not exist, and he and Lori were concerned that busy and beleaguered "Uncle Warren" might never get around to assigning them a new wife. The most senior leaders of the FLDS are sometimes referred to as "Uncle" by other church members. The honorary title is meant as a show of respect and endearment, even if the man it refers to is evil to his core.

So the Chatwins began an almost antique flirtation with a sixteen-year-old girl, passing notes back and forth like moonstruck kids in a high school study hall. Lori kept the letters in a small cardboard box and allowed me to look through them. None contained any mention of passion or sex; most were just innocent "I love you. Do you love me?" notes. The girl they were courting suffered from severe health problems and was probably wondering about her own prospects of marriage. To the delight of the Chatwins, their prospective bride thought that marrying them was such a good idea that she suggested including one of her girlfriends. That could mean a *multiple* plural ceremony.

The Chatwins had foolishly hoped to spin the arrangement in a manner acceptable to the prophet, who, more than anyone, they believed, should understand how God requires a husband to have numerous wives while on earth in order to ascend to higher positions in the celestial hereafter. They could hardly have made a bigger mistake, and at exactly the wrong time. Only a few weeks earlier, Warren had successfully crushed troublesome opponents to his reign with the mass expulsion of twenty-one men and taken away their homes and families. Even before the dust had settled, this new challenge of an unauthorized bride had arisen seemingly out of nowhere. The manic Jeffs concluded that Ross was part of a wider conspiracy to topple him from power, so the prophet announced that satanic influences were being spread among his people, and then excommunicated Ross.

Ross was instructed to write out a complete list of his sins, which Jeffs would compare to a "true list" of transgressions that had been divinely revealed to him by God. It was an exam no one could pass. "My list of sins obviously did not match up with the list of sins that Uncle Warren put together," Ross told me with a rueful grin.

On Wednesday, January 14, FLDS stooge and UEP trustee James Zitting drove out to the Chatwin place and delivered the final verdict: Ross was out. The order was crushing. He was no longer welcome anywhere in Short Creek and must leave his home immediately. Lori was to drop him, and even a good-bye kiss might jeopardize her own salvation. She and the children were to be reassigned. There would be no divorce, no custody hearing, and no due process of law; just the absolute command by the prophet to "leave [his] family and home and repent from a distance." He was not to write or call or try to make contact with the family in any way but was required to continue paying tithes and offerings to the church. The girl the Chatwins had been courting would soon be married off to someone else.

James Zitting growled that he had come over just to deliver the ultimatum, not to listen to any explanations from the Chatwins. Ross replied that he fully understood.

"Good," Zitting said. "So let's get doing it." He left, believing his mission had been accomplished. I would later discover that Zitting had had a special reason for being forceful that day. He had recently been cautioned by the prophet to shape up. Fail in this task and he might be the next one gone.

The word spread swiftly throughout Short Creek not only that Ross had been excommunicated, but also that he and Lori were refusing to knuckle under. Lori was a most unusual FLDS wife. Although trained from childhood to be subservient and obedient—to "keep sweet" no matter what—she had a rather independent personality. She could be outspoken and assertive and her words carried weight with her husband. "I love him, not Warren," she told a reporter. She would stick with Ross.

There was a small number of other so-called apostates in town who had gone or were going through the same painful process of excommunication, but who had not left the area because it was the only home they had ever known. The outside world was petrifying and foreign to them. The Chatwins would be joining this subculture of the dispossessed.

Ross explained to me what had happened next. Poverty-stricken and incredibly naïve, he had found an envelope containing some $220 on his doorstep over the weekend. Also in the envelope was a handwritten note asking Chatwin to mail copies of an enclosed letter to FLDS members who were still faithful to the prophet. He could keep any change left over from the costs of copying, envelopes, and mailing. "I guess whoever left the note knew I needed the money," Chatwin later told a reporter.

So Lori and Ross had sat down and addressed envelopes to about five hundred people, and then he had mailed the letters. The text of the letter claimed that "Uncle Rulon" Jeffs, the late father of Warren, had appeared in a revelation to an unnamed dissident and announced that Warren was not the prophet after all! This bombshell of a letter claimed that an older man named Louis Barlow should be in the top position. Barlow was one of those who had been excommunicated in Warren's abrupt "cleansing" of the church.

Warren Jeffs is remarkably adept at monitoring and micromanaging almost every person, business, shop, gas station, and home in Short Creek, and it did not take long for news to get back to the prophet that Ross Chatwin was spreading unauthorized visions about who the true leader of the FLDS was.

Ross was not yet finished, for in this unprepossessing man, the apostates had found a spokesman with nothing to lose and a lot to say. They pitched in to help him stage a front-porch press conference on January 23, during which he stood before news microphones and charged, "This Hitler-like dictator has got to be stopped before he ruins us all and this beautiful town." He also accused "Uncle Warren" of recklessly wasting more than one hundred million dollars of UEP assets, a portion of which was being squandered on building a secret new compound, a hidden place known within the FLDS only as "Zion." Very few of the rank-and-file membership knew it even existed, let alone where it was.

"We need your help to stop Warren Jeffs from destroying families, kicking us out of our homes, and marrying our children into some kind of political brownie-point system." It had been that open plea that had piqued my interest. Was the prophet truly running a whole town in modern-day America by using these despotic techniques? It seemed impossible to me.

During the three hours that I listened to Ross and Lori, I stayed in professional mode and carefully sifted through their words. Were they lying? Were they vague or inconsistent on important details? Were they just after money or media attention? Did the timeline hang together? Was there any proof? They had lent me their love letters to the girl, allowed me to copy the entire hard drive of their computer, and answered all of my questions without hesitation. Those were not the actions of people trying to hide information. I started to believe them.

I finally had to halt their astonishing narrative to explain a sticking point, one they seemed not to fully comprehend: In addition to polygamy being illegal, the girl they wanted to marry was only sixteen! That would be illegal on its own, regardless of any equally illegal polygamous relationship, and Ross could have been prosecuted not only for bigamy, but for child abuse as well.

It was strange having to explain to a couple of adults that there was a huge, sprawling nation beyond the boundaries of Short Creek and that, like it or not, they were part of the state of Arizona and the United States of America and subject to the laws of the land. Living in their little theocracy had blinded them to the values and laws of our society.

"So you understand that the legal age for marriage is eighteen," I finally said, raising my eyebrows to elicit a promise. "Right, Ross?"

Ross said nothing. Lori remained silent.

"Eighteen! Right, Ross?" Stronger this time. It was a deal-breaker for me. There was a soft groan of acceptance as he mentally discarded an important card from his life. "Uh, okay. Right. Eighteen."

It was time for me to make a decision. I had found no inconsistencies in their story, but to work on their situation as a private investigator, I had to be paid for my services in order to invoke the protection of client confidentiality, the same as with a doctor or a lawyer.

"I think I can help you, Ross. But first you have to officially hire me."

"I don't have any money," he said.

"Just give me a dollar," I said. "That's enough."

"Ok, but, uh—I don't have a dollar."

I pulled out my wallet, removed a one-dollar bill, and slid it across that laminate table. Ross put his finger on it and slid it back. Transaction complete. I was on the job.

CHAPTER 3

"Uncle Warren?"

That initial meeting with Ross and Lori Chatwin left me trying to sort out a host of questions, with only a minimum of information. I had the nagging feeling, common among private detectives, that the case needed to be made stronger. After a lot of consideration, I made myself a promise: If I found one single thing screwy with Ross's story, I was gone.

One thing that bothered me was that I had known some FLDS people for years, and they in no way resembled those who were perpetrating this outrage against the Chatwins down in Short Creek. I could not imagine them wanting to rip a family apart and throw them out of their home in the middle of winter.

In my construction days, out there building houses on scalding hot concrete pads, I had become friends with a number of FLDS men. Although, at times, their social skills left room for improvement, they excelled in construction. Most were hard-working, decent guys. They were polite and wore clean jeans, with their women in modest prairie dresses and the small kids scrubbed squeaky clean. They kept to themselves, worked hard, did not bother others, and lived far away. Under those tame circumstances, their practice of polygamy was generally viewed as a minor annoyance; I assumed that grown women were making a conscious decision to marry a man who had other adult wives, all living according to the precepts of their shared faith. Weird, but not really a big deal. Some religions play with rattlesnakes. The FLDS had been around the area for so long that they were accepted as just another part of the scenery. Those people—my friends—didn't seem to be a bunch of religious lunatics.

Still, facts were facts. The FLDS church leaders indeed were heartlessly trying to dump the Chatwins out into the cold. My personal scale of justice had tipped in favor of Ross and Lori because of the evidence and their frankness, but perhaps that was just because the other dish on the scale was empty. After years in the area, I realized I didn't know much at all about this religion and its practices. I wanted to know more. *Who was Warren Jeffs, what was the FLDS, and why were they doing this?*

Figuring out who was who in that zoo would have to wait; I had the more immediate concern of trying to keep the Chatwins in their home down in Short Creek. I put Ross in touch with the Mohave County Attorney's Office in Arizona, which steered him to a legal clinic in Kingman that provides assistance to those who cannot afford to pay for a lawyer. The hardship eviction case was then assigned by the Arizona Community Legal Services to a lawyer named Joan Dudley. I couldn't have planned it better if I had tried.

Joan embodied many things that the FLDS despised about the outside world. It was well known that in FLDS schools, teachers trimmed pictures of people of color out of the textbooks. Joan was African American. In the FLDS, women are always subservient. Joan was in-your-face aggressive. Women were not to be highly educated. Joan was smart as a whip. I knew she was unafraid of any legal nonsense by the United Effort Plan attorneys or the FLDS and would not back down an inch in the coming fight. She actually seemed to be looking forward to it.

While she took charge of the legal side, I went back to Short Creek because Ross was telling me that he and Lori were afraid to set foot outside their house. Apparently, the church was just waiting to pounce and move his brother, Steven, into the unfinished upstairs portion. In my world, that made no sense. Although the church's UEP Trust had issued an eviction order, the unsettled civil case was in dispute and headed for court. Joan Dudley, active as an officer of the court, wrote a "to-whom-it-may-concern" letter that spelled out that the property was in dispute and no action could take place involving the Chatwins' home until the matter was ruled on by a judge.

Steven had no claim whatsoever on the property, which made the threat to move him into the house seem absurd; still, Ross had grown up in Short Creek and knew the way things worked there. I was willing to take his word for it, and in part to help them feel a little safer, I went back down with construction tools to help him finish off the basement living quarters, install new locks, cut an access to the upstairs area, and build a stairway that would finally connect the two parts and make the place a single, livable house.

I began to understand why the Chatwins were scared. No longer was the mean, sharp edge of the FLDS hidden to me. I had lived for years right up the road, only an hour away, and was in the law enforcement business not only as a private investigator, but as a bail bondsman and bounty hunter. But like most residents of Utah and Arizona, I had paid little attention to goings-on in obscure little Short Creek. The FLDS and its members might as well have been a community of invisible ghosts. Now the town was turning ugly right before my eyes.

As I had started paying attention to them, they had also figured out who I was. When I rolled into town this time, a convoy of overgrown pickup trucks with menacing, dark-tinted windows roared into my rearview mirror. Then they were right on my tail, gnawing at my bumper, apparently trying to force me off the road. They cut around, boxed me in, slowed down, then sped up and sprayed gravel from their big tires. The tiny rocks peppered my car like bits of shrapnel. It was like being the main character in a *Twilight Zone* episode, the unaware stranger who has just driven off the map into a strange parallel dimension known as "Short Creek."

Being alone in a situation that had turned unexpectedly threatening did not really bother me. I had encountered much riskier moments as a bounty hunter. The drivers of these trucks were just bullies. I kept going and eventually, they peeled away. Still, I was annoyed enough to tell the Chatwins what had happened, and they explained that it was not really all that unusual; this was a standard greeting committee of souped-up trucks called "plyg-rigs." The dark-tinted windows made it impossible to identify the occupants, which helped strangers clearly understand they were unwanted by scaring the heck out of them.

There is nothing like personal experience to help an investigator form a conclusion, and the scales tipped farther. There was no way to ignore this latest episode, because it had not happened to someone else; I had been the target. There was nothing subtle about it at all. I had to start thinking about the FLDS in an entirely different light.

The empire struck back a few weeks later. I was still in bed early on a Saturday morning when Ross called to let me know that church-assigned work crews were gathering outside his house. They intended to move his brother Steven and Steven's family into the upstairs portion of the home. Steven was blindly loyal to the church and was assigned the task of harassing Ross into wanting to move. I grabbed a copy of Joan's letter and made it to Ross and Lori's place by 7:30 A.M.

The scene looked like a convention of contractors. About fifty men were already on site, readying their tools and unloading building material from their pickup trucks. I parked and got out, determined to get them to back off. The problem was that these Short Creek workers were unfamiliar with concepts like due process of law, constitutional rights, liberty, independence, and being master of your own fate. These men simply did whatever the prophet commanded them to do—end of story. Consequently, the letter that I showed them, which would have been taken very seriously at any other job site in America, only served to puzzle these people. They paused to await further orders from church leaders.

In Utah, even in Short Creek, people are generally polite, and the confused workers were in a quandary; they had been taught unwavering obedience from the cradle, and to live their religion. They also knew that not following their leaders' orders held dire consequences. Any of them could become the next Ross Chatwin if they did not follow their instructions exactly. I had presented them with an unexpected legal gauntlet that went directly against the word of the prophet. Their response was to call for help: the town marshals.

Up drove Sam Roundy Jr., the town's chief marshall, a six-footer who weighs in at over three hundred pounds and wears a badge and gun, but dresses just like any other FLDS member. His shirt stretched tight across his belly. He and a couple of deputies took charge. Now it was my turn to be puzzled.

I immediately asked Roundy why he was there in the first place. This was a civil dispute in which he had no authority other than to keep the peace and possibly arrest anyone who might try to break into the Chatwin home. Under state law, the police do not have the authority to become involved in civil disputes between private parties. To intervene would quite possibly violate the Chatwins' constitutional rights, which meant the cops would be the ones breaking the law.

On the other hand, I was glad to see them arrive because at least they were sworn law enforcement officers. They could interpret the legalities for the workmen and settle the situation.

I made some introductory private investigator–to–police officer small talk to put them at ease, then handed Roundy the letter from Dudley. Roundy was trapped. He didn't even pretend to be a real cop. The marshal pulled out his cell phone, hit the speed dial, and his first words were, "Uncle Warren?" He turned away from me and read the letter aloud over the phone.

When he hung up, he deliberately threw the document to the ground. "This doesn't mean anything to me," he snapped, and turned to the men standing around. "You men get to work. Go on in," he told them.

When Roundy ordered a deputy to break off the locks on the door, Ross handed over a key. The front door opened, and about fifty workmen jammed inside. It was a disturbing and unreal sight. In that other world, where the rest of America lives, police cannot just show up and send people into one's home without a warrant and have them literally tear the house apart. This was breaking and entering, vandalism, trespassing, and about a half dozen more criminal offenses, but worst of all, it was a violation of what most Americans consider to be their absolute constitutional right to be secure in their persons, places, and things. It was a grotesque intrusion by a government agency into a U.S. citizen's home under the color of law—the first of many illegal actions by the Colorado City town marshals' office that I would witness in the years to come.

While I was protesting to Roundy, one of his brothers, who was also a deputy, told Ross to get into the police car. "Hey, he's arresting me!" Ross called out.

That quickly got my attention. I was outraged, and barked, "Why are you arresting him? What has he done? You can talk to him, but you can't detain him. It's his home and property!" Unable to cite any charges, they backed down and let him go. The officers had been ready to snatch a private citizen into custody simply because they wanted to. The entire morning had become a legal circus.

From inside the house came the pounding of hammers and the whine of power saws. The carpenters were already busy. I pulled my video camera out and began recording the crime in progress.

Racking my brain about how to stop the madness, I pointed out the absence of building permits. The contractors claimed that they were working off the original permit, which I knew was five years old and would have long expired. Another call was made, and within minutes, the building inspector, David Darger, was on the scene.

He arrived with a fresh extension for the expired permit and a set of plans for the original house, claiming that the workers were just there to finish the job and bring it up to code. It seemed clear to me that no matter what legal obstacle I could come up with, they would simply take whatever steps were necessary to accomplish their orders. The inspector remained on site throughout the day and night, handing out any needed approvals and doing so-called inspections as the work rolled along, as well as chipping in to finish the job. He reclassified the structure as a duplex so the two halves could not be joined. The staircase that I had helped Ross build was condemned and the inspector actually helped seal it up.

By two o'clock the next morning, their work was done. The crew had covered the new stairway with joists, laid out new flooring, installed plumbing, spread carpet and linoleum, dry walled and painted, and put in counters and countertops. Steven Chatwin and his family moved in.

I could only shake my head in disbelief. There was nothing left to do. The FLDS and its United Effort Plan had ignored basic civil rights and built an apartment right before my eyes as the cops stood by to enforce the will of the church, while ignoring the laws of the land. It would have been fruitless to call for help from another police agency. The nearest real cops were in the county seat of Kingman, Arizona, five hours away, and a request to try to get them to sort this out would probably have been shrugged off with some comment like, "It's Short Creek. What do you expect?"

I was coming to understand that every official in town might be willing to blindly follow church leaders and that ignoring the truth was a normal practice of the FLDS hierarchy. It had been done that way for many decades in their parallel universe. I was furious, but I was also hungry, and I suggested to Ross that we go get some breakfast.

"Okay. We can go down to Hurricane."

"Why?" I asked. Hurricane was twenty-one miles down the road.

"No restaurants here are going to serve you, because you're a gentile, and they are definitely not going to serve me." To Ross, that made sense, but in this country, restaurants don't get to choose their customers.

That made up my mind. I drove with Ross over to the Vermillion Cliffs Café, went inside, and could almost feel a shock of surprise ripple through the place. Ross grew pale. I checked off our orders on a pad at the front counter, paid, and sat down, silently daring anyone to try and kick us out. It took a long time to cook those eggs, but the meal was eventually, although reluctantly, served.

It was a small victory at the end of a very long day. Waiting for the meal had only managed to further harden a decision that I had reached earlier while the saws had whined and the hammers had banged and the marshals had broken the law and the building inspector had lied: I was going to treat Short Creek like any other town in America.

CHAPTER 4

UEP v. Holm

I was hooked. The drive home to Cedar City in the freezing dark of that winter night was almost dreamlike and somewhere along the road I crossed the imaginary divide that separates Short Creek from the United States. The episode that I had witnessed that Saturday would not appear in the morning paper, nor on the evening news, because even if the editors heard about it, they would not deem it important enough to dispatch a reporter to cover. And for the Short Creek inhabitants like Ross, it was not really news at all; it was just another day in the Crick. Happens all the time, he said. That and worse. The difference this time was that a gentile who worked with law enforcement had been on the scene to witness it. By now, my doubts and hesitations had evaporated like mist rising from a field with the dawn; something was very wrong down there. I reminded myself not to let emotion get ahead of professionalism. My primary concern was still to keep the Chatwins in their place; it was no longer their house, but the lower floor of a duplex, a basement apartment. But sooner or later, I understood that whatever I uncovered was going to end up in a court of law. I would dot every *i* and cross every *t* to make the case watertight.

A few days later, I paid another visit to Short Creek, once again prepared to be greeted by the reception committee. Sure enough, as soon as I got into town, the plyg-rigs emerged out of nowhere and were on me. This time, when they closed in and started to buzz around like big mosquitoes, I let them force me to the side of the street, at which point I suddenly stopped, threw open my door, and jumped out. In my hands was a 35-millimeter still camera with a long black lens, and I brought it up and started snapping pictures of license plates and startled faces, bounding toward them like a determined Hollywood paparazzi after a starlet. I yelled, "Hey, get out and come on over here and talk to me!" *Click-click-click.* "Come on, guys. Let's talk!"

There was a long moment of hesitation. They had not been instructed about anything like this and just sat there, dumbfounded, in their trucks with the big engines idling as they realized the game had changed. Then they hit their gas pedals and scattered like chickens. I lowered the camera and allowed myself a chuckle as I began to realize how scared they were to be photographed. I could almost envision them speeding over to some place like the friendly Vermillion Cliffs Café, and trying to figure out what had happened over a cup of coffee. *The guy had a camera! He took our pictures!* Like most bullies, they were mostly about posturing, and if you faced up to them, they didn't know how to react. My camera was scarier to them than a gun. Eventually, I grew used to their antics; after all, when you go to the circus, you expect to see clowns.

I took some groceries over to Ross and Lori and their kids. They no longer had any source of income, and they were living like refugees trapped in a town that treated them as if they had the plague. No work, no money, no food, so I would try to help when I could. My dad had taught me that when you help others, you are really helping yourself, and it gave my spirits a boost to see the family hang tough while the FLDS tried to crush them.

In return, the Chatwins became my guides into the tangled lore and skewed history of the FLDS. Through them, I began to meet other FLDS dissidents, the apostates, who had heard about the private investigator who was standing up to the cops and the thugs. As I developed additional sources, all paths eventually led to one person. The border towns were completely under the thumb of FLDS prophet Warren Jeffs. I listened carefully, but I wasn't there yet. I had never even seen Jeffs in person. My job was to find ways to help Joan Dudley fight the eviction, and to help the Chatwins keep their home.

In long conversations with the Chatwins and my growing circle of apostate sources, I found an unexpected nugget of legal leverage, a precedent that had been decided less than a year earlier, in May 2003. After three years of litigation, the case, *United Effort Trust v. Milton Holm*, had ended with a half-a-loaf victory for both sides. The court ruled that the UEP did rightfully own the property, but also that Holm had made substantial improvements to it over the years and the UEP would be "unjustly enriched" by taking it without proper compensation for the work and money Holm had put into the 3,600-square-foot house. The FLDS refused to pay a cent, so Milton Holm was granted a "life estate" in the property, which meant his family could continue living there for the rest of his life. When he died, the family could be legally evicted.

That was definitely something to pass along to the lawyer, Joan Dudley. It was a recent legal decision that applied to the Chatwin case. But there was more to the story than just property rights. As Ross related what had happened in his calm voice, it left me reeling in disbelief. The property title dispute faded almost to an afterthought as I was swept up in the tragic saga of the Holm family. What had happened was so unbelievable that I couldn't just take Ross's word for it. It took some time for me to piece the facts together with a lot of background work and interviews with other people. Incredibly, Ross had been right all along. It was all too true.

The story involved child abuse, rape, kidnapping, extortion, smuggling minors across international borders for sexual purposes, and the astonishing fact that law enforcement agencies all the way up to the state level, the Federal Bureau of Investigation, and the Royal Canadian Mounted Police had known what was going on and had looked the other way.

Four years earlier, on a warm summer morning in 2000, Lenore and Milton Holm, a couple with thirteen children, were summoned to the office of Warren Jeffs for a surprise interview. That alone had set them on edge out of fear that he was going to accuse them of doing something wrong, and they had no idea where they had strayed from being loyal. Instead, the lanky Warren informed them that they were to surrender their fifteen-year-old daughter Nicole to be a wife for Wynn Jessop, who was twenty-three years older, married, and had children.

The wedding was already scheduled for the following day, when Nicole would turn sixteen. The parents, who had not been alerted in advance, were taken by surprise by the instruction but were relieved that they were not being punished for some unknown transgression.

They automatically agreed to the decision, just as they had been trained to do.

As they went home, terrible memories flooded back to Lenore Holm of her own forced first marriage. She recalled her first wedding night, to the man to whom she had been assigned before she married Milton, as nothing less than a brutal assault. She couldn't bear the thought of the same thing happening to her own little girl, and by the time she and Milton arrived back home, they had changed their minds. They solemnly revoked their consent.

Warren was furious. Within ten minutes, he called up Milton and told him that he had "lost priesthood" for allowing his wife to run the family, that they were no longer members of the church, and that they should immediately leave their residence.

Shortly afterward, the Holms began receiving visits from more cordial church leaders who urged them to trust the will of the prophet and yield their daughter in marriage. When they still refused, all pretense of cordiality was dropped and the visits from FLDS leaders became threatening, promising that dire judgments of God would befall the family if they did not (illegally) place their teenaged daughter into servitude. Within minutes of their final decision, the Holms were served with an eviction notice drawn up by the FLDS's favorite lawyer, Rod Parker of the law firm of Snow, Christensen and Martineau in Salt Lake City, ordering them to immediately vacate their six-bedroom, three-bath house.

Friends and neighbors they had known all their lives ceased speaking to them. The city turned off their utilities and their trash was no longer picked up. The community that had been their whole lives only the week before, now seemed determined to crush them.

But that wasn't the worst of it. Suddenly, Nicole, the pretty little daughter and targeted bride, disappeared as if she had been part of a magic show. Poof, and she was gone without a trace. A distraught Lenore pleaded with the local law, Chief Marshal Sam Roundy, to find her daughter, and he agreed to take a look. Weeks went by before Roundy reported back that he had spoken with Nicole, but did not know where she was. The girl was safe, the chief said, and had voluntarily run away from home. Lenore did not believe him. She believed that her child had been kidnapped and was probably now married to Wynn Jessop.

Lenore notified the Washington County sheriff's office in Utah, the Mohave County sheriff's office in Arizona, and the attorneys general of both states. All promised to open investigations, and Nicole eventually was located in the FLDS community in Bountiful, British Columbia, Canada. Lenore knew that her daughter did not have a driver's license or a passport, so there was no legal way for her to have crossed that international border without parental permission or the appropriate documentation, particularly since she was a minor being transported for the purpose of being married against the wishes of her family. Lenore filed complaints with the Royal Canadian Mounted Police in Canada and the FBI in the United States, and once again she was promised investigations into the disappearance of the girl. Nothing came from any of it.

Nicole was indeed in Canada and had been secretly married to Wynn Jessop, to whom she had been presented like a gift. The powerful FLDS had outmaneuvered the family. Nicole, brainwashed since infancy to obey the prophet, did just that, and was convinced that her parents were wrong. She saw nothing unusual about being assigned at her young age to an older man who was already married to someone else. But since Nicole was a child in the eyes of the law, it had not been her decision to make, and if sexual relations were indeed involved, it was clearly rape, no matter what she said or wanted or believed. The church arranged it and then ran interference for her.

Nicole refused to speak to her mother, stating that if any attempt was made to call or contact her, it would not be reciprocated. Expelled from the church for their actions, and ordered to leave their house, the parents sued.

From that came the *UEP v. Holm* case that had finally been settled the previous May. It was not really about property issues at all. The real crime was that Milton and Lenore had broken an unwritten FLDS law by challenging the word of the powerful prophet. Therefore, they had to be punished.

The Chatwins and the Holms provided a hint at what might lie ahead. Nicole was only fifteen when church leaders tried to place her in a so-called marriage. Ross and Lori had been thinking about marrying a sixteen-year-old until I stopped them. There had always been chatter in the surrounding gentile communities about young girls being married off within the FLDS, but much of it was chalked up to rebellious farm girls tiring of their restricted lives and running away from home in search of love. That happened every day somewhere in this country. But how young was too young? How low would they go within the FLDS when deciding who was ready to be married? And if little girls were involved, what about the little boys? I was just beginning to grasp the true extent of the complexities of the case.

CHAPTER 5

Big Willie

With a court appearance looming to defend the Chatwins, we assembled a list of key FLDS players who could either be deposed or appear as witnesses. The biggest name on our list was the prophet Warren Jeffs himself, and this time when I returned to Short Creek, I was carrying more than a camera, or a hammer and nails: I had a satchel full of subpoenas. The cloistered community was shocked when I started dropping the papers on them and denting their confidence that they were exempt from such legal trifles.

I began with Sam Barlow, who had been the first town marshal. Some twenty years earlier, both Utah and Arizona had decertified him as a peace officer for lying to the Washington County sheriff about a cache of some 180 semiautomatic rifles that he had secreted in a cave. He had emerged unscathed from that decertification, and as far as the church was concerned, Barlow was a key behind-the-scenes figure when any legal trouble popped up involving the gentile world.

It was not hard to find him. A sign on the building directly across the street from the police station read: SAM'S OFFICE. His big Chevy Suburban was parked outside, indicating he was present, so I went in. The whole building seemed to start breathing in and out as I told him I was serving him. The obese man's face reddened in outrage, as if he were about to explode. Barlow did not want to touch the subpoena, but I didn't care. He had been legally served, and he knew it, so I laid it on his desk and walked out.

I served several more subpoenas over the next few days, but the one that I was most looking forward to delivering was the one bearing the name of Warren Steed Jeffs. I parked about a block away from the ten-foot-high wall that surrounded his compound and settled down to watch.

The enclave, which consists of several homes, is modern and well kept, and is in stark contrast to the poverty that surrounds it. Covering an entire city block, it looks more like a walled gated community than the FLDS command center. Several entrances in the wall allow access, and swiveling, motorized cameras scan all visitors. The big rolling electric gates opened only for approved vehicles.

About five o'clock, as the work day ended, traffic picked up outside the compound, and I watched a steady stream of vehicles make brief stops on the street. The driver would jump out of the car and thrust one or more envelopes into a metal mail slot built into the wall, then dash away so the next in line could make their deposits. Sources explained to me later that it happened nearly every day, as people tried to get their tithing money, donations, and letters of repentance to the prophet in a timely manner.

I got out of my car and walked up to the big pedestrian gate set into the thick wall and rang the bell. Nothing. I had counted more than twenty other cameras around the compound, with additional tiny cameras the size of lipstick cases covering specific areas like porches and under the eaves of the buildings. One big motorized camera had been placed right over the west entrance. I buzzed the intercom and heard the hum of the camera moving to focus its big eye on me.

A young female voice from the intercom asked if she could help me. I said I had some documents for Warren Jeffs. She went silent, so I waited a few minutes and buzzed again. The same voice asked the same question. I repeated my answer. She replied that he wasn't there.

I kept talking, trying to coax her into sending someone out to talk to me in person. In Utah, it is legal to serve a subpoena on any occupant over the age of fourteen at the address in question. The receptionist, however, just said "thank you," then cut me off. After that, she would not even answer the intercom. I smiled up at the camera, then left, going on to my next stop.

At the time, the Jeffs compound was one of the only places in town with such tight security, but that quickly changed after my first subpoena blitz. Within two weeks, new fences with security cameras and NO TRES-PASSING signs began to appear everywhere. Before, I had been able to drive directly up to the health clinic and park in a space reserved for the bishop of Short Creek, Uncle Fred Jessop, when I tried to serve a sub-poena on him. Now, the clinic was completely surrounded with a rein-forced vinyl security fence, and a guard shack perched at the newly installed gates.

On an early March morning in 2004, a fifteen-passenger white van wheeled up to the courthouse in Kingman, Arizona, the Mohave County seat. The doors opened and out spilled a small army of FLDS church leaders who would represent the church's attempt to evict Ross Chatwin. Only three or four of them had been called as witnesses, some of whom I rec-ognized because I had dropped subpoenas on them. So the others had shown up either for moral support or, more likely, to make certain every-body else said and did the right things. They were cocky. They were arro-gant and disrespectful. They were the FLDS, on a mission from the prophet.

Joan Dudley was unimpressed by this gang, and she hardly looked up from her papers as they bumbled into the courtroom, bringing along their own security team of church goons. They took seats in the row in front of me, talking loudly, and that gave me a chance to both look them over and listen to their comments. Occasionally, to gauge their response and learn more about them, I would make a calculated comment to some-one nearby. Judging from the sharp looks thrown my way, the tactic ap-parently worked. Soon, the goons were up and quietly badgering the court bailiffs to find out who I was.

The combativeness of the day came to a head when Dudley called Willie Jessop to the stand. I had heard a lot about this guy and was eager to see if the rumors were true. Jessop was a longtime FLDS bully who had wormed himself into a useful position with some of the church lead-ers who felt that his bulk and willingness to do as he was told could work to their advantage. His role was always an unofficial one that the leaders could deny, if necessary. It was Willie who later shoved a camera at me as I left my doctor's office before open-heart surgery. He had a flair for the theatrical, and when his name was called he swaggered to the witness chair to face the detested black woman lawyer.

She worked him over for a while and he dodged the questions, stalled, and gave evasive answers, trying to insinuate that he—not she—was in control. Joan tuned him up like she was winding a clock. "Are you a bodyguard for the church?" she asked, raising her eyebrows slightly.

He responded that it depended on what she meant by the word "bodyguard."

She asked if he was a bodyguard for Fred Jessop—the "Uncle Fred" who held the rank of second counselor to Warren Jeffs and was the bishop of the town. Uncle Fred had mysteriously vanished, and I had been unable to subpoena him at the health clinic. She received the same non-answer from Willie.

For the third time, Dudley tried the same question, and Willie admitted that on occasion he sometimes "accompanied" Uncle Fred.

"Were you a bodyguard for Rulon Jeffs, the former prophet?" Willie belatedly recognized that this line of questioning was painting him to be a longtime church enforcer. He dodged. She followed. "Are you Warren Jeffs's bodyguard?"

Willie fell back to saying that depended on the definition of the word "bodyguard."

But Joan had laid the groundwork, and she sprung the trap. *Want a definition of bodyguard? Okay.* She wagged a finger at him as if she were a schoolteacher with a particularly dense child and barked, "Do you guard Warren Jeffs's body?"

He refused to respond, so she asked Judge James Chavez to order him to do so. Once more, Willie began a wavering ramble about the proper definition, and Joan pounced: *"Do you guard Warren Jeffs's body?"* He still would not answer directly, so the judge ordered him to do so, and Willie arrogantly replied, "No comment."

Judge Chavez exploded. "Who do you think you are? You're not outside talking to the media." He reminded Willie that he was under oath in a court of law and that he would definitely answer the question or suffer the consequences.

I watched with great satisfaction as the top FLDS enforcer was forced to give in to a black woman and a Hispanic judge. Getting Willie Jessop to admit in court to having been the bodyguard for the most important men in the hierarchy would prove to be a valuable tool that would be used against him in the coming years.

When the hearing was finished, the FLDS had failed in its effort to evict Ross Chatwin and his family. It was a good day in court, and it took Ross a step closer to obtaining a "life estate" of his own.

Up to that point, I had never even met Willie, but his name was always popping up because the apostates of Short Creek seemed to be scared of him, and also of his smaller half-brother, Dee. The two men are muscle for the church and are not shy about yearning to be God's avengers. They live for the day they are called upon to protect the prophet and priesthood.

Willie is a large man, about six foot five and weighing probably around three hundred pounds, with brown hair that he sweeps back Elvis-style.

A man named Richard Jessop Ream, who would become one of my clients in another case, later provided me with a deeper look into Willie's disturbed psyche. In an affidavit, Ream described the time that he and some friends were chatting with some local girls at the post office in Short Creek, unconcerned by the fact that the girls were considered off-limits by the church leadership. Big Willie drove up and glowered. "Leave the priesthood girls alone," he snapped.

When Ream replied that he would talk with whomever he chose, Willie closed the conversation with the threat: "If I have to use guns to straighten you little bastards out, I am going to do just that, and Uncle Warren is going to back me up."

Ream took that seriously. He had visited Jessop's home on West Field Avenue in Hildale and knew the man owned the hardware to make good on his threat. Ream described the place as a mini-fortress, with all the windows blacked out because Willie was convinced that law enforcement had him under surveillance and that government intrusion was imminent. The basement reeked of gun oil and shelves sagged along two walls beneath the weight of cases of ammunition, reloading equipment, and gun supplies. The other two walls and some tables were laden with assault weapons, pistols, rifles, and shotguns, including a huge Barrett .50-caliber sniper rifle, which can kill up to a mile away, and nearly every kind of small arms weapon imaginable.

Ream's affidavit stated, "I asked Mr. Jessop if it concerned him that he was in possession of illegal assault rifles." At the time, those were banned.

Willie laughed and replied that "what the law didn't know wouldn't hurt them." He was ready to use deadly force if the prophet commanded it.

As if not to be outdone, Willie's brother Dee Jessop has openly stated that he would willingly cut the throats of his wives if the prophet gave the order. I have no doubt that both are serious. Together, they have a tendency to more than double the trouble, becoming exponentially meaner. They are formidable and unpredictable.

I have heard Willie brag to his admirers within my earshot about almost having had to "take [me] down." The fact is that Willie rarely comes closer than twenty feet of me and, aside from our recent encounter in the parking lot of my doctor's office, we have never had anything resembling a real conversation, but not for my lack of trying. He is invariably parked, lurking somewhere nearby, when trouble arises within the FLDS or if I have some business in the Crick. When I attempt to communicate with him, I get no response. He drives a high-dollar Mercedes-Benz SUV that is decked out with the latest police radios and scanners and even a satellite dish on the roof. I have tried walking up and tapping on the window of his vehicle and motioning for him to step outside and talk. He responds by locking all the doors and staring straight ahead.

One of the more interesting aspects of my entire investigation has been watching Big Willie evolve from being just a convenient thug for Warren Jeffs to becoming an affluent businessman and the slick spokesman for the entire FLDS religion. He is always welcome on national television shows, where he is acknowledged as the face of the cult. He is among the best I have seen at being able to lie like a thief and get away with it.

His rise to power says a lot about how the FLDS operates by instilling fear. I always make sure my guard is up when Big Willie is around. While working my way through college, one of my many jobs was training police dogs. Willie reminded me of what we called in that business a "fear-biter." When you are not looking, such an animal sneaks up from behind, yaps a few times, nips at your heels, and then slinks away. It just is not prudent to show your back to a "fear-biter" like Willie. I consider both Willie and his brother, Dee, to be very dangerous men.

CHAPTER 6

P.I.

The work in Short Creek brought up some personal and professional considerations for me. The private detective business is just that, a business, and I had to earn a living. I could not just drop everything, and my paying clients elsewhere, to constantly run down to that crazy town. I could only work for so long on a dollar. But likewise, I also could not—would not—give up on my investigation. I had stumbled into an unbelievable place and an entire culture that should not exist in this country, and many of the people I was meeting were fighting for their very survival.

My research and paperwork files were stacking higher with each visit, progress had been made to get a safe haven for the Chatwins, and it was time for me to take a breather. But I knew that I wasn't finished with the FLDS.

I seemed uniquely qualified to investigate the group. Not only was I a well-educated and trained professional in the law enforcement field, but there was something else just as important in this matter: I was a Mormon. I knew my religion, its traditions, its history, and its texts well, so I could cut through the blather of the FLDS when they tried to wrap their criminal activity with a sacred cloth of piety. Add to that the interesting fact that my great-grandfather served prison time in the late nineteenth century for being a polygamist. My grandmother was the youngest daughter of his youngest wife. When I had heard those stories as a kid, they seemed as outdated as other quirky tales from back in the age of the

covered wagon. Now it seemed that I should have paid a little more attention to my mother's family history.

My mom had made sure that her four raucous sons regularly attended
church, and at the age of sixteen, I was ordained to the position of a
priest in the Mormon Church in the small Southern California town of
Banning, a place that was so quiet and normal that it was like "Leave It
to Beaverville." As a priest, I was able to participate in the duty of blessing the sacrament, something that I took very seriously.

Then one Sunday as I knelt to say the prayer, a woman in the congregation hurried up to our bishop and whispered something. He abruptly
stopped the service and announced that a matter needed to be addressed.
I was led away from the sacrament table, and everyone in the church
stared as if I were some kind of freak during that long trip up the aisle. I
had no idea what was happening. I thought my dad had been in an accident or something equally as horrible.

In his office, the bishop said he had just been informed that I had been
seen being arrested in front of the church on the previous Wednesday night.
"She is sure it was you, and that a highway patrolman took you away in
handcuffs," he said. "If that is the case, then I can't allow you to bless the
sacrament. You have to be worthy, so we'll need to get someone to take
your place."

I was embarrassed and angry as I explained that the patrolman was
Darrell Crossman, the leader of my Explorer Scout troop, and that he
had offered me a ride in his cruiser. The bishop should not have inter-
rupted the church meeting to confront me, but he had bought into the
busybody's accusation. Now, he apologized. "Come on, we'll take you
back up on the stand and everyone will see that you haven't done anything wrong," he said. As I walked with him back toward the altar, my
mind was churning with emotion. I could not continue as if nothing had
happened. Why would I want to have anything to do with a church that
would humiliate me? I walked out, and I did not set foot in another Mormon church for twenty-six years.

I grew up as a Southern California kid bent on enjoying life.

My dad told me that everything I wanted to know had been written down in a book somewhere, awakening my curiosity and probably giving me a bit of an edge growing up during a very tumultuous period. During the summer when I was eight, I read Homer's *Iliad* and the *Odyssey*; plowed through the library's shelves of biography, autobiography, and history; and then turned to the thirty-two volumes of the *Encyclopaedia Britannica*.

Still, I was swept up in the counter-culture madness that was California in the 1960s, and I tumbled from gifted pupil to troubled youth. Out of school, out of church, and out of luck at eighteen years old, I drifted from coast to coast, always looking for the next party as I earned a living in the building trades. My motorcycle was my best friend. It had a special sheath in which I kept a pair of crutches, which I needed from having been in so many accidents. But the worst mishap came in 1979, when I was a passenger in a pickup truck that slammed into a huge rock on a mountain road. The collision broke my neck and jaw and a lot of other bones, leaving me in a body cast with steel plates in my head and face holding me together and a future of reconstructive surgeries. The doctors expected me to die. I spent several weeks in traction while undergoing multiple reconstructive surgeries and five months in a "halo," a medieval-looking metal band that encircled my head, with bolts tightened into my skull with a torque wrench to keep my head immobile. My neck was broken at the C2 vertebra, an injury commonly referred to as a "hangman's break." The purpose of the halo was to make it possible for me to move around, instead of being immobilized in a special bed that kept me in traction. The problem was, I had been in bed so long that my muscles atrophied to the point of uselessness and I had to learn to walk all over again. It took two long years to finally get my legs back under me and start feeling whole again.

That close call allowed me to believe I had been given a second chance with life, a rare opportunity to start anew, and I decided to change course. I started to really grow up, got married, and settled down to start a family. But when our kids were born, my wife and I began to realize that Southern California probably wasn't the best place to raise them. For a variety of reasons, none of them having to do with religion, we decided to move to Utah. I still had no religious affiliation, and my wife knew little about Mormons.

But when my partner in a construction business in Riverside, California, learned of our decision to relocate to Utah, he was bewildered and concerned. "Be careful," he warned. "The place is full of polygamists."

"Well, we have Crips and Bloods out here, Gene," I said. "The cops just found the body of an eight-year-old girl who had been brutalized and tossed alongside the freeway just a few blocks from my home—and you think I should be afraid of a few polygamists?" I was sick of hearing remarks about polygamists and Utah. Polygamy hadn't been practiced for more than a hundred years out there—or so I thought.

So we headed for Cedar City, a place that now seems to have been picked for us by fate. When we pulled up to our new house, people we had never seen before came over to help us unload, bringing food and instant friendship. There were Mormons and non-Mormons alike. One introduced himself as Brig Young. My wife, holding a plate of cookies that had just been brought over, blurted out, "Oh, come on—!!" Brig chuckled and said, "Yep, it's true. The first-born son is always named Brigham. It's a family tradition." He was a direct descendant.

After leading cautious lives in what had turned into a high-crime area of Southern California, we were pleased to be among friendly neighbors. Six years after our move, I graduated from Southern Utah University with a 3.87 grade point average and a degree in criminal justice with an emphasis in criminalistics and a minor in chemistry. It had taken a long time for me to get through college while working full time and raising a family, but I never give up.

Then I got down to business. Right after college, I teamed up with a friend who was a private investigator in Cedar City. The town's growth had inevitably been accompanied by an increase in crime and drugs, and I saw an opportunity in the bail bond industry, which would, I hoped, provide some additional income. Along with that, I also became a bounty hunter, legally tracking down people who had had some sort of brush with the law and returning them to the custody of the sheriff to await a court appearance.

My state license as a bounty hunter proved to be a potent tool. In most states, bounty hunters do not even need permission or probable cause to enter a dwelling, unannounced, to make an arrest. And through reciprocity agreements, if a case originates in Utah, I could follow it across state lines and go into other cities with the same authority I had at home. I became good at finding people who didn't want to be found. I learned a lot about tenacity and seeing a difficult assignment through.

Among my first jobs was a self-assigned cold-case project back in

California. Even before we moved to Utah, Larry Wheelock, one of my best buddies, had been murdered in a home invasion robbery, and the killer had never been caught. I dug out the files, pestered detectives, and discovered some new evidence by using new technologies. Within six months, Larry Donel Page was arrested for the murder. At twenty-six years, it had been the oldest cold case to be solved in Orange County history.

Because an adversarial situation plays out in just about every case, I have made a decision to be armed most of the time. I have come to the realization that it would be foolhardy to find myself—or worse, my family—in circumstances that might require having to protect ourselves against the threat of serious injury or death, and not have the means to do so. I refuse to let that happen.

As I settled more into our new home and life, I began to feel an obligation to my children, and myself, to contemplate the value of some sort of spiritual life. After years of exploring many religions, I was converted, along with my family, to the mainstream LDS Church. I had returned to my Mormon roots.

By the time I drove down to Short Creek to meet Ross Chatwin for the first time in 2004, I already had a lifetime of experience dealing with hard cases. Little did I know that I was on a collision course with Prophet Warren Jeffs and the breakaway, mysterious sect called the Fundamentalist Church of Jesus Christ of Latter-Day Saints.

CHAPTER 7

The Father

I vividly remember my grandfather's stories of leaving his home in Farmington, Utah, and riding the rails to San Bernardino, California, in his search for work during the Great Depression: Wall Street had crashed, thousands of banks had closed and wiped out the savings of millions of people, industrial production collapsed, and farmers throughout America lost their land. Utah's citizens were trying to survive, but times were hard in this rugged state. There was a great exodus of men looking for work.

However, returning to Utah from England about that time was a tall, neatly dressed twenty-three-year-old man with a nice smile and dark hair who had escaped the ruination that had been suffered by so many. His name was Rulon Timpson Jeffs. He arrived not in a boxcar but on a passenger train, and he was a loyal, practicing member of the mainstream Mormon Church. Born in 1909 in Salt Lake City, Jeffs, a highly intelligent young man, became valedictorian of his LDS high school class in 1928 and delivered the graduation address in the Mormon Tabernacle in Salt Lake City, which he recalled as a "knee-knocking" experience.

Mormon young men are encouraged to undertake a proselytizing mission for the church as they mature from adolescence to manhood. It requires that they set aside their own wants and needs and devote two years of their lives to spreading their beliefs through personal example. Brigham Young once said those called to the position must have "clean hands and pure hearts, and be pure from the crown of your head to the

soles of your feet; then live so every hour." LDS missionaries continue to
be an extraordinarily successful means of spreading the Mormon message around the world, and multitudes of people have responded to the
words and deeds of the devoted young "saints."

Rulon Jeffs began his own mission on June 1, 1930. He was sent to
London, where he became a secretary at the mission headquarters. Two
years later, he was home again and was given a secure job with the Utah
State Tax Commission, a salaried government position that included an
office in the capitol building in Salt Lake City. In June 1934, his fortunes
grew even more when he married Grace Zola Brown, the daughter of
influential LDS apostle Hugh B. Brown. That gave the ambitious Rulon
a direct link to leadership and influence. He and Zola had two children.

As I plunged into the daunting task of figuring out the structure and
history of the FLDS and its leadership, it was apparent that understanding the enigmatic Prophet Rulon Jeffs would be necessary before there
could be any hope of grasping the madness of his son, Prophet Warren
Jeffs. Was Warren an extension of his father's eccentricities and deviant
behavior? Between them, the two men hijacked the fundamentalist movement, established a position of unchecked power, and sowed chaos and
perversion in their wake for fifty years.

The Mormons' incredible record-keeping system would prove to be invaluable as I assembled the puzzle. The genealogy and family histories
of millions of individuals, soon to be billions as more databases come on
line, are available through LDS resources. I have even found and read my
polygamist great-grandfather's personal diary, digitized and available online in its original form. Starting the investigation, I began to amass material gleaned from legal documents, the churning of online search engines,
books and papers available in libraries and private collections, private law
enforcement databases, public business transactions, and information
from personal interviews and conversations. This is the kind of project
that I find particularly intriguing as an investigator; I love this stuff.

The problem was that the fundamentalists were no less enthusiastic
about their own records. They were intensely paranoid about their illegal lifestyle and did a thorough job of hiding their accounts. For a re-
searcher, that created an occasional black hole. I felt the information

must be out there somewhere, beyond my reach, secreted away in barns or cubbyholes, behind false walls or in locked rooms. I would fantasize that at some future place and time I would find my way to that hidden trove of information, or it would find its way to me.

The "Hallelujah" moment for Rulon Jeffs, his introduction to Mormon fundamentalism, came on September 25, 1938, when he took his father, David Ward Jeffs, out for a birthday dinner. David had been a closet polygamist for years, so deep underground that Rulon had been born "in hiding" to David's second wife. The boy lived for the first ten years of his life under the fake name of Rulon Jennings, although in such a society, it is doubtful he ever questioned his name change. The practice was not uncommon in other families that he knew, and that was just how things were. David allowed his son to become a faithful mainstream Mormon, perhaps because being discovered as a polygamist could have meant a jail term for the father. Now, at his father's birthday dinner, it was time for Rulon to know everything, and David presented his son with a copy of the *Truth* magazine, an underground publication put out for those maintaining the covert and illegal practice of plural marriage.

In his memoirs, Rulon wrote, "I asked Father, 'What is this?' He told me it was put out by Joseph W. Musser. I said, 'By what authority?' So he told me, and he took me to see Brother Musser [who] received me like a father into the work, and I got well acquainted with him.

"When I was told about the Priesthood Council, I said, 'Father, who is the head man?' [and the reply was] 'Well, he has to be in kind of hiding.' I said, 'I want to see him.' So I finally got to see Uncle John over on 809 East, 700 South, met him in his home there. My heart leaped for joy finding the Prophet."

"Uncle John" was John Y. Barlow, the acknowledged leader of the secret movement, who had been excommunicated by the LDS Church. After those meetings, Rulon Jeffs fully embraced the fundamentalist philosophy, casually discarding the religious faith he had practiced his entire life.

After joining the flock, he hung out with his new friends at "cottage meetings" around Salt Lake City, where they spoke fervently about the plural lifestyle and how to mold this idealistic "Priesthood Order" to oversee the breakaway faith, which was called "The Work" by its adherents.

"Priesthood" may best be described as the spiritual glue that binds together the FLDS power structure. Usually, when a boy is about twelve years old, he is ordained within the fundamentalist religion into a preparatory level called the Aaronic Priesthood. It is a means of taking on responsibility and commitment and is not too different from similar practices, under other names, with the youth in other churches. Any comparison ends there. Elsewhere, priesthood is about service; in the FLDS it is about power and control, and even the Aaronic Priesthood would be swept into that black vortex. The higher up the ecclesiastical ladder a man climbed, the more priesthood powers he enjoyed. In the hands of Prophet Warren Jeffs, "priesthood" was wielded like a magic wand. It meant whatever Jeffs wanted it to mean, and he used it as a handy camouflage and justification for his dreadful actions. To lose priesthood was to lose everything.

When Rulon told Zola in 1940 that he had found a shopgirl that he wanted to marry as an additional wife, she balked. Polygamy was no longer part of Mormon doctrine and anyone found practicing it would be excommunicated. This simply had not been part of the deal when they got married. For Zola, as with the vast majority of Mormons, polygamy was a thing of the past. Her father, the LDS Apostle Hugh B. Brown, came to the house and issued an ultimatum for Rulon to either give up his heretical ideas or be kicked out of both the LDS Church and the Brown family. Having already surreptitiously taken his new bride, Rulon refused, and both threats came to pass. The divorced Zola took their sons and moved to California. Her departure did not really bother Rulon. In the coming years, he replaced her with a harem of dozens of wives.

Polygamy had been illegal for more than sixty years by the time Rulon decided it would be his life's calling. Back in January 1879, the United States Supreme Court had heard the case of George Reynolds, a Mormon resident in the Utah Territory, who was charged with having two wives—Amelia Jane Schofield and Mary Ann Tuddenham. In a unanimous decision, the high court found Reynolds guilty of violating the Morrill Anti-Bigamy Act. The Reynolds case set the stage for the Mormon Church to discontinue the practice of polygamy and for Utah to become a state. Wilford Woodruff, the fourth LDS prophet, issued what became known as the 1890 Manifesto, which made monogamy official church doctrine.

Special provisions were eventually made into law allowing those who were already in plural marriages at the time to continue them without disruption, but no new plural marriages could be performed. That was the situation under which my pioneer great-grandfather lived, although he was occasionally hassled by the authorities for "cohabitation," or living with a woman to whom he was not legally married. He paid $150 on one cohabitation charge and noted that it was "a lot of money."

Eventually, polygamy faded from the mainstream church as most Mormons busily assimilated into the growing United States. However, the deep divide had been created with the Manifesto. A handful of die-hard polygamists refused to go along with the new direction, arguing that the church had abandoned "God's will" and that a man must possess numerous wives. The dissidents were excommunicated and driven into secrecy.

By splitting away, the fundamentalists found themselves shorn of the right to set foot in any LDS temple—and temples are extremely important to Mormons, who use them as places for special worship such as formal marriages, in which everlasting vows are taken. The rebels could reasonably substitute meetings in private homes for their normal church services, but they had nothing that resembled a temple, and this created a big hole to fill in their new brand of religion. They came up with the novel excuse that since they were the true Mormons, they were of a higher order than everyone else, and therefore did not need a temple at all. Over time, that rationalization would become a point of stubborn pride with them.

Rulon Jeffs rapidly became a big frog in the very small fundamentalist pond and rose steadily in power. He was soon an apostle, then a patriarch, and then he held one of the seven positions on the Priesthood Council (or the "Council of Friends"), who shared power and control over their loosely formed organization and everyone in it. They controlled everything. Rulon also was the protégé of President John Y. Barlow.

A demonstration of the status he was acquiring came in 1942, when the fundamentalists created a rather dreamy socialist scheme called the United Effort Plan Trust (UEP), in which they pooled their resources with the notion that everyone would share the wealth equally. While that practice had been a part of early Mormon life as the religion struggled to survive during their long westward migration, it was eventually abandoned in favor of tithes given to the church and a storehouse from which supplies could be given to the needy. The fundamentalist version would turn that original good deed on its head.

Not just tithes, but all real estate holdings and other assets would be pumped into their UEP, and its trustees would decide how to dole out the assets, as well as doling out entitlements from their own version of a "bishop's storehouse." Rulon, the financially shrewd tax accountant, was appointed a trustee of the UEP. The United Effort Plan Trust became the financial arm of the church, and grew to be worth millions of dollars. Since the United Effort Plan had no bank account—having an account might have opened the records to legal scrutiny—that fund was controlled primarily through the private Rulon T. Jeffs Trust, for which he had sole authority. The storehouse for the needy instead became plunder for the loyalists.

As Rulon prospered in Salt Lake City, a colony of polygamists under the guidance of the Priesthood Council settled in an isolated little town called Short Creek, at the far southeastern end of Utah, along the Arizona Strip. It had been mostly rough cattle ranching country up until polygamists started using it as a hideout after the Reynolds Supreme Court decision. "The First City of the Millennium" was a hundred tough miles from Kingman, Arizona, in the days before automobiles and airplanes, and was shielded on the south by the Grand Canyon. It defined raw isolation. The polygamists, anchored there by the rapidly reproducing Barlow and Jessop clans, found a home at the foot of the massive and strikingly beautiful Vermillion Cliffs, which were rechristened with a more fitting biblical name, "Canaan Mountain."

The large rebel settlement on the border and the underground movement remaining in Salt Lake City shared the same ideals, but they were far from consolidated. An effective central leadership was impossible, and there were frequent challenges between factions, when each side would "excommunicate" their rivals, flinging the term "apostate" at each other like arrows. The losing group typically would drift off and settle somewhere else, with the result that there are pockets of polygamy all over the West. Even today, fundamentalists always seem to be in organizational disarray and turf wars are frequent. The only things that all of the mutinous groups agree upon are their mutual belief in plural marriage and contempt for the mainstream Mormon Church.

John Y. Barlow died in 1949, setting off a battle for succession. There is no orderly procedure by which to promote someone to the ultimate position in the fractured religion, and Barlow had tried but failed to maneuver his own candidate, LeRoy S. Johnson, into the chair. The next prophet was Joseph Musser, and when he too sought to name his own successor years later, he also failed. Finally, LeRoy Johnson took over as president and prophet, and Rulon Jeffs was his right-hand man. They ushered in a new era of stern control, because they had both witnessed the problems that could be caused when too many people had the ability to interfere with what the prophet wanted. Uncle Roy and Rulon Jeffs became the champions of a no-questions-allowed policy called "One-Man Rule." The seven-member Priesthood Council was on its way to oblivion, leaving no system of checks and balances.

For the man who personified polygamous unions, Johnson actually had encountered problems getting married for the first time. He recalled that when he was young, he had made proposals to many women. "They all turned me down," he confessed to Joseph Musser, according to the official FLDS version. Musser responded, "Well, I will promise you this, Brother Johnson, you won't have to go out and solicit them from now on. They will come to you."

Uncle Roy made his home down in "the Crick," which had become incorporated as Colorado City in Arizona on one side and Hildale, Utah, on the other side.

Rulon Jeffs remained in Salt Lake City, as befitted a man of his stature: a professional accountant, founder of Utah Tool & Die, on the board of many companies, and president of an insurance company. He settled into a new home in Little Cottonwood Canyon outside of Salt Lake City. The main house, with columns at the front, sprawled over 8,300 square feet per floor, and featured two kitchens, twenty-three bedrooms, and ten baths, as well as the Jeffs's Sunday school, which had a baptismal font. An adjacent "smaller" place had another twenty-two rooms, and the entire property was enclosed by a huge concrete wall, a reminder for the rest of the world to keep out.

Warren Steed Jeffs was Rulon's miracle child, delivered two and a half months premature on December 3, 1955, in Sacramento, California, after a difficult pregnancy that jeopardized the lives of both the infant and his mother, Merilyn Steed, one of Rulon's four current wives. He kept his other three in hiding, spread out in Arizona, Utah, and New Mexico to confound the law. Rulon was in Salt Lake City when he received word that Merilyn and the baby were in danger, and he rushed to Sacramento, arriving in time to actually help bring the boy into the world.

By itself, the birth could not have been regarded as a significant event. After all, the boy was Rulon's third child that year, and number fourteen overall, including the two by his divorced original wife, Zola. There would be many more children to come, but Warren would outshine them all. From his first breaths, Warren was favored by his forty-six-year-old father.

The spindly, far-sighted boy was born during a particularly turbulent time within the movement. Only two years earlier, in 1953, the politically ambitious governor of Arizona sent more than a hundred police officers into Short Creek to put a stop to the illegal practice of polygamy. Dozens of men were arrested and 263 children were swept into custody. The ensuing national publicity that included photographs of policemen snatching crying children from their mothers tilted national sympathy to the side of the polygamists, who claimed they were just an innocent religious minority being persecuted by an oppressive government. Like an ebbing tide, the Arizona government had retreated from Short Creek. The FLDS, however, never forgot the lessons of the "'53 Raid." Although Rulon's base was in Utah, and therefore exempt from the Arizona action, the constant fear of government was the primary reason that he scattered his wives over several states.

Even as a child, Warren automatically had a special standing within the fundamentalist community through his powerful father. Some recalled him as a spoiled brat and a tattletale, the golden boy who could do no wrong. Beyond the walls of the family compound, however, the skinny and fragile boy had a difficult time. One of his aunts described for me the day during his first year of middle school when Warren had to go to the bathroom, but was too timid to raise his hand and ask permission. He wet his pants. The telltale wet spot drew the attention of other students, who taunted him unmercifully. Such incidents contributed to his already introverted behavior.

As he grew, Warren was petrified when it came to girls. When some of his brothers tried to drag him outside to talk to some girls on a visit to a relative's ranch, he broke down crying, ran away, and locked himself in the family pickup truck. Although fearful of personal encounters with the opposite sex, young Warren was definitely interested in them, just not in normal, healthy adolescent ways. By the age of eight, he already had developed a reputation as a voyeur.

I interviewed a female relative who told me that her household had a special routine they put in motion upon receiving word that Warren would be coming for a visit. All of the girls and women taped newspapers over their windows to prevent him from peeping in, and they stuffed towels beneath their doors because Warren would try to slide a mirror underneath in hopes of catching them in various stages of undress. "He was notorious for that stuff, even at that age," she told me.

The host family could not scold the boy and order him to stop peeping. He was the favorite son and off limits to criticism, something that would become another lifelong trait. As Carolyn Jessop recalled in *Escape*, her penetrating book about her life in the FLDS, "No one stood up to Warren."

While not the physical equal of many others in public school, he was brighter than most, and he graduated with honors from high school, skilled in math and science. Warren's graduation was perfectly timed, perhaps a little too perfect to be coincidental, because his father at that moment made a decision to build a private school specifically to meet the educational needs of the growing mass of children from fundamentalist families in the Salt Lake area. Too many things that were taught in public classrooms were religiously unpalatable and in stark contrast with what the kids were learning in their homes, such as the nonsense that man had walked on the moon. In 1973, Rulon Jeffs had one of the larger buildings within his walls turned into an FLDS school with a proper, fundamentalist curriculum. It was called the Alta Academy, and it would become Warren's launching pad.

Without a college education or teaching credentials, he was hired into the original faculty of the academy and was soon elevated to the position of principal, a promotion that carried an astonishing amount of personal power for someone who had yet to see his twenty-first birthday. Inside that building, the headmaster could do as he pleased, so he did.

CHAPTER 8

Lost Boys

One stormy afternoon late in May 2004, my cell phone chimed as I was driving down Main Street in Cedar City. The water was slamming down so hard that I pulled into a parking lot before answering. On the other end of the call was prominent Baltimore attorney Joanne Suder.

She said that she was looking for a private investigator for some potential lawsuits that were in the works involving the FLDS and that my name had come up as someone knowledgeable about their culture.

One of the first things Suder wanted to know about was my own religious beliefs. When I replied that I was LDS, her next query was whether my being a Mormon would create a problem in investigating the FLDS. *How many times have I answered this question?* In the minds of many Americans, if you are a Mormon man, then you must have a couple of wives. Nothing could be farther from the truth.

"I'm not FLDS," I told her rather firmly. "I'm LDS." Then I gave her the shorthand version of the stark differences, and I ended the lesson by saying, "The FLDS are no more Mormon than Lutherans are Catholics." That made sense to Joanne Suder. She was a Roman Catholic and yet had played a lead role in exposing the rampant child abuse by pedophile priests within her own religion.

Suder was now setting her sights on abuses by the FLDS involving the so-called Lost Boys. I turned off the car and made myself comfortable.

For the next hour and a half, we discussed one of the most horrific practices within the fundamentalist organization.

The Lost Boys are former FLDS kids who committed such outrageous sins as watching television, sneaking away to see a movie, or perhaps unbuttoning their shirts at the neck. Others may have been caught experimenting with drinking or flirting with a girl or having an attitude about something. Or perhaps the prophet may have seen them in a bad dream. No matter what the reason, such offenses are deemed not to be harmonious with how God wants them to behave, and the wayward boy can be excommunicated and literally abandoned by a roadside by his own family and ordered not to come back to Short Creek.

Girls are handled in an entirely different manner. A polygamous society needs a lot more hens than roosters. Girls, because of their potential as brides and child-bearers, are a valuable commodity. In almost any other town, the male-female ratio is about fifty-fifty, but the plural marriage system creates its own mathematical certainty; if the older men harvest the child brides, what is to be done about those strong sons who were raised doing hard farm and construction work? If young girls were allowed to choose who they wanted to marry, they would invariably pick husbands near their own age, cutting out the good ole boys and the aging church hierarchy. That would not work within the FLDS caste system. The gender ratio had to be turned on its head.

The first step was to keep all of the children, boys and girls alike, ignorant of sex education and normal marital intimacy. Sex was and is never discussed with FLDS children, and unless they grow up on a farm where they can witness animals breeding, they have no idea about sexual relations. Instead of receiving education, the children are admonished to avoid any physical contact completely and treat the opposite sex as they would poisonous vipers. For many a little bride, her first intimate encounter is in the form of abuse by her newly assigned husband.

The girl's parents hope to place the bride in a prominent church family, which would raise the status of "Father" (in the FLDS culture, the male parent is always referred to as Father) in the eyes of church leaders, resulting in more business and religious connections. A son always walks a much narrower path, but if he is obedient, finds some way to contribute, and is just plain lucky, he may last long enough to be assigned a wife by the prophet, and a plot of UEP land on which to build a house. Perhaps he will be brought into the family business, where his cheap labor can result in more revenue for church coffers, and again increase the social standing and financial prospects of Father. The new couple is expected to have children and their success within the group depends on their repeating the cycle of building wealth and prominence through procreation.

If the fortunate younger man continues to be obedient and contributes enough to differentiate himself from the pack, he may be blessed with another wife. That means more children, and suddenly he is considered the "Father," and will sire even more male drones to work in the family business and more young wives to marry into prominent families.

Now firmly on the path, he may be assigned the important third wife, which is his ticket to salvation. FLDS doctrine teaches that it takes three wives to reach the highest kingdom of heaven. It also allows him to have still more children. Depending on how he plays the hand, and if he stays on the good side of the prophet, he will continue to secure his place in God's kingdom. The FLDS believe that the only way a woman can reach heaven is with her husband or "priesthood head," so women are eager to ensure their place in eternity. If her husband is considered to be a less than stellar person by the church authorities, a wife is doomed to share her husband's fate and accompany him to a lesser glory.

The entire FLDS structure is supported by how many children can be contributed to the system, so the abusive cycle is repeated, time and again. The more wives a man is assigned, the richer he will become both on earth and in the hereafter. Women and children are considered chattel and the measure of a man's success.

The path is slippery for any boy trying to be obedient and climb the ladder of success. Church leaders, under the guise of religious piety and love, go to extraordinary lengths to protect the bride pool for the older men. The slightest misstep by a boy can be cause for instant banishment.

The age at which the boys enter the danger zone starts at about only eleven years and they remain at risk until adulthood. Extensive testing has shown that most of the Lost Boys are lucky to leave school with a third-grade education. Everything depends upon their obedience level and what kind of skills they can contribute to the hive. At a time when normal parents would give their kids extra support and work with them through mistakes, the church leadership looks for opportunities to expel the young offenders. They are mostly used as drones to be cast aside when their usefulness is exhausted.

Back when I worked on construction sites, I would see FLDS kids (some barely old enough to read a tape measure) unroll their power cords at dawn, work all day beneath a broiling Utah sun—totally buttoned up and wearing the traditional long underwear beneath their jeans and shirts—and not pack up again until dark. Most of their salaries went to their fathers. It is illegal in most states to have children younger than about sixteen or seventeen on a construction site, yet I have seen and photographed kids who appear no more than eight years old finishing concrete, driving heavy equipment, walking I-beams on the top stories of steel buildings, and working commercial construction projects. They are so short that the handles of the hammers dangling from their man-size tool belts drag along the ground. To me, it looked like slave labor. Banishing boys comes at a cost. The youngsters form an essential part of the FLDS economy, and their cheap labor helps FLDS businesses out-bid their legitimate business competition. But the threat they pose to their elders far outweighs their labor value and is constantly watched to maintain the proper equilibrium between males and females.

One boy who was only twelve years old recalled his experience for me. It was a story that I have heard far too often. He arrived home from a construction job, and Father told him to take a shower and clean up because they were going out to dinner. After a great meal at the Mark Twain Inn, his father broke the news. Uncle Warren had decided that the son was a "bad seed" whose evil actions were endangering the rest of the family. To protect the eternal salvation of his siblings, the boy had to be cast out not only from his home, but from the entire community before his evil influence could spread like a plague. Father already had packed some of his son's things. He drove him out to the highway and left him there with the suggestion that perhaps he could find shelter with another banished family member.

The boy also was given the same warning that I would hear repeated over and over, so often that it is burned into my memory: "Don't call: if you try to do so, we will not accept your calls and will hang up on you. If you write, we will destroy your letters without reading them." One day a boy can be in the bosom of his community, protected by the prophet and family, and the next, he is out on his own.

It is hard to imagine the terror of a youngster without much education, and with very few coping mechanisms or life skills, deliberately abandoned by his parents and his church and flung into a world he barely knew existed and has been trained to fear and hate. But the FLDS has callously tossed hundreds of boys, mostly in their mid-teens, aside like garbage over the years to keep the church's perverted gender scales in balance and reduce the chance that a girl might lose her heart to someone her own age. A son can be easily replaced because the wives of the FLDS have been taught that their sacred obligation is to reproduce as quickly as possible. Many females produce twelve or more children within a fifteen-year time period. They are always churning out new generations. It is a baby mill; a human assembly line.

Being the son of an FLDS leader does not automatically exempt a child from being thrown away. As Warren Jeffs recounted in his Priesthood Record, even some of his father's own sons were cast out, dismissed with the words, "You are a bastard and not a son."

The favorites are kept around and for some transgressions are simply told to repent and not to do it anymore. They are needed to replenish the family gene pool. It is a way of setting aside breeding stock, like prize bulls, in order to continue to replicate the family genome.

After our long phone conversation, Suder decided to move forward, and we agreed to get together in Salt Lake City for a face-to-face meeting. I was disturbed by the lawlessness that I was discovering in Short Creek, but I didn't know how long I could continue working without pay. I hoped my meeting with Suder would be more than just an information session for some attorneys who would politely thank me for my time, and that would be it.

I arrived at the Grand America Hotel, the best in the city, on a bright June day two weeks later, wearing my usual jeans, boots, a loose shirt, and an old ball cap. I considered putting on my Sunday go-to-meeting clothes, but I didn't feel a need to fabricate a facade to impress people. What you see is what you get. Besides, this was Utah, where my outfit doesn't normally draw a second glance. I called upstairs and a few moments later, a genial guy named Shem Fischer came down to meet me. He explained very little as we rode up in the elevator, although I could see him sizing me up.

Joanne was waiting in the luxury suite and the three of us made small talk for a while. Then she looked me up and down, as if noting that she was a long way from Baltimore. Having already tried a dark-suit-and-tie-guy private detective who hadn't worked out, she may have figured that a cow-country investigator might be just what was needed for the job. She smiled. "Well, I think we ought to hire you," she said. "Shem? That okay?" I didn't realize until later that I was being offered not one paying job, but several, which would eventually lead to even more new clients!

Shem hired me on the spot to help with case preparation and serve legal process in his own suit against the church and its financial operation. He had been fired from Forestwood Products, a cabinet-making company in Hildale, after being expelled from the FLDS by Warren Jeffs, with the usual accompanying orders to surrender his home and his family. But when Shem decided to fight that decision, he chose a novel course by bypassing local and state jurisdictions entirely. Instead of taking the chance that the FLDS and the UEP might get the upper hand in a lower court, he filed a federal suit that alleged his First Amendment rights had been violated because the church had blacklisted him.

It was while working on Shem's case that I first observed Warren Jeffs's bizarre strategy in dealing with the law. After being humiliated on the witness stand in a child custody battle, in which he had expelled a man by the name of Jason Williams, Warren left the courtroom making the comment that he would never again subject himself to the laws of man. He *never* responded to legal complaints.

Warren preached that when Jesus Christ was questioned by Pontius Pilate prior to being sentenced to crucifixion, Christ "answered him nothing." Warren equated all contemporary law enforcement with Pilate and trained the faithful to follow what he said was Christ's example and his own and avoid any inquiries by those from the outside world.

As a result, Shem Fischer eventually won his suit by default because Warren did not respond to the complaint. In years to come, I would marvel at watching the FLDS march from defeat to defeat in various courtrooms, most of the time preferring to lose rather than break Warren's firm edict to "answer them nothing."

CHAPTER 9

Headmaster

LeRoy Sunderland Johnson became a beloved figure in Short Creek, although he was not loved by everyone. The leadership of the polygamist movement had been unsettled for a number of years, and "Uncle Roy" was almost defrocked in 1979 when he suffered a debilitating case of the shingles, which left him bedridden and vulnerable to opponents who branded him a false prophet. Because of Rulon's closeness with Uncle Roy, his own influence and future also were in jeopardy, but he stuck by his friend and mentor. The old man was comforted with large doses of morphine and slowly recovered. The wilderness years came to a dramatic end on February 12, 1984, when Uncle Roy was helped to the pulpit and challenged his major foes, J. Marion Hammon and Alma A. Timpson.

"The Lord gave you men five and a half years to change your thinking on this principle of having one man holding the sealing powers in the earth at a time, and you have made a mess of it," Johnson told them in front of the congregation. Hammon and Timpson were expelled.

Among those in attendance on that momentous day was the twenty-nine-year-old headmaster of the Alta Academy, Warren Jeffs. He likened the experience to a holy wind rushing through him, and was so thrilled that he wept with joy. That was the way to lead! That was how *he* would do it!

Hammon and Timpson did not exactly leave town. They just started their own rival fundamentalist sect only two miles away on the other side of Highway 59.

To ease some of the confusion between the uneasy neighbors, Colorado City and Hildale became known within the FLDS faith as the First Ward, and the new group of Hammon-Timpson dissenters in "Centennial Park" would be the Second Ward. It was all still the Crick.

Uncle Roy died two and a half years later, in November 1986. This time, there was no question of succession. Rulon Jeffs and Uncle Roy had laid down the law of one-man rule within the fundamentalist movement, and Rulon grabbed the golden ring, becoming the new "prophet, seer, and revelator."

Rulon's most fervent supporter was his son Warren, who was by then in full manhood at the age of thirty-one. Warren had spent his entire career since graduating from high school—thirteen years—teaching and being the principal at the academy. He already had the addictive taste of power on his own lips.

Alta Academy was not only a school for elementary school children, but also a learning institution where Warren would hone his skills as a predatory monster.

Each day started with Warren's flat, hypnotic monotone either being delivered in person in the gathering hall or being broadcast over speakers to classrooms. The children would be quizzed on what he said. The FLDS educational process was so totally skewed toward strict religious dogma that many kids graduated still unable to speak or write in whole sentences. For most, the ability to properly read a list of food ingredients or a tape measure at a construction site was deemed adequate. Many teachers were hired based on their loyalty to the extremist faith and obedience, rather than credentials of a college education. There was no need to be certified by the state in an FLDS private school. Some of the students would roll right into the position of teachers, perpetuating the low educational standards and toeing the religious line. The instructors taught that the outside world was devoid of honor and not to be trusted, and gentiles were, of course, excluded from the faculty. Gentiles were bad, but apostates were worse. Students must "keep sweet" no matter what they were required to endure, even physical abuse. It was not education, just a thorough theological brainwashing.

The academy had several labor and delivery rooms on the second

floor designated for the use of a midwife to attend the births of new babies, which reduced the need to expose fundamentalist wives to the prying
eyes of gentile medical staff members in public hospitals, where family
names and dates of birth were routinely sought. It was symbolic of how
the breakaway fundamentalists withdrew from the scrutiny and norms of
the world.

A former student by the name of Mike recalled for me the day when
he was eleven years old and Uncle Warren singled him out for punishment. The youngster was made to stand in front of the classroom and
drop his trousers to his knees so Warren could savagely beat him with a
yardstick. Other former students echoed Mike's experience with their
own stories of what happened in the downstairs room containing the
baptismal font. If a yardstick broke, Warren would continue beating
them with the remaining portion. He spouted religious diatribes about
committing his young victims over to the judgment of God as he circled
the boys, ogling and brushing up against them.

My contacts among Jeffs's former students would reveal that it wasn't
just the boys being subjected to his psychotic behavior. Warren was the
self-appointed dress code enforcer and young females would recall standing numb and frightened beside the principal's desk as he pretended to
check their dress length to see if it fell to the appropriate height above
the ankle. While doing so, Uncle Warren's hands wandered over their
bodies and beneath their clothing.

Total obedience was mandated. If a child dared to complain about
the abuse at school, the parents would most likely take the side of Warren
against their own children. In interviews with parents who had left the
religion, I would discover that most of them could not fathom what kids
had to endure within their culture. They would continually struggle with
the fact that they had been complicit in the abuse and hadn't recognized
what was going on around them. Any parents who forgot that Warren
was the favored son of Prophet Rulon Jeffs and dared to protest could
count on incurring Warren's enmity for many years to come, the potential for future public humiliation compounding like interest in a bank.

The more parents and former students I spoke with, the more I heard
the same story over and over again. For Warren Jeffs the Alta Academy
was more like the mountain chateau of the Marquis de Sade than a
school. The only person who really learned anything there was Warren

Jeffs, who earned himself a post-graduate degree in the use of unchecked power.

My first personal look inside Warren Jeffs's shop of horrors came shortly after I was hired by Joanne Suder in 2004. It was even worse than I had imagined.

This particular case involved the family of Ward Jeffs, one of the prophet's many brothers. Ward was among those who had been banished years earlier by their father, Rulon, but he had refused to give up his family. Although once a polygamist, he now lived only with his wife Susan. They were waiting for me at their home, along with their three grown sons: Brent, Brandon and David.

A fourth son, Clayne, had endured a tormented life that eventually had led to a tragic death by his own hand. Shortly after Clayne's death, his therapist revealed to his family that he had been treating their son for a horrifying trauma he had experienced as a very young boy. Clayne had confessed to the therapist that he had been repeatedly raped by several of his uncles, including Warren Jeffs. As these tragic details came to light, his brothers Brent and Brandon courageously admitted the secret that had been haunting them for years: They also had been victimized by the same deviant relatives.

During the following week, I interviewed each family member separately, paying close attention to their stories and looking for inconsistencies. I found none. Both young men held fast to their accusations that when they were just little kids, between the ages of five and seven, they had been repeatedly raped and sodomized by Warren and several other uncles for more than a year.

The abuses that I learned about from Brent and Brandon had taken place at the Alta Academy. I had already heard about Warren's terrifying methods there, and I felt I needed to see the place first-hand. Brent mustered the incredible strength to give me a guided tour, although it meant having to relive his childhood horrors. He has since described it all in his book, *Lost Boy*.

The Alta Academy had closed shortly before the turn of the millennium and the compound eventually would house a charitable organization known as Common Thread, which provides services to people awaiting organ transplants. It was heartening to learn that the building was no longer linked to the church and had been put to a worthy purpose.

Brent led me downstairs to a room that had been used as a nursery for the young children while the others attended worship services upstairs in the main hall. Behind that door, the disturbing shadow of Warren Jeffs still lingered. Brent painfully recalled how when he was only five years old, his uncle Warren would come into that room and fetch him out by the hand. He would lead the child through the narrow corridors to a children's bathroom where happy paintings decorated the walls, and in which all of the sinks and toilets were at a low level to be accessible to the kids. Once the bathroom door was locked, the helpless little boy was folded over the edge of the bathtub and Warren and a few more of his uncles, all grown men, took turns raping their nephew. Brent described the pain as being almost unbearable.

Warren would be keyed up tight in his lust and babble continuously that it was part of the boy's secret initiation into the priesthood. He warned that if Brent ever told anyone about their "sacred rite of passage," the boy and his entire family would be plunged into hellfire. Decades later, Brent was still struggling to come to grips with the brutality he had endured, but he did not flinch in reconstructing the horrific events.

One of the most painful experiences for victims of abuse is to summon the courage to tell of that abuse, anticipating that a backlash is certain. Sure enough, when Brent told his story, he was demonized by his former friends and family members and called a liar. Defense attorneys for the church used every trick in the book to try to discredit him, but he was no longer a little kid who could be led around by the hand and coerced. He was a grown man who was determined to tell the truth.

It was a disquieting story, to say the least. This wasn't my first case dealing with child abuse, but as the father of three children, I always find it tough to hear those stories, and I have spent many sleepless nights trying to put them out of my mind. My task, though, was to nail down information for possible litigation, so to substantiate the facts I made another trip to the academy, this time with Brandon, who brought along their other brother, David, for moral support.

There is no such thing as a "typical" victim of child abuse, and Brandon was a good illustration. At twenty years old, he stood six feet four and was solid muscle, a soldier home on leave from the U.S. Army prior to being deployed to the Middle East. But that hard toughness began to evaporate the moment we entered the building and he led me step by step toward that evil bathroom. As he described the horrors he had endured behind that door, tears tracked down his cheeks and his voice shook. Before my eyes, this soldier was reliving those scenes from his childhood, tormented by the memories of what he had endured at the hands of his trusted teacher and uncle. His chilling descriptions were almost identical to those of Brent, but with a few differences, which convinced me that their stories were unscripted.

Finally, it was too much for Brandon. He staggered, sobbing openly, and David grabbed him in a bear hug. Both were crying. Then David looked solemnly at me and admitted, for the very first time, "It happened to me, too."

Visions of my own children raced through my mind, as well as intense rage for a monster that could do something so unspeakable to any child, much less a family member. I turned away from the scene to avoid losing control of my own emotions. All four boys had been raped as small children by their pedophile uncle: Warren Steed Jeffs. I promised David I would keep his secret and I did until after his untimely death only a year later. Now, two of Warren's nephews had succumbed to the lifetime of torment inflicted on them by the hideous headmaster of the Alta Academy. To my way of thinking, Warren inflicted a slow and tortuous death on Clayne and David just as sure as if he had plunged a knife into their chests.

The shy and awkward principal's extreme fear of girls had not improved as he matured. The situation was finally addressed through someone else's intervention, and it was remarkably similar to the experience of Uncle Roy when he had been a young and single future leader of the FLDS. Warren chronicled what happened.

"When I was eleven, I thought I would never get married. At seventeen, I was sure of it. I got up to twenty-three . . . and I thought, 'Oh, well.' Then father walked down to my bedroom. Knock, knock, knock. He said, 'Uncle Roy wants you to get married.'"

His brother, Lyle, rushed excitedly into the room to offer congratulations. "Warren! Do you know who you are marrying? . . . She is a dish!"

His first wife was a beautiful girl he didn't even know. He learned later that her name was Annette Barlow. She was from an independent polygamist clan, and it was an arranged marriage, almost politically feudal in its roots, a joining of the clans. Love was unnecessary. Annette was just the first of his many brides, and her sister Barbara loomed in the wings.

By the time of the rapes of his nephews, Warren was married to two women. Strangely enough, he seemed to feel no remorse; he could go home after raping a little boy and have a calm Sunday family dinner.

CHAPTER 10

Coup

Rulon Jeffs was an imposing figure: tall, supremely confident, charismatic and commanding. "If we had ten men like you with us, we would turn this world upside down," the old prophet John Y. Barlow had written to his protégé almost forty-five years earlier. With dark hair that he combed back in a suave pompadour, Rulon was also fastidious and vain, spending long periods before a mirror, re-knotting his tie over and over to get it just right before stepping outside of his home.

Following the death of Uncle Roy in 1986, Rulon was the sole authority over everything in the FLDS—the "Keyholder, the Prophet, and Mouthpiece of God." In the FLDS, being recognized as the mouthpiece of God on earth automatically quelled any dissent, for who can argue with God? The blind obedience that was hammered daily into the membership, combined with his financial savvy, allowed Jeffs—unlike his followers—complete freedom to do as he wished. But as the British historian Lord Acton wrote, "Power tends to corrupt, and absolute power corrupts absolutely." It was a perfect description of Rulon Jeffs. Simmering just beneath that smooth surface, the prophet was a philanderer, a fraud, and a drunk.

He made sure that alcohol was usually nearby. Several of his grandchildren and people close to him told me that during family get-togethers, kids were warned, "Don't touch Grandfather's water!" Of course, that only heightened their curiosity and compelled them to sneak a sip. Most never went back for a second sampling. The ever-present "glass of water" was actually a tumbler of vodka. At dinners, he frequently would consume glasses of wine. As his secret drinking became more noticeable, the prophet sought to condone it by redefining a long-standing Mormon doctrine known as the Word of Wisdom. Rulon declared the Word was only a guide, and that drinking, in moderation, was acceptable. That allowed him to put his stamp of approval on his own alcoholism. I was surprised to discover that many FLDS members have followed his example, resulting in a culture of closet drunks who deceitfully hide their alcoholism from their neighbors.

Fueled by alcohol and unlimited power, Rulon Jeffs began to indulge his deviant urges with abandon. During his sermons, he would focus his attention on a pretty girl out in the congregation and later, while everyone filed out at the close of services, he would give her hand three gentle squeezes. That was the signal for her family to prepare this daughter for marriage to him. Eventually, he would have between fifty and sixty brides.

The families did not object. Most young girls considered it an honor to marry the prophet, and it meant added prestige for her mother and father. Truly fortunate families might have several daughters in Rulon's stable. Any hesitancy on the part of the inductee or her family would be looked upon as questioning the will of God and would result in severe reprisals, not only by church leaders but also by neighbors, friends, and other members of the extended family.

But even the easy harvesting of new wives to do his bidding was not enough to tame Rulon Jeffs's compulsions.

A ranking member of the church who eventually left the FLDS described for me what happened when he caught one of his daughters with a neighbor boy in the back of his van. What had been taking place was apparent by their lack of clothing. The distraught father believed that in order to confess and repent, the youngsters should seek the counsel of the prophet. "Rulon first spoke with my daughter, alone, then summoned the young man to hear his version of the transgression," the father recounted to me. "I had never imagined him using such language, graphically referring to body parts and sex acts unnecessarily by their common names and trying to extract all of the sordid details, over and over again."

The flustered parent listened in astonishment as Rulon quizzed the children, asking for explicit details about sexual positions and intimacies that the parent himself didn't even know existed, having been raised with the church's strict teaching that sexual contact was solely for the purpose of procreation. As the interview progressed, Rulon became more and more excited, "as if he was on drugs or something," and had a wild look in his eyes, "like he was on a high." The father's sadness over his daughter's sexual transgression turned to disgust at the lewd interrogation, and his own faith wavered. He began exploring thoughts of leaving the church rather than follow such a perverted prophet.

No matter what Rulon did, he was able to rationalize his disturbing behavior to his obedient followers; it was he who was really the one suffering—sacrificing himself before God in order to protect and prepare them for the imminent day when the world would end. They could either be lifted up with the righteous or burn with the wicked. "We are living in that great and dreadful day, the great day of the Lord when all the prophecies will be fulfilled concerning the last days, the dreadful day because of the judgments that must come, and will come to try our people," he would bellow, looking straight into their fearful hearts. "They are coming upon the House of God first." Such prophecies of doom often poured from "God's mouthpiece."

In addition to performing hundreds of marriages, Rulon started reshuffling FLDS families. He would take wives from men whom he deemed unworthy and place them instead with men he decided had the ability to lead new concubines to the celestial kingdom. He performed this pimping and pandering for his favorites without fear or hesitation. He did not ask the people involved what they thought. Even Warren was amazed. "We had never seen anything like it," he said.

A shift in the center of power was taking place within the FLDS. Although people not born into the faith were never welcome, the church had grown substantially over the years through the multiple wives who kept producing children. In Salt Lake City, when the flock became too numerous to continue meeting in Rulon's living room, they met in the more spacious rooms of the Alta Academy.

Although the Jeffses remained in Salt Lake City, the population was growing even faster down in Short Creek, and the faithful there built the LeRoy S. Johnson Meeting House, a sparkling structure of 42,000 square feet with an ornate pulpit area and an organ to supply the music for up to four thousand people.

The splinter group finally took a name in 1991, when leaders of the First Ward congregation founded a corporation, and chose a name that virtually parroted that of the mainstream Mormon Church, creating a great deal of confusion that continues to this day.

The Church of Jesus Christ of Latter-day Saints—the mainstream LDS Church—has nothing to do with the polygamous sect. Nevertheless, the breakaway group made some minor changes to the name and the Fundamentalist Church of Jesus Christ of Latter-Day Saints, the FLDS, was born.

In many other religions that have broken from an established church, such as when Martin Luther led his followers away from Catholicism, the new movement attempts to separate itself from original ideology or doctrine. However, the ragtag group of excommunicated fundamentalists in Short Creek did just the opposite. The adherents to polygamy considered themselves to be living according to a higher spiritual calling than the regular Mormon faith. They claimed the mother church had drifted from its true purpose, leaving the FLDS as the true Mormons. At one end of the spectrum, the fundamentalists try to convince people that they are Mormons, thus riding the coattails of LDS legitimacy. At the same time, they denounce the mainstream church as being filled with heretics. On any given day, whether they claim to be true Mormons or Mormon-haters depends upon what agenda they happen to be promoting at the time.

By the time of Rulon's ascension in 1986, the FLDS was firmly under one-man rule. The advisory council created in the formative years to put checks and balances on the actions of the president had been reduced to a "First Presidency" made up of the president (Rulon) and his first and second counselors, Parley J. Harker and Fred Jessop. The two ancient men held no real power.

Unofficially and behind the scenes, Rulon's son Warren had become his father's closest advisor, although he held no office within the church.

He was merely the school principal in Salt Lake City, but he held the confidence of the prophet.

Others spoke. Warren listened. He knew the people, the inside workings of the church, and could spout scripture and give trainings with the best of them. He carefully followed his father's path and step-by-step became the power behind the throne while his father savored the good life.

Rulon's appetites were insatiable. He had dozens of women, indulged freely in alcohol, and he was also a glutton, making almost daily trips to the home of his friend Ron Rohbock, who laid out feasts of rich foods accompanied by overflowing glasses of homemade wine from Rohbock's excellent vineyards. The aging patriarch began to put on weight, and by the time he realized his health was in trouble, it was already too late.

In 1997, Uncle Rulon suffered a series of minor strokes, and the following year, he was incapacitated by a major one. That same year, First Counselor Parley Harker died, and Warren readily stepped into that vacated leadership position. With his father crippled, Harker dead, and Second Counselor Fred Jessop old and compliant, Warren grabbed the reins. Many members who lived down in the Crick, primarily in the large Barlow clan, grumbled about this usurpation of power, but none stepped up to contest Rulon's favored son up in Salt Lake City.

After all, the prophet wasn't dead, so he was still the prophet. They remembered how Uncle Roy had been laid low for years by illness, only to return to power. Rulon might recover.

It took only about a month before Warren publicly flexed his new muscle by announcing with cold certainty, "My father has the mental capacity of a child. I am now my father's mouthpiece."

Although his statement carried no legal standing within the church, it served to cap an audacious coup that could only have worked among a subservient people trained in total obedience.

Since everyone in the faith already acknowledged that Rulon was "God's mouthpiece on earth," and Warren was now his father's mouthpiece, sitting on his bed and talking with him daily, the implication was clear: God was now communicating directly with Warren through the broken vessel that was Rulon.

The great Uncle Roy had declared that, "Only one man at a time holds the keys and power of the sealing power, and those who act during his administration are only acting under a delegated authority." That provided Warren with plenty of cover to exert control without actually having to fight for leadership. After all, he was only helping his ailing, revered father. He remained polite and respectful in his dealings, and still did what he wanted, bulldozing his way through all obstacles by claiming that "Father" was still calling the shots. He actually took over Rulon's big desk, leaving no question about who was really in charge.

Rulon required constant care, and the handling of those personal needs was up to his doctors and his many wives. Warren decreed that seclusion was necessary to protect his father from the troubles and burdens of daily life and leadership. He had become an invalid confined to his bed, with great trouble articulating words, and then dementia set in due to brain damage caused by the stroke. Warren would translate for him.

From Rulon's bedroom, the first counselor issued a series of dire pronouncements that guaranteed the followers would look to him for guidance: The world was coming to an end!

God would lift up the FLDS faithful, scour the world with fire, and then replace the chosen ones back down safely in the holy city of Zion, Warren declared. The date was set for September 1998, but when that came and went without incident, it was reset for October, which was another failure. A new forecast naming December as the time of reckoning also did not work out, but that did not stop Warren from continuing the drumbeat of doom, insisting the predictions came from his father. With the FLDS penchant for anniversaries, another, more certain end-of-the-world date was set for June 12, 1999, which would mark the 111th birthday of the late Uncle Roy.

It was a big day in Short Creek, and at dawn, thousands of the faithful crowded into the meeting house for a special service. After a prayer circle, they trekked over to Cottonwood Park. All day long they waited, along with the groceries that were to sustain them during the unknown temporary time that they would be up in heaven. Nothing happened. Warren said his father was disappointed that the believers still were not strong enough in their faith to deserve this blessing.

There was hope, however, because God was ready to grant them yet another chance. The close of the twentieth century was at hand, so they had been given another six months to sort out their behavior. If they strengthened their beliefs, the new millennium could really be the end of the planet, spelling death and destruction for everyone who was not a member in good standing of the FLDS church. This series of cataclysmic pronouncements was successful in one sense, however: it distracted the faithful from anything as insignificant as worrying about the ambitious Warren. They apparently never saw the pattern.

CHAPTER 11

Diversity

Shortly after being hired to investigate the FLDS in early 2004, I received a disconcerting phone call from Carson Barlow, one of Warren Jeffs's more ardent supporters and a business associate from my construction days. We had always had an affable relationship and I thought highly of him as a hard-working family man. But he had recently been kicked out of the church, losing everything he had, and I could not imagine the inner turmoil he must be enduring. Carson was furious—but not with Warren; with me. "I'm just warning you. Get off the case or you are going to get hurt." Getting a little testy, I asked if it would be him or Warren Jeffs administering the hurt. My bitter, broken friend kept ranting until I asked why he was still following a madman. The shock of my question quieted him for a moment, then in a quavering voice that sounded ready to cry, he said, "I reverence Warren Jeffs the same as I do God."

I had gotten to know special agents in the Salt Lake City office of the FBI, and I gave them a taped copy of the thinly veiled threat from Barlow. After my initial introduction to Short Creek, I was already in the habit of keeping them informed of what was happening, and of notifying them in advance when I was heading down to the Crick, just in case. I wasn't worried about some conspiracy within the church leadership to take me out, but a troubled member who had been cast out of the FLDS just might try something on his own in order to get back into the good graces of the prophet. It was better to be careful than sorry.

Barlow would have been much more upset had he known what we were really doing.

Normally, a lawsuit seeks justice in the form of monetary compensation for wrongs committed against the plaintiffs. This case was different. Our clients were not after money. Most just wanted to renew the relationship with their parents and siblings instead of being forced to live as sinful outcasts. If that could not be accomplished, then they hoped to eliminate or reduce the possibility that other young men and women would be subjected to the pain, humiliation, and loss they had endured.

Not all of them had been kicked out just for having a shirt button undone; the FLDS burrowed much deeper than that. A number of them had left home of their own accord, although out of fear that if they did not go away peacefully, something terrible would befall the family—a sister might be married off to an old lecher, or the parents would lose their home. It was not that they were wicked bad apples; they just ran out of options. It was a subtle but highly effective form of extortion.

So our lawsuits would not be just the usual attack on polygamy; in fact, polygamy had nothing to do with it. We were going after Warren and the FLDS and the United Effort Plan in civil court but would name them as defendants for criminal acts: the rape of Brent Jeffs, and racketeering violations under the Utah version of the federal RICO statutes (spelled out in the Racketeer Influenced and Corrupt Organizations Act of 1970). The Feds had created this tool to fight the Mafia; now it could be used in the lawsuits against the FLDS, which I considered to be a criminal organization.

For many of the Lost Boys, the only beacon of help was the Diversity Foundation and an extraordinarily kind man by the name of Dan Fischer, a brother of my new client, Shem Fischer. Dan had once been a polygamist with three wives, but he had abandoned the practice and left the FLDS fold more than a decade before we met. He now had only one wife, but as honor dictated, he continued to help support the other two. During that decade, Fischer had become financially successful by inventing and patenting teeth-whitening systems, and he had created a nonprofit organization known as Smiles for Diversity. The organization recruited dentists and orthopedic surgeons to fix the teeth of children in Third World countries.

Because of Dan's reputation for helping people, desperate Lost Boys began finding their way to his doorstep. With Dan, they didn't have to explain; he understood what they had been through and wanted to help. At first, he fed and clothed the shattered youngsters and gave them a safe place to sleep, and when all of the bedrooms of his home were filled, he converted a big maintenance garage into apartments for extra capacity. He helped them gain a sorely needed education and life skills so they could begin to understand the outside world, become independent, and move on.

When the constant exodus of boys being exiled from their FLDS homes eventually got too big for Fischer to rescue them all on his own, he turned Smiles for Diversity into the more wide-ranging Diversity Foundation. An untold number of lives—hundreds, and perhaps thousands—have been put back together through the food, lodging, educational opportunities, and friendship provided through Diversity, under the leadership of Dan and Aleena Fischer.

For aiding the castaways and exposing many abuses within the fundamentalist culture, the FLDS and its controlling hierarchy hated Dan Fischer with a special passion. Dan refused to reciprocate the animosity, despite an FLDS campaign of smears against him. The board of directors of the Diversity Foundation was not as forgiving. They decided that something stronger was needed from a legal standpoint to protect the children, and they hired Baltimore attorney Joanne Suder.

My job for her was case preparation and process serving. The intense secrecy of the FLDS would make proving the case extremely difficult, but not impossible. There were scores of victims and eyewitnesses; I knew the evidence was out there, and I intended to find it.

Joanne warned me the investigation would be a wide-ranging one that would require meticulous work, and also that she hated surprises. Like all of the attorneys with whom I work, she demanded that an investigator provide all the facts, good or bad. It is always a relief for me to hear that; it saves me from having to turn down the case. No matter what is found, it is always imperative to keep an open mind to all possibilities. In the words of Sherlock Holmes: When you have eliminated the impossible, whatever remains, *however improbable*, must be the truth.

However, professional objectivity did not mean that I was not personally shocked and appalled by things that would come to light in the course
of my investigation, such as Warren raping children, child abandonment
and neglect, and the ordeals of underage brides and families being ruined.
I was not devoid of an opinion; very much to the contrary. But I draw a
firm line between personal views and professional responsibility.

Since Joanne was operating out of Baltimore, she needed an on-site attorney who could act as local counsel. She brought aboard prominent
Salt Lake City lawyer Patrick A. Shea. He was a graduate of Stanford
University, a Rhodes scholar, held a law degree from Harvard, and was
politically connected. Shea had run unsuccessfully for both governor and
senator in Utah and had served as head of the Bureau of Land Management under President Bill Clinton. Since returning to Utah from Washington, he had taught at colleges and universities and had written extensively
on legal matters.

Shea had his own private investigator, a local in Salt Lake City, and
we got together to make sure that I had everything that he did. I found
the guy to be a TV-style P.I., who regaled me with tales of rich and famous clients and pointed out his ten-thousand-dollar camera over here
and his ten-thousand-dollar computer over there. Everything in his office
apparently cost ten thousand dollars. I didn't care. What did he actually
have on the case? He handed over a three-ring binder enclosed around an
inch of paper. Most of the material was straight off the Internet, available
to anybody who knew how to type. The P.I. was excited. "This is going
to be a big case. Jon Krakauer is on it."

"Who?" Never having paid much attention to famous people or bestseller lists, I wasn't even sure who Krakauer was. This was a time for hard,
sweaty digging, and I had too much legwork to do to be getting involved
with celebrities.

He gave me a disbelieving look. "He's just one of the top five authors in
the country. Jon is going to pick me up in a private jet, and we're going to go
find Warren." The man apparently was not really familiar with Krakauer.
As I would later learn, jets and celebrities weren't Krakauer's thing any
more than they were mine.

Jon Krakauer had been returning from a climbing trip in 1999 when he stopped for gas near Short Creek and noticed the settlement on the other side of the highway, a hazy hodgepodge of half-built houses and trailers in the distance. It seemed like something out of a Steinbeck novel. Curious, Krakauer decided to take a closer look.

Crossing over the highway and going into town, he quickly began to realize that he had wandered into a different kind of place. Women working in their vegetable gardens were covered from their necks to their ankles in pioneer-style dresses that reminded him of Muslim burqas. All of the men wore long sleeves and their collars buttoned tight, and both men and women wore the same cheap sneakers. Then out of nowhere, a large 4×4 pickup with darkly tinted windows loomed into his rear-view mirror and began aggressively tailing him.

Krakauer is an athletic outdoorsman who loves to explore new places and is not easily spooked; he had climbed Mount Everest and had managed (barely) to make it off the mountain with his life. However, any uninvited stranger is likely to be unnerved by a Short Creek welcome. Krakauer couldn't shake the vigilantes following him and they became increasingly aggressive. The globe-trotting author had never experienced anything like it, at least not in this country, and he later described that first confrontation with the FLDS as having "scared the shit out of me." He left town in a hurry.

Since there is nobody to call for help in Short Creek, Krakauer drove on until he found a National Park ranger and reported what had happened. The ranger shrugged it off. "You were in Short Creek, the largest polygamist community in the country. That's the way it's been out there forever," he explained.

Krakauer thought a lot about the desert town as he finished the long drive to his home in Colorado. Then he did some research into the FLDS Church and realized he had stumbled onto some prime material for his next book. Krakauer spent the next four years investigating and writing *Under the Banner of Heaven*, the story of a couple of fundamentalist religious zealots who had stabbed a woman and her baby to death, believing that God had commanded them to commit the murders. The bestselling book would portray Short Creek as it really was, a place without joy that is run by a Taliban-style theocracy. It might never have been written if the xenophobic people of Short Creek had not run him out of town.

CHAPTER 12

Blood Atonement

The longed-for end-of-the-millennium day of doom finally arrived, and once again, nothing happened. Word came again from the saddened prophet in Salt Lake City, relayed through his son, that the people were still too sinful to be worthy of entering God's sight.

Again, they accepted the explanation. No matter what went wrong, the membership was at fault and the poor, stricken prophet would no doubt have to suffer even harsher consequences to atone for their sinfulness. The end-of-the-world date was recast once more, this time for 2002, when gentiles from all over the world would descend on Utah for the Winter Olympics based in Salt Lake City.

Meanwhile, the world lived on, and so did the stricken Uncle Rulon, with his scheming son at his side.

Rulon had been something of a diplomat who had often ventured forth from Salt Lake City to visit the flock in Short Creek and in Canada. Some trips would be made aboard a chartered jet, others in luxury cars or a large mobile home, and after his mix of strokes, he traveled in a long white Lincoln Town Car towing a portable toilet on a trailer.

The autocratic Warren lacked such diplomatic skills, but he was a shrewd politician who could count noses. Only a few hundred FLDS members still remained in Salt Lake, while thousands resided in Short Creek. If Warren was to consolidate his power and fight off future challengers, he needed to be nearer the heartbeat of the religion; a move to Short Creek would be required. Luckily, the Lord had given everyone an additional two years to prepare for Armageddon, which was plenty of time for him to engineer an exodus.

All FLDS members in Salt Lake City were told to sell their homes and businesses, even if it meant taking substantial financial losses, to go into debt, to max out their credit cards because they would never have to repay them anyway, and herd together down in Short Creek. Alta Academy was closed, shuttered, and sold.

One of my sources, Debra Dockstader, who eventually bolted from the religion, recalled for me how her family had been ruined by that decision. Her husband and his three wives had docilely obeyed the order, gathered their children, sold everything, run up debt, and moved from their nice house in Salt Lake to a mouse-infested singlewide mobile home in Short Creek, where they lived crammed together and destitute. Such was not the case for the Jeffses. Rulon and Warren moved into a spacious new walled compound that was built for them covering an entire city block in Hildale, on the Utah side of the Crick.

The overall effect of the FLDS abandonment of Salt Lake City was to slide the members even farther away from the rest of civilization and build a wall of empty miles between themselves and the rest of America. Warren settled in and got back to solidifying his position. He was the first counselor, but he quietly chafed at the popularity enjoyed by the second counselor, the amiable Fred Jessop, the bishop of Short Creek. Uncle Fred had accumulated a lot of influence during his long lifetime; and he was a calm listening post in sharp contrast to the mercurial Warren, who had to consider Fred a potential rival as a successor to Uncle Rulon. A formal photograph of the three men from that time shows Rulon seated in the middle, with Uncle Fred to his left, while at the prophet's right hand sat Warren, the unquestioned arbiter of all affairs. Fred would prove to be no match for the vigorous, much younger Warren.

A more serious challenger, in Warren's mind, was Winston Blackmore, the bishop of the 1,000-person FLDS enclave up in Bountiful, British Columbia, just over the U.S.-Canadian border and about 900 miles north of Short Creek. Blackmore had an almost rock-star status within the religion, in which he was known as "Uncle Wink." With a large family of his own, an unshakeable faith, an outgoing personality, and a loyal following, he tried to live as an example of what he believed the FLDS was really all about. In sharp contrast to the Jeffses, Bishop Blackmore eschewed any extravagant lifestyle.

Winston had been a close friend of Uncle Rulon for many years, and he answered only to the prophet. He was not about to give in to Warren's strong-arm tactics. The two men were on a collision course that would play out across many months, and the issue was one of life or death for a teenage girl.

Most FLDS members and leaders are superstitious to the point of mysticism in their beliefs. Legends and old wives' tales are passed down among families as truths. Poultices are preferred to doctors, and the members even have a formal ritual for the blessing of the brakes of their pickup trucks. Taking an archaic notion out of history and molding it to suit their skewed agenda is common practice. One of the most brutal elements handed down over the generations, "blood atonement,"—the doctrine that states a sinner must pay for his or her offense by shedding his or her own blood—has been around for many years. I believe it is still practiced today within the FLDS.

More than two decades earlier, in a legal action to strip Short Creek marshal Sam Barlow of his badge, polygamist Harold Blackmore had sworn in an affidavit:

> While being instructed in our duties and responsibilities, we were taught the "Divine Law of Retribution," commonly called "Blood Atonement." I listened to Guy H. Musser teach this doctrine with a quivering and doomful voice to a large assembly of men as follows: "You brethren, you have got to learn to give strict obedience to every request made of you by this priesthood council. You have to prepare yourselves to the point where you will shed the blood of any one of your brethren if we tell you to for the sake of his salvation as atonement for his sins and to prove your faithfulness."
>
> . . . I have listened to Rulon T. Jeffs . . . preach along the same line with passionate fervor:—"you brethren, you have got to learn to submit and take direction. You have got to learn to obey anything we tell you to do without the slightest mental reservation—right or wrong!"

Without exception, every single former FLDS person I have interviewed concerning the practice has expressed the unequivocal belief that it is considered a true principle of the religion. By the same token, I have yet to talk to anyone who has actually witnessed such a bloodletting. But I believe, just as the Utah attorney general's office did, that Warren Jeffs wanted, but failed, to have a father bring his daughter home and face death in a religious ritual in the year 2000.

That they totally believed in the bizarre ritual is beyond doubt. A widow of Rulon Jeffs described for me a time that she and one of her sister-wives came across a passage they did not understand while studying a book that Rulon had written, "Purity in the New and Everlasting Covenant of Marriage." It was mandatory reading for all wives, and in it, Rulon claimed that Brigham Young had announced in a sermon more than a century earlier that some sins were so heinous that even the atonement of the Savior was insufficient to pardon the transgressor and gain salvation. The only possible remedy that might bring redemption would be for the offender to shed his or her own blood.

Rulon wrote that blood atonement was an act of love and duty. He left no doubt that he was not talking about pricking a finger, but about murder. "I could refer you to plenty of instances where men have been righteously slain, in order to atone for their sins. I have seen scores and hundreds of people for whom there would have been a chance [for salvation] if their lives had been taken and their blood spilled on the ground as a smoking incense to the Almighty, but who are now angels to the devil, until our elder brother Jesus Christ raises them up—conquers death, hell and the grave. I have known a great many men who have left this Church for whom there is no chance whatever for exaltation, but if their blood had been spilled, it would have been better for them . . . This is loving your neighbor as yourselves; if he needs help, help him; and if he wants salvation and it is necessary to spill his blood on the earth in order that he may be saved, spill it."

This was heady material for the two wives. Fortunately, while they sat puzzling over the book on the stairs inside Rulon's home, Warren came walking past and they asked if he knew anything about it. Yes, he replied. It was "a true and correct principle." He not only endorsed it, he described his vision of the ritual for them in frightening detail.

The sinner had to be bound to an altar of stone, preferably in a sacred place such as a temple. A rope of a specific size would be blessed by a ritualistic prayer, and then tied to certain areas of the body in the manner

with which Abraham lashed down his son Isaac when God had commanded Abraham to slay the boy as an offering.

As he warmed to the impromptu lecture, Warren told the women that
everything was done in accordance with holy ordinances, and each step
of the process had a special meaning. For instance, special ropes and
knots were required, and the event should be done in a basement to sig-
nify the subject rising from the terrestrial kingdom and overcoming hell.

When the subject was secure, a mask was placed over the face of
the condemned person, and a special knife was used to cut the throat
of the victim in a proscribed manner. After that, some of the blood was
saved to be drunk by priesthood members in attendance, to seal their
oaths to keep the sacred procedure a secret, even if it meant their own lives.
The rest of the blood was to be burned so that the smoke could rise to the
heavens as a burnt offering and hopefully be accepted there by God.

He ended the hair-raising lesson by saying it had to be kept a strict
secret because the outside world would not understand and would try to
stop the practice if it became known.

I got to know Winston Blackmore during the Lost Boys investigation,
and he became one of my most knowledgeable guides into figuring out
what made Warren Jeffs tick. He would personally tell me the story of a
troubled girl named Vanessa Rohbock, a daughter of Uncle Rulon's old
dining and drinking buddy Ron Rohbock.

She had been given without her consent to be the third wife of a man in
Short Creek. "I about died," she had confided to Blackmore. "I was only
sixteen and I didn't want to marry that guy, but I was told that if I did
not do it, there would be nothing more for me . . . ever. What could I do?
When my mouth said 'I do' my heart was screaming 'NO! NO! NO!'"

She ran away to stay with a sister who had already been expelled from
the FLDS, then had second thoughts and returned to her father's home.
Soon, she began to sneak away again to meet a boyfriend about her own
age. He would turn off the lights of his truck and coast up to the house,
where Vanessa would jump in, and they would go share a pizza. The
couple was followed one night, caught, and hauled before First Counselor Warren Jeffs. He decided that since Vanessa was a married woman,
even though she had not wanted to wed, she must bear total blame. It

was decided to let her influential father, Ron Rohbock, take her up to Canada for a cooling-off period. The extraordinarily lenient decision was a good example of the benefits that can accrue to a loyalist within the inner circle.

Warren telephoned Winston Blackmore to tell him the teenager would be coming for a temporary visit, adding that she was on antidepressants and had to be considered suicidal. Blackmore agreed to take her in, and soon Vanessa responded to the distancing of herself from the tumultuous situation in Short Creek. She was persuasive enough in her apology that Uncle Rulon extended a further favor to his friend Ron and gave Winston Blackmore permission to forgive the girl's sins through rebaptism, which Winston did.

Vanessa, now with a clean slate, then upset everything by announcing that she wanted to get married again, but to her boyfriend, someone of her own choosing. Warren exploded in rage during a heated telephone call to Blackmore. "There it is!" Warren said. "I told Father, 'If you let this girl get rebaptized, then the next thing she will want to do is get remarried, and there it is.'" He could not overturn Rulon's decision to forgive her, but he had a different idea. "Her baptism did not work," Warren ordered. "She shall not be remarried. There is nothing left for her to do but to come [back] and have her blood shed for the remission of her sins! You are instructed to tell her to gather up her things and to go away. You and Ron [Vanessa's father] are instructed to pray night and day for the Lord to destroy her from the face of the earth!"

Warren was condemning the girl to death. "No trial, no mercy, no defense, and all while Uncle Rulon was in his bed and asleep," Winston recalled for me in a halting voice. The horrified Blackmore would have no part of it.

Rohbock showed up in Canada, under a strict order from Warren to retrieve his daughter. "Ron Rohbock was the meanest man I've ever met," Blackmore told me. "He said that he was the one who had brought Vanessa into this world and it was his priesthood duty to take her out of this world. He was ordered to love his daughter enough to carry out the edict in order for her to have a chance at salvation." Blackmore refused to hand the child over for retribution. He kept her secreted away in a distant house, and her father returned empty-handed to Short Creek.

The confrontation escalated as time passed, and Warren sent Rohbock back to Canada two more times, including a trip on which he was backed up by Warren's brother, Leroy Jeffs. Blackmore not only refused their demands, but notified the Royal Canadian Mounted Police, which contacted the FBI and the Utah attorney general's office. The word went out: If Warren did not stop this mad crusade against the child, the law would intervene. Warren backed off, but he never forgot.

Vanessa eventually married the boy she originally wanted, and against all logic, they settled in Short Creek. I have seen that same decision made repeatedly by outcasts, because it is so difficult for residents to give up the only way of life they have ever known. Blackmore observed that so much official attention had been focused on her situation that Vanessa probably was the safest woman in town.

Warren Jeffs would later insist that his words had been misunderstood. However, I am convinced that without the intervention of Winston Blackmore, Vanessa would have been sacrificed in a "blood atonement" ritual.

Ron Rohbock's failure to deliver his daughter for punishment earned him a place on Warren's blacklist. As far as Warren was concerned, his father's old buddy was expendable. Punishment would be years in coming, but when it came, Warren would destroy Rohbock.

CHAPTER 13

Death in the Family

The mind of Rulon Jeffs wandered, spinning off in the middle of conversations onto subjects as arcane as how his own father used to call him "Rudy Pergucious." Warren's quicksilver brain took up the slack. As the effects of the strokes and dementia continued to marginalize Rulon, Warren was the puppet-master, able to get his father to do anything.

Warren would occasionally take his feeble father to the meeting house to preside over a church service. A microphone would be rigged around the neck of the seated old man, then Warren would whine out a long sermon and graciously turn to Rulon and say, "Let's hear what Father is thinking. We would like to turn the time over to the Prophet to hear the word of God." Silence would smother the crowd for long minutes while Rulon, mouth agape, would struggle to put together some words, eventually blurting out some accusation such as, "The judgments of God are upon you! Do you understand?" To which the congregation would respond with a unanimous, *"Yeesss!"*

The father definitely still had usefulness in Warren's plans. In one of his boldest moves, Warren persuaded Rulon to give him the management of the United Effort Plan Trust. Warren personally supervised the revision of the trust documents, then steadied the feeble old man's hand as he signed away his authority. That meant all of the UEP holdings, an avalanche of assets and property in the United States and Canada, now shifted to Warren's direct control. A required board of trustees was made up of hand-picked loyalists, but he made all of the decisions and held veto power. Millions of dollars were generated annually, and it all would be administered by Warren.

All comments about business were carefully phrased by Warren to get Rulon to make the right choices. In one of his more lucid moments, Rulon apparently realized that he no longer ran the empire. He broke down at dinner, pounded his fist on the table, and shouted, "I want my job back!" Warren swiftly soothed him. It was too late for Rulon. Warren had control, and he never gave up anything.

Perhaps to calm murmurs from dissidents that he wanted to take over everything officially, Warren spread a secret: Rulon was going to live for hundreds of years to come. Even Rulon had not known about this until the thought came tumbling out of Warren's rambling imagination. In an interview with me, one FLDS member described paying a visit to the ailing old man one day. The ever-present Warren asked if the visitor would like to hear of a vision that Rulon had experienced. "Sure," said the visitor, and Warren pulled out a little notepad that he scribbled in. At 2:30 one morning, said Warren, his father awakened him to describe a vision in which the Prophet Rulon had seen a beautiful large valley filled with young women and children, and he had understood it to be his own future. The vision placed the valley more than three hundred years in the future and Rulon was to reach it without ever tasting death.

It was such a startling idea that Uncle Rulon whispered, "Did I say that? I don't remember a thing of it." The visitor then watched in astonishment as other church officials came and went, and Warren related the same fable of longevity to each in turn. His father continued to say he didn't remember anything of the sort.

"Very soon, that was all that Warren wanted to talk about," the visitor confided. "We heard it in church, we heard it in private, and there soon became a great fervor." The big lie, relentlessly pounded home by Warren, became accepted as truth. That was when Warren began thrusting young girls upon Rulon, allegedly to make sure that the prophet would have the "ladies" needed to procreate with him through the coming centuries. In reality, Warren had a much different plan in mind, one that only he knew. Until the time was ripe to unveil it, marrying the girls to Rulon would remove them from the market of brides available for other men.

While his mind might be slipping, the stroke-crippled Rulon still had a sexual appetite, or at least imagined that he did, at ninety-two years of age. Sometimes, a new wife would be shocked to get a wet French kiss from the old man after the evening meal. When one girl proved reluctant to comply with the elderly Rulon's wish for some unconventional sex, Warren set her straight in a hurry: God's command was to "give yourself to your husband mind, body, and soul." In other words, do whatever Rulon wanted. To do otherwise would jeopardize her status as a mother in Zion. Since there is no such thing as sex education within the FLDS culture, when a young girl was placed with a depraved older man, it would usually be a confusing and crushing experience. She often had little or no idea about sex. Warren, acting as his father's self-appointed pimp, kept track of what was happening, and he would be furious if the concubines did not "keep sweet" and comply with the arranged sexual liaisons.

On a visit down south from Canada, Winston Blackmore was shocked at the fresh new crop of young girls ranging in age from twenty-one down to fifteen entering the Jeffs family. The bishop asked what was going on. Rulon replied, "I don't know. Ask Warren. Why am I being married to all these young girls?" Uncle Rulon married some of them while he was abed, delirious and unaware of what was happening. Marriage licenses, of course, were not required; simply a "sealing" ritual by someone in the church hierarchy who was authorized by the prophet to conduct the ceremony was sufficient. The ceremony had absolutely no legal standing, especially since it was usually performed in conjunction with the crimes of child abuse and/or polygamy.

Warren continued placing new spouses with his father up until only six months before the decrepit prophet's mortal ministry came to an end. It finally took a direct, desperate plea from Rulon himself—"No more wives!"—to make Warren stop.

On the surface, the purpose of the onslaught of marriages was to benefit Rulon. Underlying that fact was Warren maneuvering toward a completely different and sordid purpose: He intended to marry some of his stepmothers into his own growing harem when the old man passed away.

Another myth that has come down in FLDS lore is that the final destruction of the earth will be so complete that "not a yellow dog will be left to wag its tail." In the summer of 2001, that nightmare would come true in Short Creek.

With Uncle Rulon physically fading, Warren needed to test his own support. Was it real? Had his incessant "trainings" and sermons programmed the believers strongly enough to ensure that they would follow him automatically? Could he count on their blind obedience and loyalty when he took the ultimate leadership role? A horrible tragedy provided the opening for him to test them. Best of all, the target of this grim scheme was one of the rare gentile converts in their midst, who I will refer to as Mike, so not too many people in the Crick really cared much about what happened to him or his family. No matter how devout their beliefs, converts are never really accepted as anything more than second-class citizens.

In June 2001, a chained-up guard dog that was used for breeding attacked, mauled, and killed the family's baby boy. Soon afterward, at the meeting house, Uncle Fred Jessop told the congregants that Prophet Rulon had received a heavenly revelation that pets had no place in the Kingdom of God, not among the pure and clean people of the priesthood. Henceforth, no dogs would be allowed. Everyone understood that this was really Warren talking. Warren didn't like dogs.

Uncle Fred was passionate from the pulpit that day. Not giving up your pet would be an act of disobedience, proving that you lacked faith. Your standing in the priesthood would be in question, which could lead to expulsion from the church and community. Citizens of Short Creek would be given some time to rid themselves of their pets voluntarily, but after that, assigned crews of churchmen led by that peculiar pair of enforcers, Willie and Dee Jessop, would be called on to finish the job.

Local law would not be involved in the massacre. Although the cops were thoroughly in service to the FLDS, this nasty piece of work fell to the church's hooligans without badges. To be called to service in such a position was a rare opportunity for these men to distinguish themselves from the rank-and-file membership. They could move about the community and force compliance from the disobedient, which meant that now they were somebody!

When the grace period expired for people to have disposed of their pets, the gang came in to round up the dogs that had not been given away. They started with the strays, but soon they were snatching pets from the arms of their owners. Dee Jessop went through the streets like a destroying angel, fulfilling his macabre mission. Willie would often be parked in a conspicuous spot nearby to intervene if there was any backlash from a brokenhearted family member.

The captured dogs were driven in trucks out of town to the far side of a sylvan setting known as Berry Knoll, where dusk almost always brings a double sunset as the sun slides down two mountains that nearly touch at Canaan Gap. Not only is light magnified out there, but so is the sound. Residents of the Crick would hear the squeal of a pickup truck's tires on the pavement in town, then not long afterward would come the wail of a dog, as if through a megaphone, followed by a gunshot out by Berry Knoll.

Finally, the guns were deemed too noisy for the job and the killers came up with the idea of clamping jumper cables from the powerful batteries of big pickup trucks onto the animals to electrocute them. Instead of gunshots, the howls of the tortured dogs rent the night air.

There are no more dogs or cats to be found in Short Creek or other Jeffs-run FLDS strongholds to this day. For Warren Jeffs, it was a diabolical test of loyalty: If he could get people to surrender their pets to the executioner, he could continue pushing the envelope and demand even greater sacrifices. The ready-made scapegoat, Mike, was left to shoulder any emotional blame. After all, it was his dog and his child that had precipitated the drastic measures. Warren threw him out of the church and nobody cared.

Rulon Jeffs was aware throughout 2002 that he was barely clinging to life. One day as he shuffled along on his walk with a group of wives and children assisting him, the prophet told them he was tired of living, and the helpers would not be burdened with this escort duty much longer. He struck a fist on his chest and called out, "I am so sick of this decrepit body! When do I get to go?"

The answer was: not yet. He still had some usefulness for his heir apparent.

The reign of Winston Blackmore as the prophet's right-hand man in Canada ended abruptly with a single phone call from the ailing Rulon in the summer of 2002. Blackmore was in his truck with a visitor from Short Creek, Ezra Draper, who heard every word over the speakerphone, and Winston himself later confirmed the incident for me.

Winston was well aware that his old friend Rulon was no longer mentally stable, but although the old man stumbled as he groped for words, he laid down the law: Blackmore was dismissed as the bishop of Bountiful. He was instructed to surrender his wives, was removed as a UEP trustee, and was ordered to turn all of his business assets over to the UEP.

Draper said that after each pronouncement, there would be a pause in the conversation, and they could hear the voice of Warren Jeffs in the background coaching his father on what to say next. The old man would repeat those words verbatim. "Rulon Jeffs didn't even know who he was talking to," Draper recalled. "Warren told him what to say, sentence by sentence."

When Ezra Draper returned home to Short Creek, he feigned innocence and asked Warren how the dismissal of the Canadian bishop had gone. Warren beamed with pride. "Ezra, Father handled that situation all by himself."

The blood-atonement attempt involving Vanessa Rohback was a side issue by then, but Winston's defiance had been remembered by Warren. His revenge for that embarrassment was to engineer the removal of Blackmore as a potential rival for leadership of the FLDS. Warren later dispatched his "God Squad" enforcer Willie Jessop up to Canada to make sure that Winston understood that he no longer "held priesthood." Blackmore, though, was unafraid of the bully and refused to recognize Warren's claims of authority.

There was fallout anytime someone crossed Warren Jeffs, who kept track of every perceived trespass in his little notebook. He eventually expelled both Ezra Draper and his brother, David, and told them there was no hope of their getting back in. Ezra managed to leave with most of his family intact, but David was devastated at losing his family and everything he had. Ezra made a luncheon appointment to talk with his distraught brother, but David did not show up. His body was found in the wreckage of his truck at the bottom of Hurricane Mesa, about twenty miles from Short Creek, along with a suicide note. As Warren's appetite for power grew, so did the body count of devastated victims, both literally and figuratively.

That the end was near for Rulon was probably obvious to his scheming son; in fact, it couldn't have been going better if he had actually personally planned it that way.

Several years would pass before I was able to piece together the dramatic final sequence of events through personal interviews with people who were there, recordings of the services, and the descriptions detailed in Warren's Priesthood Record. It was a macabre glimpse into the final days of a religious monarch and the rise of his ambitious successor.

Rulon Timpson Jeffs finally died on September 8, 2002. He was rushed to the hospital in septic shock from an obstructed bowel and was in such dire condition that doctors estimated he had only a five-percent chance of survival if they performed surgery, and no chance at all without it. "It does not matter what they say, the Lord is in charge," Warren told his brother Isaac. The old man's blood pressure was very low, but suddenly it rose enough for the doctors to operate—a miracle. "We knew he was going to walk out of there. No question," said Isaac.

Rulon was grimacing on a respirator as the medical staff wheeled him to the operating theater aboard a gurney. When he was returned to the intensive care unit, his heart began to stutter. Family and friends knelt in prayer circles as CPR, then electric shock treatment, were performed. Warren was on his knees on the floor at his dying father's bedside. "I could not think of anything else but his renewal in this life. But as I witnessed his final breath and his heart stop, and I wanted to cry unto the Lord to intervene now, but the good Spirit whispered, 'Peace. This is the Lord's will.'"

Still, the actual death seemed to surprise almost everyone, as they waited patiently for Rulon to be renewed into his former youthful self. It had become a matter of faith that Rulon, as the living prophet, would be the one who would finally hand the keys of the kingdom over to the returned savior, Jesus Christ. In reality, all he did was die. And the keys were snatched away by his conniving son.

The legion of shaken wives had believed the promises made to them of eternal life, that Rulon would be changed in the twinkling of an eye back into his vibrant prime. God had raised the dead in the Scriptures; surely the prophet deserved the same blessing. "There was no doubt in my mind that he would just come back," one of the many widows told me. "God would touch him and he would be made young in every sense of the word. He would be able to walk around with us and know our names, and have time for us and things like that."

When Rulon was buried four days later, their faith still had not wavered. "At the funeral it was just so freaky and so hard," a wife remembered. "When they shut the casket for the last time, it was like . . . No, you can't do that! He's going to bang on it and say, 'What the hell are you guys doing?' We truly expected that."

With angelic sweetness, a choir of wives sang an original five-minute composition entitled "Our Prophet Is Caught Up," which included the words, "He shall come forth again to earth and lead his people on." Warren stood tall beside the grave, and some of the women said he was aglow with heavenly brightness.

His long wait for power was over.

CHAPTER 14

Stepmothers and Wives

Warren Jeffs wasted no time grieving for his father; he had a religion to run. It was also time to start cashing in on his aspirations, and his first item was taking the women he wanted from his father's harem. He stepped before a special leadership meeting two days after Rulon's death and coldly announced: "I'm here to tell you men, hands off my father's wives!"

He explained, "Now I understand what father was doing, building up his family, so I could carry on." He had first choice, and the rest would be reassigned to loyal men whom he selected—and who would then be stuck with the financial responsibility of caring for the less desirable wives and children.

By announcing his intention to wed many of his own stepmothers, he broke a taboo, which shook the entire FLDS. Many contended that it was a violation of the Biblical Law of Moses, which stated that a man shall not marry his father's wives. Those accusations led Warren to formulate rambling rationalizations and revelations from God, which he would dispense to the flock as needed, like scattering feed before chickens. "People are searching the history, and they can't quite match up the present situation with anything else," he said, according to a section of his Record.

If people did not understand his logic, it obviously was their fault because their hearts were dark. Opponents were warned that they were "treading down the path to apostasy" by criticizing his work toward the "celestialization of this earth." What he was really saying, in words cloaked in piety, was that opposing opinions would be dealt with swiftly and severely.

Many of Rulon's wives reeled at what they perceived to be incest, so Warren sweet-talked and perplexed them with revelations from beyond the grave. "Every one of you ladies, my mothers, are worth more than worlds to Father. Through you he will bring forth sons and daughters that will become gods here and in the spirit world, and those gods will create worlds upon worlds."

It was confusing. Warren had a way of speaking in tangled sentences that meant nothing, but slowly they understood that he intended to bed and have children by them because that was "Father's and God's will." He was speaking in the present tense, as if Rulon were standing in the room. Trained throughout their entire lives to be docile in the face of a man's authority, most eventually agreed.

One absolutely refused. "Lorraine" had been married to Rulon for seven years and was an anomaly among FLDS women. She had somehow managed to grow up with a mind of her own, and she was willing to challenge Warren's advances toward her and her sister-wives. She would not be bullied. Warren wanted this beautiful woman badly, but she was equally adamant about having nothing to do with him. Finally, in a fit of frustration and desperation, he glared at her with maniacal fierceness, wagged his bony index finger in her face, and promised, "I'm going to break you, young lady."

At that point, Lorraine knew her life would become a living hell if she did nothing to protect herself. That very evening, she decided to leave the FLDS rather than endure the punishment certain to come her way for refusing to marry the demented son of her late husband. Lorraine literally went over the wall of the Jeffs's compound and escaped.

Another special wife was Mary Fischer, the nurse and sister of Dan Fischer, who had constantly tended Rulon prior to his death. She knew everything about both Rulon and Warren, and Warren was concerned that Mary would turn against him, like her brothers Dan and Shem. He could not risk losing "Mother Mary" to the world and having her reveal her secrets to the authorities, so he persuaded her to marry him. Afterward, he kept her in hiding, virtually as a voluntary prisoner. She, like many other women, had become a victim of circumstance, and she had nowhere else to go. She would only emerge occasionally, when her nursing

skills were needed within the closed society, and then she would be ferreted off to a new hiding place to avoid detection.

Polygamy is the heart of FLDS doctrine, and Warren Jeffs was going
to see to it that he had more wives than anyone else, even if it meant
marrying his mothers. I have personally counted more than eighty wives,
and others peg the number at better than ninety. Within a few years of
seizing power, he would brag in a sermon before a huge gathering of
FLDS members that heavenly father had revealed to him that he would
have one hundred wives.

After throwing a fence around his stepmothers, Warren turned his attention to consolidating his leadership. He would later write, "All of the
people are asking, 'Who did Uncle Rulon appoint?' "

Warren acknowledged that within the governing body of the church,
there was nothing to show that he was the legitimate heir. The FLDS
has never had an organized right of succession—no rule book and no
protocol to fall back on—and so historically, an internal fight would
usually ensue when the top position came open. Warren knew that he
had to be smarter, faster, more ruthless, and quicker on his feet than any
rival.

His closest potential rival was the faithful Fred Jessop, the bishop of
Short Creek. Uncle Fred had been around a very long time, and had
earned a loyal base of followers. Dissident Flora Jessop, the daughter of
one of his half-brothers, described Uncle Fred in her book *Church of
Lies* as "a mover and a shaker in the FLDS and rich to boot."

During the reign of Rulon Jeffs, Uncle Fred handled affairs concerning the town, including the collection of church tithes, 10 percent of
everyone's income. The tall, quiet man had remained as the faithful second counselor without protest when Warren had usurped the position of
first counselor back in 1997.

Uncle Fred, however, was tragically flawed by something that would
never permit him to be the official leader of a cultish religion that ex-
pects men to be the fertile producers of squadrons of youngsters. He was
sterile. Physically unable to have kids of his own, Fred built his own large
family of reassigned wives and children, widows, and orphans. The
package was a stew with many ingredients, and the residents of Short

Creek loved him for being such a benevolent benefactor. Warren had to tread lightly in dealing with Uncle Fred.

According to the Priesthood Record, the two men had a private meeting in which Warren swore to follow Fred "if the Lord wants you to lead." Fred answered that God had given him no such instruction, but that he had somehow seen a vision of "Uncle Louis."

That would be Louis Barlow, the patriarch of a large and influential family in the Crick. This "vision" was unsettling news for Warren, who wanted to hear Uncle Fred declare undying support for him. Fred, in his nineties, probably just wanted to spend his last years in peace, not in a religious gang war. Under pressure, and knowing that he was no match for the conniving favorite son of the dead prophet, Fred wavered and promised to submit to whoever the Lord chose. Given my experience, I can imagine that the old pioneer was wise enough to realize that going up against Warren's ruthless ambitions would end up in a public bloodletting in which he would likely lose everything at a very vulnerable time in his life. Warren silently put old Louis Barlow on his private list of enemies to be dealt with at some future time.

Just putting Uncle Fred in his place was not going to be enough to persuade everyone to follow along. Warren needed witnesses if he was to cement his power play.

Although he did not trust her, Warren brought Mother Mary, Rulon's former wife and nurse who knew all of the secrets, to the pulpit during a meeting. She had been at the dying prophet's bedside night and day and had witnessed all the details of Rulon's last moments in mortality. Now totally dependent upon Warren for her existence, Mary dutifully testified that the prophet had indeed expressed a fervent wish that Warren follow him as the next leader. Women, however, have no standing in the FLDS, which weakened her testimony substantially, and the old-timers were grumbling that there was no priesthood authority to testify of Rulon's last wishes. Warren needed the backing of a priesthood man.

His brother Isaac assumed that task, and in the future, he would be richly rewarded for his choice. Isaac stepped forward and announced that all the way back in August of 2001, he had heard Rulon speak about Warren during a meeting, saying "The finger of the Lord is pointing to this man." Isaac further testified that as they drove home on that eventful day, he had heard Rulon tell Warren several times, "I want you to accept the presidency of this church to take my place." Isaac did not stop there. He emphasized that Rulon had repeated his decision about thirty times on that one day. Even when his wives and Isaac helped the prophet to the bathroom, the old man had closed his eyes, bowed his head, then looked at the wall and declared, "Warren is going to be the next leader of this people." Back in his bed, he said it again and again.

During the crucial weeks after the death of Rulon, Warren would repeatedly cite Isaac's testimony to justify his claim of FLDS leadership. He was careful not to mention that his brother's remarks as a witness had not surfaced until after the old man was dead. No one seemed to recall that during the time Rulon allegedly made the important comments, Warren had stated that Rulon had the mind of a child. It had been obvious to those close to him that Rulon often hadn't even known what day it was, so perhaps he would have found it difficult to express opinions on intricate church matters. Rulon never wrote down his wishes designating a legal successor to follow him as president of the FLDS church.

Because there were no rules for succession within the FLDS, the combination of questionable personal testimonies from Isaac and Mary, plus the nod of the cowed Uncle Fred, had to be good enough, and Warren named himself the new prophet, seer and revelator. It wasn't in writing, but that, too, was about to be remedied.

The only real problem left was the uneasy situation in Canada, where the decision to fire Winston Blackmore as bishop had caused a deep split. Some strain had always existed between the FLDS groups in Canada and the United States. Despite mutual claims of friendship, those living in the Crick believed the Canadians were much too lax in discipline. The Canadians felt the Americans were much too rigid. As long as the friendship existed between the late Uncle Rulon and Winston Blackmore, differences could usually be worked out. Not so with Warren at the helm.

As a private investigator, I am always on the lookout for possible sources of information, so I contacted Blackmore by telephone in 2004 and introduced myself, and, to my surprise, he agreed to speak with me. I found him to be an affable man who could communicate easily with people in the outside world, while still maintaining his strong unconventional beliefs in polygamy. A key difference between Winston and the

FLDS brand of polygamy was that he no longer condoned the practice of underage marriage. Although admitting to having taken at least two underage brides while still a member of the FLDS church, he said that he had come to the realization that the practice was wrong and illegal, and he would never promote, condone, or participate in the practice again. In the months to come, Blackmore and I would have numerous intense discussions about polygamy and the differences between his fundamentalist and my equally strong mainstream Mormon beliefs. Fortunately, I did not have to agree with his views, nor he with mine, in order to establish a rapport and talk openly about issues that might be beneficial to my investigation. My job was not to convert him; he was a source who willingly opened a window for me into the hierarchy of the FLDS. He became a knowledgeable guide into the intricacies of his fundamentalist religion, which he never abandoned, and of the dark side of the FLDS religion, which he had abandoned.

He told me about his basic disagreement with Warren. "One of the most frequent questions asked is about a power struggle between me and Warren," Blackmore said. "Now I don't know what that is, but I will tell you about my own struggle. I had to struggle when I was told that there was not enough time left to help anyone repent. I struggled when I saw men who had been restored and forgiven in the days of Uncle Roy and Uncle Rulon, and now have their families swept away from them and their homes given to another. I struggled when I saw men's wages given to the church, and then see their boss go buy a new Lexus. I can't imagine why anyone wouldn't struggle trying to believe there could be anything 'Mormon' about what was happening."

Blackmore said that he had come to dread being summoned down to Short Creek by church leaders, because he never knew in advance if the purpose was to sign some business document, have a meeting with Warren, simply to visit Rulon, or to marry another wife. "I'm telling you, it is a not a good feeling thinking that you may be coming home with some young girl," Blackmore observed. "A lot of people think it's about having sex with a new girl, and maybe for some people it may be, but the reality of it is, there's nothing pleasurable about it." A new young bride meant disruption of the status quo of the household, more in-laws with whom to deal, and an added financial burden. Winston Blackmore had developed a more pragmatic view of polygamy, and of life. My personal views of whether or not Winston was being forthright with me concerning his change of heart regarding child abuse were only relevant to me with respect to his credibility. If I were to have found out he was lying to me (which I have not), I would still have maintained a relationship with Winston, because that is my job. When I make contact with a junkie that is willing to share with me his experiences and provide me with information that will be beneficial to my case, I do not refuse to speak with him if I find out that he is shooting heroin. Winston helped me to gain a more complete understanding of the dark side of the FLDS church and its leaders, and for that I remain grateful.

After being dismissed by Rulon during the Warren-coached telephone call, Blackmore was replaced as the bishop of Bountiful by a quiet and obscure mechanic named Jim Oler, a staunch Warren loyalist. About half of the membership stopped following Blackmore, or listening to his sermons, and followed Warren's substitute, Oler. The rest stuck by the defrocked Blackmore. Winston's wives ignored Jeffs's warning to either leave Blackmore or be doomed to hell and never see their families again.

It was a typical FLDS schism, dissidents within dissidents. Blackmore remained in the Bountiful area as the minister of his own congregation and provided a safe haven for people who had run-ins with Warren. One of their few alternatives was to get to Canada and seek solace from Uncle Wink.

Warren Jeffs would always remain angry with the continuing influence of Blackmore, regarding it as a poison. An "uprising of bad feelings started in Canada and [it was] filtering through the people," he would repeatedly state. Blackmore no longer presented a true threat as a political rival, but that did not mean he was not dangerous in other significant ways; in contrast with Warren's maniacal hatred of the law, Winston Blackmore chose to cooperate smoothly with a number of law enforcement agencies, including the FBI.

CHAPTER 15

Predator

Fifteen months would pass between the time that Warren Jeffs took over the FLDS and the time I first set foot into his private world with my initial visit to Short Creek to meet Ross Chatwin. That interval seemed to close fast.

Over the years I would spend investigating him and his church, I became fascinated by his strange behavior, particularly during that transformational period after his father's strokes. I am not a psychologist, so I pulled out my old college texts and talked to some professionals to satisfy my curiosity about how this man, once he obtained unlimited authority and power within his religion, had changed from a quiet behind-the-scenes manipulator into a runaway, destructive locomotive.

Warren Jeffs possessed all the outward signs and symptoms of narcissistic personality disorder, but narcissism was the lesser of deeper and more frightening emotional problems. I have dealt with many sociopathic criminals over the course of my career, and I can say that Warren was a sociopath too. He is unable to emotionally bond with people, and with his own feelings paramount, he feels none of the pain he inflicts on others.

His feigned love for God and his fellow man were a means to an end, something that he fabricated to gain the trust of his victims and maintain his guise as a man of God. The pain and struggles of other people seemed to bring him great pleasure, and watching his gullible followers willingly suffer at his command gave him a short-lived rush. I would never cease being amazed at the depths of his depravity.

As the FLDS case expanded before me over time, and evidence mounted concerning the behavior of Warren Jeffs, I began to view him as an evil sexual predator who took satisfaction at exercising power not only over children, but anyone under his control.

To the narcissistic sociopath, a sexual experience is not about sex; it's about having complete control over his victims. They satisfy their sick compulsions by preying on vulnerable victims who they feel can most easily be manipulated and are least likely to expose their crimes.

Warren needed the FLDS even more than the rebel religion needed a leader. His specialized psychosis was dependent on a unique religious hook that just would not work in the general population. In the outside world, he would never have been able to convince anyone to take him seriously. But with the FLDS predilection for blind religious obedience and submission to authority, he had the willing, captive audience that he needed, like a scientist needs lab rats. They believed everything he said and would do whatever he wanted.

Add to that volatile mixture another insidious mental illness for which there is a treatment, but no cure: schizophrenia. It was well known within the FLDS community that some members of the Steed family, the line from Warren's mother, had suffered from the disease. It was not uncommon for voices, which Warren would claim were heavenly beings, to interrupt sermons or meetings. It is highly probable that Warren had picked up the family trait. As the boy grew up, he appeared to be constantly teetering on the brink of either genius or insanity. When he became a man of great power, he also became increasingly irrational. Out of this brew of compounded mental illnesses grew a bizarre phenomenon that Warren termed "heavenly sessions," in which he claimed to commune directly with God, and also with his dead father—sometimes being transformed into a heavenly being himself!

Many members of the flock also would come to believe that Uncle Warren could actually undergo a transformation that allowed him to literally walk and talk with God in the flesh, and then resume his mortal form.

These sessions could strike at any time, whether he was resting in bed or just reaching for a doorknob. He would collapse into a trance-like fit of quivering and mumbling and regularly miss scheduled meetings, or excuse himself from other people because he could feel a heavenly session coming on. It might pass like a gentle rain shower, or he might go storming on for hours, apparently sound asleep but contorting like a dervish.

When he awakened from a trance, Warren would pass along what he had learned from the Lord in his usual droning, unemotional voice. The recipients of the edicts would therefore receive very bad news in the belief that it was a wrathful God, and not their kind and loving Uncle Warren, who was dispensing it. Instructions revealed to him by the Almighty during these sessions were nonnegotiable.

I spent much of the early summer of 2004 trying to break through the FLDS code of silence, their strong self-imposed shield of secrecy that kept the rest of the world at bay. I had to throw a very wide net and not rely just upon the apostates in Short Creek, because I didn't want to take the chance that their viewpoint might color my conclusions.

Through my independent sources, cops and law enforcement personnel in Utah and Arizona, I was able to find people in outlying communities, so I drove out to see them, looking for insights into the FLDS culture. Even out in the boondocks, the men would suddenly develop amnesia when I approached. Some may have taken young brides themselves, or have been part of some questionable FLDS business scheme in the past, but the main problem was that they believed their salvation would be in jeopardy if they communicated with me, and they were petrified of Warren Jeffs. Most were curious about who I was and what I was doing but did not want to take the chance of having anything to do with me.

I also started talking with merchants and contractors who hired FLDS members, and even they knew little about the people with whom they did business. The church guys would bring their own lunches, stay to themselves, and appoint one member of their group to communicate with the outsiders. Medical personnel, car dealers, and home builders all told me similar stories of the icy separation they felt when dealing with the FLDS. It was even hard to gain the trust of many apostates, and I would have to win them over one at a time through keeping my word and following through on my promises.

I was searching for people who might be potential witnesses and might be willing to travel with me up to Salt Lake City to meet with Joanne Suder, where we arranged a hotel suite in which to conduct interviews and secure affidavits about what they had experienced and knew. It took a lot of persuasion, because they were frightened about who could potentially read their statement, if they had done something wrong themselves, if a family member might chastise them, and how their leaders would react. I discovered that there were very few Ross Chatwins around, people willing to speak their minds.

It was during that process that I first met the firebrand dissident Flora Jessop, who was more than willing to talk. Flora drove the FLDS crazy, but not without reason. As they say in the army, she had earned her stripes. She had two mothers and twenty-seven siblings when she tried to escape the religious web at the age of only thirteen. She was caught, and an apathetic judge sent her back to the family, which kept her a virtual prisoner for the next three years.

Not only had Flora personally been persecuted and brutalized by the FLDS theocracy into which she had been born, but her sister Ruby had endured a similar ordeal. Ruby was "sealed" at the age of fourteen to her older stepbrother Haven Barlow; she was raped by him and almost bled to death before being taken to a hospital emergency room. When Ruby later tried to run away, she also was caught and eventually returned by the Utah Child Protective Services to her so-called husband, the very perpetrator she had originally accused of the horrible rape. Knowing what had happened to Ruby pushed Flora to make the decision to become a child-abuse activist.

Flora finally broke away from her family for good at the age of sixteen, choosing a rough life in the gentile world over spending one more minute under the thumb of the FLDS. Eventually, she got her life back in order, and today says she is not a victim, but a survivor. Flora never forgot her experiences within the intolerant church, and she remains outraged by the sense of apathy that is so often displayed by the authorities in Utah and Arizona dealing with the "plygs."

Detested by many in her family as well as the FLDS leadership, she did not care what they thought. She would take on anyone, anytime, to help a child in need. As a private investigator, I was happy to have her open up to me about her experiences. Her zeal might sometimes lead FLDS apologists to brand her as an over-the-top activist, but Flora had a deep well of knowledge of what the FLDS is capable of doing. In our meetings, she kept worrying that something had happened to Uncle

Fred, the former bishop of Short Creek, who was missing. Flora thought that Warren had probably kidnapped and killed him, a conclusion that seemed a bit edgy at the time but would prove in the future to be eerily close to the truth.

The idea that lightning-rod personalities such as Flora Jessop were talking to a high-powered legal team in Salt Lake City was unsettling to the FLDS church leaders, as it should have been. As we listened to those stories, we understood that we were dealing not just with child abuse, but with downright atrocities.

Any evidence or indications of crimes that we might discover during the interviews were reported to the proper authorities, and I was working to raise the awareness of the officials and authorities involved. Politicians and law enforcement agencies are busy people and would occasionally need to be jolted into probing the ongoing atrocities within the FLDS and its hierarchy, so briefing various lawyers became another regular aspect of my job.

Alongside the Lost Boys matter, we were also tightening up the Brent Jeffs case, a civil court action in which Warren would be accused of rape and sodomy of a child. We had no powers of arrest, but we hoped that law enforcement would step forward to file and prosecute those charges; but none did. Warren was never charged with those crimes, despite the incredible testimony that would have been available from the victims. Nevertheless, both of our civil cases were strong, and we worked to make them even stronger.

Also on our docket was trying to do something about the corruption within the church-controlled legal structure in Short Creek. To that end, we hoped to expand our targets to include members of the town's crooked justice system—a difficult task because judges and police have a built-in immunity.

In all, it was an ambitious undertaking, and the outcome was uncertain. But our clients were dedicated to the task of trying to rectify some of the wrongs that continued to take a toll on their family and friends, and so was I.

I returned to Short Creek with another subpoena in hand. Uncle Fred Jessop had been replaced as the bishop of Short Creek by William E.

Timpson. It took a while to figure out, because the name game is kept intentionally muddy in the FLDS as one more obstacle to be faced by anyone trying to figure out the culture. Timpson was his last name by birth, but his mother had been reassigned to a new husband, none other than Uncle Fred Jessop, when Will was already an adult with a family of his own. Not only was Will given that new last name, one of the most common in town, but the surname also was bestowed upon his own numerous children. As a result, Will (Timpson) Jessop became routinely confused by outsiders with the notorious FLDS spokesman, Willie Jessop.

By becoming the bishop, Will also had inherited the position of registered agent for the church's legal entity, which meant that I could now subpoena him. His legal address that was listed with the Utah Department of Commerce was 1065 North Hildale Avenue, which I knew was within the town's health clinic compound. That meant that serving the subpoena was not going to be easy. Following my earlier visits, the compound, which occupied about two full blocks, had become a securely fenced and guarded area.

Because of rugged, mountainous terrain, it was nearly impossible to approach the property from the rear. In front, Hildale Avenue dead-ended directly in front of the clinic's two big gates attached to a sturdy fence whose hollow vinyl shell had metal bars hidden within. Between the gates was a concrete barrier with an intercom and cameras. Behind that was a guard shack. I felt it would be foolish to try and gain entry on my own, because what would have been a routine process service anywhere else in the United States could turn into an actual physical battle in Short Creek. Any such perceived challenge to priesthood authority is treated as if you just sucker-punched one of their kids.

I decided to call for some assistance from another Cedar City private investigator, my old friend Jeff Lennert. There was no use asking for help from the Short Creek cops, who not only would warn anyone I might be looking for, but probably would actively try to stop me from serving the subpoena. Instead, I notified Washington County deputy sheriff Matt Fischer about what I was going to do, so he could be on patrol in the vicinity in case of trouble.

Jeff and I observed the clinic from a distance and noted there seemed to be a strict protocol for vehicles entering and leaving the grounds, whether for medical care or for an appointment with the bishop. When a car approached, the guard would view it first through the cameras stationed at the gate and along the perimeter. Once the car was cleared for entrance, the sixteen-foot-long motorized gate would slowly open just enough to allow the visitor to drive inside. Then the car would stop to prevent any other vehicles from coming in behind it, while the gate hummed back into place and shut tight. Getting out was just the reverse. This was extremely tight security for a health clinic that accepted federal funding and was supposed to be open to the public. But any security can be penetrated.

The chance came when Jeff and I saw a car getting ready to come out. When the gate opened, Jeff quickly drove up and stopped. I jumped out of the passenger's side and ducked through the opening gate, as Jeff called Deputy Fischer to alert him that the service was in progress. Before anyone emerged from the guard shack to try and stop me, I made a beeline for the front door of the clinic, surprising a young receptionist wearing a blue pastel dress with a white medical smock over it. The name tag identified her as another one of the Barlows.

"He's not here right now," she responded when I asked to see the bishop. I handed her the papers and thanked her for her help while she stammered, "I . . . I can't take these!" It was a valid service, and I left the building as fast as I had entered.

I had been inside less than two minutes, but by the time I came out, two police trucks were at the scene, one of them already in the compound. Out of that truck stepped Sam Johnson, one of the newly hired cops who, livid with anger, told me that I was trespassing. I shot back that I had every legal right to be there serving a subpoena on a registered agent of the church. Then I added, "You know what? It's a misdemeanor for you to interfere with the service of legal process. A Washington County deputy sheriff is outside the gate right now, so I'll talk to you out there."

I walked away and yelled at the guy in the guard shack to open up. The gate slid back just enough for me to step outside, with Sam Johnson at my heels, threatening to arrest me. The other cop, Helaman Barlow, had blocked the clinic's entrance with his car to stop Deputy Fischer from coming in to assist. As we stood outside the gate, talking to sort things out, a flurry of papers was flung over the fence by an inside guard. It was the subpoena, fluttering to earth. I got a kick watching Johnson scurry around picking the pages off the ground and then try to hand them to me.

"I don't want those," I said, trying to hold back a laugh.

"You can't serve this here," he replied, turning in a circle, as if lost.

"I've served them already, and the person named on it can do whatever he wants with them. It's not my business anymore."

Frustrated, Johnson slapped the subpoena down on the center dividing post between the gates, where the breeze soon sent the loose papers sailing about again.

In July 2004 we sent out a news release to announce a press conference at the state capitol, at which details would be given concerning the filing of a racketeering lawsuit against Warren Jeffs and the FLDS church. The second thunderclap aimed at the FLDS came only came a week later, when we filed another suit on behalf of Brent Jeffs, charging his Uncle Warren with those brutal rapes in the children's bathroom at the Alta Academy.

Since the church's beginning, the FLDS fundamentalists have been plagued by legal problems of one sort or another, involving internal power struggles and external issues associated with polygamy and underage marriage practices. The standard response from the FLDS leadership to outside challenges was to raise the "religious persecution" flag and claim the gentile world was just trying to defame an unpopular religion. Our assertions were significantly different and more focused. The target was not their religion; this country provides everyone the right to worship as they please. Although our cases would be handled in the civil courts, we were alleging outright criminal activity, and we were going after the prophet himself as the leader of a criminal organization that practiced systemic child abuse. Now all I had to do was find him.

CHAPTER 16

The Record

At the time Warren Jeffs took over as FLDS leader, his flock was estimated at ten thousand people or more, a huge number for any breakaway sect, but that number is deceptive. The membership cannot be truly measured, because their records are kept hidden in hideouts and "places of refuge" throughout the country. The FLDS exists not only in Arizona, Utah, and hidden colonies across the United States, but also in Canada. After generations of secretive growth, the actual number of members and hidden compounds is unknown. Even most FLDS members don't know how many of them there are. Compounding the problem is the FLDS mistrust and refusal to cooperate with any government entities, including the U.S. Census. Any estimate of precise numbers is no more than a best guess.

Despite media reports such as one in the *New York Times* and the February 2010 cover story in *National Geographic* magazine, Short Creek is not the orderly, spic-and-span utopia molded by a fastidious, fervently religious colony of quirky little worker bees as is so often portrayed. Overzealous reporters often fall into the trap of trading editorial control of their piece in exchange for a promised "exclusive glimpse" of life in the secretive FLDS culture. I know of at least a half dozen of those so-called exclusives that were, in fact, a successful attempt to dupe the media into placing a positive spin on the cult and ignoring the real facts. In fact, both of the twin towns are shabby and continue to deteriorate. The immaculate mansions that belong to the church hierarchy are surrounded by half-finished houses, raw basements covered by crude roofs, and trailers that seem about to topple over. Much of it is nothing more than a run-down trailer park with chickens pecking around fancy pickup trucks. Abject poverty and squalid living conditions are a sad contrast to the unique natural beauty out of which sprouts the most lawless town in America.

And yet, despite the down-at-the-heels appearance, it is not a community of cartoonish hillbillies or throwbacks to the nineteenth century. There is money in the pipeline—plenty of it. It all goes to the prophet.

For decade upon decade, the FLDS faithful struggled to tame this piece of wild land in hopes of being self-sufficient. Orchards and farms flourished from water that was brought in by irrigation systems they had built, and Warren had recently dedicated a Bishop's Storehouse that could hold 45,000 sacks of potatoes that would be brought in from FLDS farming operations in remote Beryl, Utah. FLDS members own and operate a number of businesses, in several states, that deal in everything from timber to cattle to motels and that have done double duty as hideouts for Warren and as FLDS rendezvous points.

Big FLDS construction companies such as R&W Excavation, Tonto Supply, and Paragon Contractors build public-works infrastructure for cities and towns throughout the country and act as subcontractors on other projects. Other smaller, ever-changing FLDS companies are nothing but fly-by-night operations that are suddenly created, get loans for new equipment, then default on the debt, stealing the new gear they had bought in the hope that the finance company will never find it.

FLDS members are involved with not only bricks and mortar businesses but also with modern, specialized production. They have high-tech companies that have a record of doing business in Washington, D.C., developing ideas as sophisticated as top-secret night-vision components and experimental "smart clothing" for soldiers. FLDS businessmen have also made extensive contacts in the legislative branches of government and the Pentagon. Perhaps the most well-known example is the history of Utah Tool & Die, a business founded by Rulon Jeffs in 1968, which grew into HydraPak, Inc., established in 1976 in West Jordon, Utah, while Rulon Jeffs was on the board of directors. The company found a niche in the lucrative aerospace industry and became the sole subcontractor producing O-rings for the aerospace giant Morton Thiokol. After the space shuttle *Challenger* blew up, killing all seven crew members, in January 1986, a formal government investigation blamed faulty O-rings for the fiery disaster. Rulon's name was soon removed from the board of HydraPak, but the company maintained its strong FLDS links, and his son Wallace Jeffs took over. HydraPak changed its name to Western Precision and moved to a huge building that was hastily constructed as a United Effort Plan work project in Short Creek in only thirty days. In August 2006, when the FLDS came under pressure from the courts seeking UEP assets that had been used to finance the company, Western Precision vanished overnight, moving to Las Vegas, it is now called NewEra Manufacturing, Inc.

Some of the FLDS people are trained as professional grant writers in order to bilk great amounts of cash from federal and state agencies and gain preferential minority treatment on government contracts. Trusted wives are listed as officers of a corporation in order to receive minority preference points for the bidding process. For the FLDS community, success in business is more than just a livelihood and means to support their families. It is a religious calling, and they know all of the angles, which they pursue with great zeal, as if their salvation were dependent on it.

Short Creek's water department exists on paper only. The fire department and search and rescue squads have been formally charged with misappropriating taxpayer money to support local businesses and church members, and are still under investigation. It is almost impossible for a building contractor to win a project on which the FLDS is also bidding, because the church membership has such a vast pool of free labor, using their own young kids to bypass minimum wage and tax laws.

The companies and the contracts are privately held but are secretly consecrated to the church to support its massive legal fees and the extravagant lifestyle of the church hierarchy. Even the wages of the boys are donated to the church. Legitimate business and government entities are unwittingly helping maintain the FLDS leaders' lavish lifestyles, supporting illegal underage marriage, and participating in the abandonment and neglect of young boys by doing business with a criminal organization that openly thumbs its nose at the laws which the rest of us live by.

Since all of the property and living arrangements in Short Creek were assigned by the United Effort Plan Trust, which was headed by the prophet, the majority of residents literally live there by the will and good graces of their religious monarch. However, the Utah Attorney General stepped in to protect the beneficiaries of the trust in the spring of 2005, and seized control of all its assets. A battle continues to this day by the FLDS, challenging the government's intervention to secure the homes on behalf of all the people in Short Creek, FLDS members and apostates alike. But the prophet wants the trust back so he can continue to use the people's homes as leverage to compel them to obey the will of God.

Many of the large polygamist families exist primarily on government-provided food stamps and other means of public welfare support. As far back as 2002 an Arizona judge characterized Short Creek as a "taxpayer emergency." Not much has changed since then, other than the fact that residents have become more experienced and polished in their ability to squeeze money from government treasuries. They willingly take from the federal and state governments they hate and distrust, but they go to extraordinary lengths not to give anything back, claiming that such avoidance is their religious duty. Author Jon Krakauer would famously observe that FLDS leaders refer to the practice as "bleeding the beast."

Short Creek has long been a drain on the welfare and educational systems of Utah and Arizona, diverting funds that would otherwise be available for sorely needed services elsewhere in those states. Colorado City routinely comes in on the top three cities in Arizona for amounts of money received through homeland security grants, and the town received such high-tech equipment as heat-sensing night-vision goggles costing about $25,000 apiece. If there is a government grant available, the FLDS will find it and take advantage of it.

With no housing or upkeep expenses, the locals are free to sink their cash into pricey vehicles such as the "plyg-rig" trucks, shiny new off-road monsters with dark tinted windows that ordinary construction workers can only dream about. The church permits it because those vehicles can be used in business operations, which, of course, also builds church coffers.

Warren Jeffs now had everything he wanted, but as he surveyed his dusty kingdom, he grew agitated. The Priesthood Record would eventually reveal insights into Jeffs's twisted thought processes, showing that the more power he held, the more he feared it was slipping away; he saw rebellion, desertion, apostasy, and the devil at play wherever he turned, and particularly in wicked little Short Creek.

He felt pushed by the velocity of the changes he had wrought, and the thing he feared most was a revolution among the people. He was determined to quash any perceived movement before it started. The tool he would use to fight this evil was the priesthood, redefining the term to represent a rather mystic authority that covered whatever he wanted. It was not as if all of the high priests could gather in some holy clubhouse and discuss or vote on things, and the so-called Priesthood Council, or the Council of Friends, had withered beneath years of one-man rule.

Priesthood originated as a gift from God to be used to bless people's lives, and it meant everything, but now it was an elastic term defined by Warren, and he was ruthless. Those who were half-hearted would have to prove themselves, and if they failed, they would be removed and lose priesthood.

Members were now terrified of somehow screwing up, making Warren angry, and thereby losing the revered status of holding priesthood. If they made a decision on their own, they might be accused of stealing the prophet's authority. By the same token, if they did not act, they might just as easily be in trouble for not showing enough faith. Either choice contained risk, and the FLDS men were constantly begging forgiveness, making it clear that they only wanted to do the prophet's and God's will in all things. Contritely, they willingly bowed to "accept any corrections" that might be due them.

Because Uncle Warren *controlled* priesthood, loyalty to him was ever more paramount. Back in 1989, Uncle Rulon once was asked to explain the Priesthood Council, and had replied simply, "I am it." Now Warren was.

Even the most devout had reason to feel as if they were standing at the edge of some cliff, with Warren's fingertips pushing gently on their backs. The prophet could dispense blessings, or he could retract them. He examined his people constantly and seldom found that they were "keeping sweet" as required, even while they strove to meet his impossible standards of absolute purity and obedience in all things at all times.

To enforce his will, the prophet found a source of willing muscle in the teenage membership of the novice Aaronic Priesthood and in the higher-ranking and more mature Melchezidek Priesthood. In a normal world, young men would perform routine church functions. Warren seized the opportunity to steer these youngsters into being his snoops among the faithful. They would enter private homes at will and make sure the inhabitants were being obedient to the prophet, had his picture properly displayed on a wall, and were following his edicts, much as Hitler's Nazi youths had spied on their own families. Any indiscretions discovered were reported through the priesthood line of authority all the way up to Warren Jeffs, who would deal with the offenders. To not allow the "Sons of Helaman," as Warren referred to them, into your home would be considered an act of disobedience and would be dealt with sharply. The prophet insisted that it was all simple missionary work.

Only a week after his father passed away in September 2002, Warren stepped into the pulpit at the meeting house for the usual Monday morning session to warn the flock: "The outward signs of evil are among us." Younger people were going to the movies in other towns, buying television sets, and listening to rock music. He sternly chastised them, "When you choose to put in that disk or that tape, and the booming music is taking place, you are denying God, and you are participating in devil worship." What he called cowboy music and easy rock were equally pernicious. "It grabs hold of you, it puts a beat inside of you, and it makes you lose your ability to pray." Books and magazines and flashy clothes were works of the devil, and partaking of such evils set bad examples.

Even as he delivered that puritanical lashing, he noted that a lot of his targeted audience—the youth of the community—were not at the service. "Maybe some of them slept in this morning," he said with heavy sarcasm. He did not tolerate, forget, nor forgive such absences. Such behavior signified disobedience.

As he was micromanaging every aspect of the lives of the FLDS members, he began to preach that Short Creek was hell-bent and needed stern correction. His hammer already seemed to have fallen everywhere. There would be no flying of the American flag, no sports, no organized get-togethers, dancing, or holidays; even Christmas was abolished. No one could wear the color red, because Warren claimed that to do so would be to mock Christ, who he predicted would return in red robes. No television, no books other than approved Scripture, no magazines, and no toys. He seemed intent on erasing all of the happiness and joy from life in order to implement his warped vision of a "pure" society. And he was just getting started.

On October 7, 2002, one day shy of a month after Rulon died, Warren took the controversial step of marrying seven of his stepmothers, chosen because they were the most compliant with his wishes. The "sealing ceremony" was held in the room that had once been the office of their late husband. Warren claimed that he had twenty more ready to be sealed to him for their remaining time on earth, after which they would be reunited with Rulon for eternity. In attendance were Uncle Fred and Wendell Loy Nielsen, who would soon be elevated to fill the first counselor vacancy that had been created when Warren became president. Also present was Warren's brother Isaac, whose duty apparently was to parrot not only the information that Rulon had chosen Warren to succeed him, but also that Rulon had publicly condoned the marriages of the widows. That was important because the FLDS had long believed that Scripture required at least two witnesses to validate decisions of major significance. Warren used himself as one witness and Isaac as the other.

Nielsen, a businessman, understood that the sudden unions would not be embraced by everyone in the faith. "I have a strong feeling that Uncle Warren's life will be in danger," he said. Then he emphasized the importance of the ceremony which had just been performed, because Rulon was "hand selecting spirits that can come to the earth now that will be very powerful spirits that will come and live and give themselves to God and grow up without any gentile traits or influence, being just fully Priesthood." Translated, he meant Warren could father perfect children by these women who he had been calling his mother less than a month earlier. With that, Warren Jeffs was "sealed for time" to Paula Jessop Jeffs, Naomi Jessop Jeffs, Ora Bernice Steed Jeffs, Patricia Keate Jeffs, Kathryn Jessop Jeffs, Melinda Johnson Jeffs, and Tamara Steed Jeffs.

This was the moment at which the prophet also decided that the time had come to write everything down, expanding on what he had always done in his trusty notebook, but on a grander scale. It was time to record the reign of Warren Steed Jeffs. He would write his own version of history, as it occurred. Not only God, but also the deceased Rulon would help him dictate. Warren now claimed to have become his father's living memory; in other words, the dead prophet—Rulon—was still able to regularly communicate his will through the living prophet, Warren. Specially selected wives would be his "scribes" and record his decisions and words, keeping the notebooks and computer disks hidden under tight security at all times. His new favored bride Naomi was one of the first to take on the task, and by doing so, she would gain significant influence over Warren.

So began the elaborate and meandering journal filled with a careful mixture of fact and fantasy, doctrinal references, and declarations to prove that everything Warren did was proper and for the good of the people and his religion. Much of it was simply gibberish. It was stilted, archaic, and out of whack with truth and reality—the world seen through the eyes of a madman. He would even document the terrible, unrelenting abuse of young girls in much the same manner as a demented serial killer will take souvenirs of his atrocities from a crime scene in order to continually relive the horrible event.

CHAPTER 17

Whirlwind

Serious problems were bubbling to the surface, one after another, faster and faster, and Warren was discovering that he could not handle it all. The year after his father's death, 2003, would prove to be a terrible year.

A few of the women who had escaped the FLDS grasp were breaking their silence, and church secrets began spilling into the gentile world. Drawing public attention could only spell trouble for the cult.

A taste of what was to come surfaced on April 22, when Carolyn Jessop ran away. She had been assigned to a top Warren confidante named Merril Jessop as his fourth wife, when she was eighteen and he was fifty, and had borne eight children. But with Warren now pushing hard for underage marriages within the FLDS, Carolyn was terrified that her fourteen-year-old daughter was entering the danger zone, and that her kids would become more fodder for the FLDS abuse mill. So she packed all of them, including a handicapped son, into a broken-down van and sped away from Colorado City in the middle of the night with twenty dollars in her pocket. She was thirty-five years old.

Women and girls who try to break away from the FLDS are always vigorously pursued, and if caught, they are usually returned to the family from which they had fled. Carolyn Jessop could not expect much help from anyone, particularly the church-run Short Creek police. She knew they would be coming after her, and they did, but this courageous woman somehow beat the odds.

"When I first fled, I felt that I had landed on another planet," she would later testify before the United States Senate. "I had only limited exposure to the outside world I had been brainwashed since birth to believe was evil. My rights to my own life and liberty were taken from me when I was forced to marry Merril Jessop. I never knew what it meant to be safe."

For the prophet, her disappearance was not a huge difficulty in itself, but it fed into his churning imagination as additional evidence that control might be slipping away. At the time, he knew only that Carolyn Jessop had become another enemy. What he did not know was that she was going to tell everything. Four years later, she published what became a bestselling book, *Escape*, that offered a shattering portrayal of life within the radical polygamist cult.

One important thing for a private investigator to do is just to listen: What are people saying? One story circulating around Short Creek concerned a set of twins born to Ora Jeffs, one of the late Rulon's wives, in April 2003—seven months after the old man died. That required some fast and fancy coverup work, because the ailing, wasted Rulon could not possibly have been the father. The newborns were kept out of sight in another location so as not to be noticed by the faithful, who might count the months and notice that the arithmetic of gestation was slightly off.

It is not uncommon for FLDS children to receive birth certificates later in life, if at all, and those documents were finally issued for the twins a few months later by the church's doctor, Lloyd Barlow. They only muddled the picture. The supposedly genuine papers claimed the two children were not twins at all, but were born to the same mother, Ora, with Warren listed as the father. The birth dates were a few months apart, the timing adjusted to cover the normal gestation period, but still quite impossible. It was a typical FLDS dodge of fabricating paperwork, especially birth certificates, to cover up whatever was necessary.

In May 2003, without asking Warren's permission, the Barlow family unveiled a historical monument, a library, and a museum in Short Creek to house books and artifacts from the historic 1953 Raid in which the State of Arizona had sought to crush the FLDS. That government intrusion had famously backfired when the national press had published pictures of children being taken away from their mothers, and public opinion had swung against the state and in favor of the polygamists. The Barlows emphasized the roles of their own ancestors in the historic event while cutting out the Jeffs.

Warren was furious when he discovered what had been done, and he ranted in a meeting that the people of Short Creek were idolatrous and were worshiping their ancestors and a graven image instead of God. He ordered that the artifacts in the museum and library be burned, and that the stone monument be smashed. Its dust was scattered to the winds that whipped around the striking red cliffs that overlook Short Creek.

The Barlows were enemies.

Next in 2003 came an unexpected source of outside pressure with the publication of *Under the Banner of Heaven: A Story of Violent Faith* by Jon Krakauer, who once had been run out of Short Creek. *Banner* was an immediate bestseller, although it had almost no impact on the lives of ordinary FLDS members. Since Short Creek residents were not allowed to read books, magazines, or newspapers, watch TV, or listen to the radio, most never even knew that the book had been printed. Church leaders tried to dismiss it as just another example of religious persecution by the world outside, but the story opened an unwanted window through which their private world could be examined.

Krakauer was placed high on Warren's ever-expanding list of enemies. He was a nightmare to them—a well-known journalist they could not control—and they were in for a disappointment if they hoped that Krakauer would disappear once the book was finished. A lot of things had happened in the four years since his first wild ride through Short Creek, and the author had no intention of walking away from it all. He would later tell me, "After being so closely involved with the tragedies that were occurring continually from within the FLDS community, I found it impossible to turn my back on it. I had made the transition from author to activist. I knew too much."

That summer, the State of Utah scored a significant victory against the FLDS by convicting one of the Short Creek cops, Rodney Holm, of bigamy and unlawful sexual activity with a minor. For the first time since the '53 Raid a government had moved against the polygamist religion, but this time the state had won.

Holm had been thirty-two when he took sixteen-year-old Ruth Stubbs, against her will, to be his third wife in 1998. The assigned marriage had been arranged by Uncle Rulon, with Warren by that time lurking close by, and since Holm was more than ten years older than his underage bride at the time, it was a third-degree felony under Utah law. After having two children and while pregnant with a third, Ruth had escaped; and, for a change, the law paid attention and brought charges.

"At the age of sixteen, I was pressured to marry Rodney H. Holm, under the rule of the [FLDS] church," she would testify later in a child custody case. "Since that time, I have lived in a controlling and abusive environment common in the community. The 'sister-wives' were physically and emotionally abusive to both myself and my children. I have scars on my face from one beating. Children were beaten and locked in rooms. On several occasions, younger children would be smothered by one of the mothers until they choked or gasped for air. I was required to work and leave my children with the other eighteen in the care of the other two mothers."

Holm was found guilty and spent eight months in a work-release program at Purgatory Correctional Facility and three years on probation. That sentence appeared to be not much more than a slap on the wrist for a man who had abused a sixteen-year-old girl, but it was generally in line with a case of statutory rape for someone whose presentencing report showed him to be a first-time offender and a former police officer with an otherwise clean record. His religion, in which such treatment of women and girls was commonplace, was not a factor, although it should have been. Holm had no remorse for the crime he had committed and the chances that he would repeat the offense were one hundred percent, if called upon by the prophet to do so. Instead Holm became a hometown hero for taking a hit for God and the prophet.

Still, it was a shattering blow for the polygamists. Utah had broken through the threadbare argument of religious freedom to convict an FLDS loyalist of a crime concerning underage marriage. A lot of men in the priesthood suddenly recognized that the threat of legal action was real.

Fresh off of that courtroom victory, Utah attorney general Mark Shurtleff convened a "Polygamy Summit" on August 23, 2003, in St.

George, assembling government agency representatives from Utah and Arizona to start a serious discussion about crimes that might be taking place within communities that practiced polygamy. The attorney general rattled the prophet with the comment: "I don't mind telling Warren Jeffs that I'm coming after him . . . We have seen compelling evidence that crimes are being committed, children are being hurt, and taxpayers are footing the bill."

A morose and angry Warren Jeffs struck back by declaring that Short Creek, which had for so long been a religious haven for the FLDS, was unworthy of further protection by the priesthood, which was his quasi-religious doublespeak way of saying that he was washing his hands of the place, and he slipped out of public view.

He was not quite finished with the town, however, and did not slow his frantic drive to marry off its young girls. Instead, he hastened to do even more, and much faster.

Warren was ripping through the families of Short Creek, searching for tender daughters who could be given to older men, along with his permission to immediately start having sex with them. The Priesthood Record painted his perverse goal with shocking clarity in November:

> The Lord is showing me the young girls of this community, those who are pure and righteous will be taken care of at a younger age. As the government finds out about this, it will bring such a great pressure upon us, upon the families of these girls, upon the girls who are placed in marriage . . . And I will teach the young people that there is no such thing as an underage Priesthood marriage but that it is a protection for them if they will look at it right . . . The Lord will have me do this, get more young girls married, not only as a test to the parents, but also to test these people to see if they will give the Prophet up.

It was an ultimate trial of faith. Would they cooperate, or would a disloyal mother or father turn him in to the gentiles? As always, they cooperated without fail.

The prophet intended to practice what he preached. When his brother Lyle approached Warren with questions "about [Lyle's] 16-year-old wife—should he wait until she is 'of age' so-called before he goes forward with her and has children? I told him he should live the [Celestial] law now. He didn't get married to not live the law!"

Then on November 25, Warren summoned his staunch ally Merril Jessop to inform him of a new revelation from the Lord, a shocking dream in which wicked men wanted to destroy certain young girls, including Merril's thirteen-year-old daughter, Ida. She was in mortal danger! The prophet said that if he stood aside and did nothing, he would be held responsible for the terrible things that would happen to her—kidnapping or even death. Merril scurried home and fetched the girl back so she could be saved. With her father looking on proudly in a hurried evening ceremony, Warren Jeffs married Ida Vilate Jessop in the presence of his henchmen, Uncle Fred and Wendell Nielsen.

"She will be raised up as a daughter and gradually as a wife," the prophet promised Merril. He added an extra comment in his private diary: "But she looks like a natural wife, already." Being only thirteen years old was not going to protect her. Within two weeks, Warren would turn forty-eight. The child was almost like a birthday present to himself.

The following day, Wednesday, November 26, spelled the end for Ron Rohbock, who never knew what hit him. The prophet had a revelation that showed Rohbock had to be removed from the FLDS. It sent a message to the entire membership. If a ranking confidante like Ron Rohbock could be summarily axed, then no one was safe.

Rohbock was the father who had been so obedient that he had been dispatched to Canada to fetch back his runaway daughter Vanessa to be blood-atoned, although he had failed in that mission. He was Uncle Rulon's old winemaking and dining buddy and was considered by some to have been the former leader's bodyguard. He had taught at Alta Academy and knew the entire family well. But during the new revelation, Warren discovered a "subtle deception of Lucifer" had crept into Rohbock. The prophet designated him a "son of perdition," ruling that "Ron Rohbock and his son John do not hold Priesthood . . . and they are to be sent away . . . and not be among the people and repent from a distance." Rohbock was out, along with John, who had defended his father.

All ties were broken. Rohbock lost his place among the blessed priesthood and was excommunicated. Warren called a special meeting of FLDS leaders to say that anyone who sympathized with the heartbroken castaway would receive the same treatment. Even generous Uncle Fred, out of fear of being flattened by Warren's momentum, turned his back on Rohbock and demanded the return of a down-payment he had lent Ron to buy a pickup truck.

As is usual with FLDS men who are expelled by Warren, Rohbock genuinely did not understand why he was being booted out of the church and losing his home and family. Warren never explained anything more than to say it was a revelation received from God. When Rohbock asked his old friends to help him understand the decision, he was shunned. To Warren, questioning the decision proved that Rohbock was a master deceiver trying to worm his way into the hearts of the people. When Ron tried to confess his sins, the prophet judged that the sinner did not admit to some of the "immoral" things that the Lord had unveiled.

My investigation eventually would show there was more to the story. Some sources told me that Rohbock's real sin had been catching Warren in bed with a couple of Uncle Rulon's young wives while his crippled father was confined to another room. With the marriages to his stepmothers causing such controversy, Warren did not want Ron to have any sort of political leverage against him. But there was more.

Rachel was a daughter of Uncle Rulon and a sister of Warren. She was a troubled creature who daringly sought help from a professional therapist outside of the FLDS, but eventually could not bear the abuse she had suffered and would succumb to a drug overdose that many thought may have been suicide. Upon learning of Rachel's death, Warren slid coldly into one of his pious ramblings about how that was the sort of thing that could happen to women who strayed from the faith.

Released from confidentiality by the death of his patient, the therapist finally shared Rachel's story with ex-FLDS family members and friends outside of the church, who told it to me. The cause of Rachel's troubles, according to the therapist, was that she had been sexually molested as a child by her father Rulon and by her brother Warren Jeffs. As Rulon's confidant, Ron Rohbock apparently knew this and kept the abuse she suffered quiet. Connecting the dots, it all made sense. Warren would later admit to having immoral relations with a sister and daughter. He used Rohbock to demonstrate in the harshest terms that he practiced neither mercy nor forgiveness, even when it came to his most loyal followers. And any protest would only prove that God had discovered his black heart.

Later during my investigation, in the summer of 2005, I worked through a contact to set up a possible meeting with Rohbock. Knowing his background, I was not optimistic, but I had to try. He had the potential to be a very valuable source of information. A deal was arranged: We would go to a restaurant, where I would sit on one side while Ron and my contact sat at a table on the other side. If Ron was comfortable with the idea of talking, the contact would wave me over. But the wave never came, and I never made personal contact. Even after being ruined by the FLDS, he could not summon up the courage to speak out against the prophet and the church.

The stress of all the negative attention, the sudden awakening of government law enforcement, the relentless threat posed by his enemies, and the requirements of running the entire FLDS all by himself overwhelmed the prophet. Danger lurked everywhere. He expected to be arrested or assassinated, and he routinely prayed for "fire from heaven . . . to keep all evil powers and spirits away."

"No one knows how many times you have been through this mortality," his stepmother-wife-scribe Naomi cooed sweetly to comfort him after watching him twist and turn in his bed all night, burning within rings of fire. "You were foreordained to come back to earth at this time . . . You are a God."

She always knew what to say, but this time soft words of praise were not enough. He needed a way out from under his mounting problems. Warren was flying blind, relying on an instinct for survival. "I ain't got all the answers, 'cause I ain't been asked all the questions. So don't demand all the answers right now, because all the changes ain't takin' place yet," he told his scribe. "I am taking it as it comes."

He thought discord was spreading within the FLDS, and had even wormed its way into his own household. Jealousy was breaking out as earlier wives were forced to make room for the new ones, and one even had the audacity to become upset when she discovered him groping and kissing a new wife. None of this slowed down his acquisition of young girls. In a single eight-day span, he zoomed from twenty-five to forty-two new victims in his stable, with still more undergoing religious "trainings" before being officially corralled. At least one was given a double wedding ring to prove she was married to both Rulon and Warren.

Troubles mounted throughout 2003. Legal actions were being filed, less than half of the original congregation in Canada remained, and the law in Arizona and Utah, according to Warren, was telling "terrible lies against [him]." He likened the accusations to a Mafia novel because authorities gave their sources pseudonyms to protect their identities, even as Warren himself became more and more like the Mafia dons he professed to abhor. He hauled along a full security detail when he shared breakfast with ninety women and children in Cottonwood Park.

It was becoming too much for him to handle, and he decided on a unique solution: simply to disappear. "The Lord has directed me to move away," Warren confided to some wives after a revelation. Scouts were dispatched to seek isolated locations across the nation in which he and those loyal to him could find shelter when the world finally came to an end. In reality, they would be a series of emergency bolt-holes in which he could hide from the law.

A place in heavy forest about twenty miles outside the little town of Mancos, in southwestern Colorado, was the first selected, and the first of several parcels of land there had been purchased on July 11, 2003, through an FLDS shell corporation called Sherwood Management, under the guise of being a corporate hunting retreat. The mountainous and thickly wooded terrain reminded Warren of the grand family estate that had been abandoned in Little Cottonwood Canyon when they had all moved to Short Creek. Mancos was given the code name of Refuge One, or R-1, to avoid disclosing its location. Specially chosen work crews were dispatched to start building there in great secrecy, and orders were placed for truckloads of Canadian logs from the FLDS colony up north that would be turned into cabins. The hideout was to be in operation by the last day of November, a tight deadline that Warren promised could be met because angels would work alongside crews, even when they were only putting up sheetrock.

After a good deal of work had been put into the Mancos project, another even more attractive possibility was found down in West Texas, a state that was very light on zoning and building restrictions. Texans tended to mind their own business, and the state's marriage laws had not changed since the nineteenth century; girls as young as fourteen could still legally be married there with the consent of their parents. It looked very promising, and FLDS front man David Allred was authorized to buy 1,371 acres of rural land outside of the town of Eldorado, in Schleicher County. Several hundred more acres would be purchased later. "Thanks unto the Lord for His bounteous blessings in acquiring the land in Texas," Jeffs sang out with great joy on Sunday, November 23.

This presented a whole new set of problems: how to get construction under way in Texas even as the R-1 refuge in Mancos was still incomplete. Warren set unrealistic deadlines, saying it was a "life and death" matter to finish the houses in Colorado by November 30, so that he could send four men down to Texas to begin foundation work there. He said the workmen should not be concerned about the breakneck schedule because "attending angels" would be helping them pound the nails and put up sheetrock.

When they were not actually building in Mancos, the chosen workmen underwent intensive new spiritual training for their sacred new calling at the Texas site that Warren was calling both "R-17" and "Zion." They were already loyal FLDS members and skilled workers, but now they had to be elevated to the exalted rank of "temple builders," a title never before heard within the FLDS that carried great prestige as well as secrecy.

With his master escape plan coming together, the time had come to slam the hammer down on his Short Creek enemies. Warren would later report that God delivered specific instructions on what had to be done during a special revelation on December 24, the night before Christmas 2003. When he returned from Texas, he would follow those instructions and take care of one last important piece of business in Short Creek.

CHAPTER 18

Twenty-one Men

Warren Jeffs blew into Texas on a lie. A single entity buying more than thirteen hundred acres of land at once was bound to draw attention, even in rural areas of Texas. A curious neighbor who watched the new activity while leaning on the fence at the eastern boundary was told that a private hunting lodge for rich men was to be built on the ranch and that construction workers and their families were coming in to get things under way.

The first time that Warren went walking alone on the Texas property, on Sunday afternoon, January 4, 2004, he followed a dirt track to the northeast and got lost in the sprawling, empty sameness of it all. He wandered back south and was gone for two hours, until found by an FLDS man driving a dump truck. The next day, undertaking a wider exploration with a guide, he bounced along aboard a small and rugged four-wheeler and got a better lay of the land. Zion blazed in full glory in his churning imagination, as he charted out where God wanted the temple to be built, as well as the houses, the barn, the dairy, and the manufacturing and agricultural areas. He saw deer and antelope and got the worst case of hay fever he had ever had.

But he could not linger. Claiming to have an important Saturday Work Meeting to conduct back in Short Creek, he headed back to Mancos, Colorado, leaving behind his hand-picked cadre of twenty-five men, twelve women, and sixteen children to start the Texas project. They would live for now bunched into a large camper trailer, a motor home, and four tents. The motor home had a bathroom and the tent dwellers shared a portable toilet. The living conditions were really much too Spartan for a man of Warren's delicate sensibilities.

An eerie scene unfolded shortly after dawn on January 10, 2004, at the cavernous LeRoy S. Johnson Meeting House in Short Creek. The tall, slender Prophet Warren Jeffs had arrived in the empty hall at 6:40 A.M. and was standing alone at the speaker's platform when the FLDS faithful began to show up. He was not smiling. God had finally identified his enemies and shown how they were to be handled. On this day, Warren would prove to the FLDS, once and for all, that it was he who held the reins of power in their lives.

As usual, it was an FLDS members-only affair. But over time, and through many interviews, listening to tape recordings of Warren's monotone tirade, and finally reading his own version of events in the Priesthood Record, I was able to piece together exactly what happened that morning, and the hazy initial reports smoothed into crystal clarity. Warren manhandled them.

Dan Barlow, the town's mayor and fire chief, was one of the early arrivals at the meeting house, and he approached Jeffs and shook his hand. The prophet edged Barlow to the side and quietly confided that he had been instructed by the Lord to deliver a public correction to Barlow; the mayor could either stay in the audience or listen in private from an adjoining room. Barlow chose to stay. A number of other men received similar quiet, personal warnings as they arrived with their families, and they also chose to remain in the big central chamber.

The women and girls were as usual dressed modestly in long, pastel-colored prairie dresses, and their long hair was swept up in the unique fashion that is standard within the religion, but that outsiders call a "plyg-do." The men and boys wore their long-sleeved shirts buttoned at the wrists and collar, for any display of skin would be frowned upon. The children were well-behaved and squeaky clean.

Jeffs conducted the service with authority, reading forcefully from church doctrine that men who would spread even the least doubt among the faithful must be cast out. For an hour and a half, he flailed them in a voice that carried no more inflection than the drone of an air conditioner. One by one, he expelled seventeen men, dropping his ax on many whose families had carved the town out of the wilderness before Warren was even born. He commanded everyone to rise.

"The Lord has revealed to me that these men no longer hold Priesthood. They have been tested of God and found wanting and Heavenly Father, through the Prophet, will have me handle these men in order to begin a cleaning up of his kingdom before the great and dreadful day of the Lord. We love these brethren and await the day that we can welcome them back into the brotherhood of the Lord but until they have been sufficiently humbled before God and bow before the Lord with a broken heart and contrite spirit, the Lord God will have me send them away to repent from a distance!"

There was a pause as the congregation seemed to be holding its breath as they soaked up the startling decision. Warren pushed ahead.

"All those who can validate this action as the will and word of God, please so manifest by raising your arm to the square. Any in opposition may so manifest in the same manner." Of course, there were no dissenting votes. All in attendance raised their hand in support of the prophet. Even the surprised victims reacted with reflexive obedience and raised their right hands as if swearing in court, to affirm the decree. He then dismissed the exiled men from the meeting, with instructions to return to their homes and prepare to leave Short Creek as soon as possible. They accepted the abuse like meek little lambs.

Among those Warren expelled were four of his own brothers: David (who was confined to a wheelchair due to polio), Hyrum, Brian, and Blaine. In the complicated Jeffs family tree, Blaine's youngest wife was also his stepdaughter.

(As strange as it seems, that is not an uncommon practice within the FLDS. When a man is thrown out of the church, the prophet automatically dissolves all of the transgressor's previous marriages. The freed wives and children are assigned by the prophet to someone else, so new kids are frequently being brought into established families. The prophet may later reward the new father for displaying great obedience in taking on the responsibility of someone else's family by assigning one of the new stepdaughters to be another wife. The girl thus becomes a sister-wife of her own mother and is available for sex with the man who is her new father.)

Of paramount importance for Warren on that momentous January day of reckoning was the opportunity to "handle" four of the influential Barlow brothers. The family responsible for the unauthorized monument, library, and museum was decimated. Mayor Dan Barlow was on the list. So were prominent businessman Nephi Barlow and Truman Barlow, an important figure financially within the church and in town tax collections and disbursements. The primary target was Louis Barlow, age eighty, who many people had thought should have become the prophet instead of Warren with the death of Rulon in 2002.

Warren accused the Barlows of forgetting God by having erected monuments to man in Short Creek—constituting idolatry—and charged that they had secretly been forming "a counterfeit government." They were ordered to write letters of confession, leave their homes and families, and to "not come in this community until they receive permission from me, of the Lord." It was the standard sentence for men and boys who were thrown out of the religion: Repent from afar.

He was not yet finished, and he now instructed the entire congregation of several thousand people to kneel before him. "I raised my arm to the square and pled with the Lord to forgive these people," he would recall later in his record of events. Then he addressed the families of the banished. "All you ladies married to these men are released from them and will remove yourselves immediately from their presence. If you don't, I will have to let you go."

Four more men also would be tossed out soon after that fateful meeting, bringing the total expulsions to twenty-one. They were stunned. Nothing had ever happened on such a scale in Short Creek; with so many FLDS families being destroyed in one swoop, hundreds of women and children were affected.

The dumbfounded congregation was instructed to begin a two-day fast as part of the repentance process. After a closing prayer, Warren brought the extraordinary gathering to a close and calmly strolled to the exit doors to shake hands with the congregants as they filed past. Happy to have dodged the bullet themselves, they eagerly declared their loyalty.

"I love you all," Warren assured them, projecting an image of unwavering love—"keeping sweet"—while having casually destroyed so many lives. The awful repercussions of that day can be measured in the suicide, death, despair, depression, misery, financial ruin, incest, and immorality that followed. The wives of the expelled men would be "reassigned" to other men, and their children would be forced to call a stranger "Father."

It was all done in the name of the Lord.

The political rivalry between the Jeffs family and the Barlows stretched back a long time, but the power struggle was now over. Warren believed that he had ended it by ripping the heart out of the Barlow clan, but he would continue to cut them even deeper in the months to come, vindictive in his retribution. There was no mercy because the people needed to understand what happens to those who dared to challenge the Lord's self-anointed leader.

The Barlows and the other expelled men did not recognize just how serious Warren was about crushing them. They thought their exiles would be temporary, and that after repenting for a couple of weeks, they would be allowed to return to their homes and regain their families. That was not the prophet's plan at all, and as time passed, my investigation would show that some of the women and children were handed around the "priesthood" like sugar candy at a party; everybody got a turn.

When the expelled Barlow men moved into a house together in another town, Warren attacked again, ruling that if they were ever to regain even the slightest chance of being forgiven by him, they could not keep each other company. If they were together, they might be tempted to commiserate about how they had been wronged and start plotting against the prophet. Once again, they blindly followed Warren's edict, obeyed his absurd rules, and separated to live alone, with no family contact whatsoever.

The unrelenting pressure, loneliness, and humiliation eventually became too much for the elderly Louis Barlow. Once considered a candidate to lead the entire religion, he now slid into depression and debt, living off his credit cards. The old man decided that no matter what had been decreed, perhaps God might accept him into Heaven after all, so he took his own life. Suffering from congestive heart failure, Louis stopped taking his medications and died of a heart attack in May, four months after having been excommunicated.

Warren even seized that tragedy to further shame his deceased rival and the Barlow clan. He magnanimously allowed a funeral to be conducted at the meeting house and a burial in the town cemetery, but he would not allow the grave to be dedicated, a traditional and vital part of an FLDS funeral service. Jeffs claimed that Louis had not fully repented before death, so was undeserving of his priesthood blessing. At the service, the dead man's former wives were ordered to sit beside their newly assigned husbands.

There was no longer any confusion about who was in charge of the FLDS and the millions of dollars of riches in its financial arm, the United Effort Plan.

Immediately after the Saturday Work Meeting on January 10, Warren Jeffs disappeared.

Only eleven hours and fifty minutes after delivering his blow to Short Creek, he was back in the Mancos hideout, rushing to lead the church hierarchy into what he called "deep hiding." Elderly Uncle Fred had been quietly removed to Mancos in the middle of the night, stripped of his title as the bishop of Short Creek, and Warren instructed Fred's wives that the old man was "gone, not to come back" to the town. Wendell Nielsen, the old ally who had filled Warren's slot as first counselor in the presidency, would also go underground with Warren and Fred, surfacing only for special missions. Jeffs ordered his own family to scatter, and they piled into waiting vehicles and took off, destinations unknown, some joining him five hours later in Colorado.

The only newspaper in Short Creek is an irregularly published community periodical from the church, but bigger papers had been watching and had developed sources in the town. The *Daily Spectrum* in nearby St. George and the *Deseret News* and *Salt Lake Tribune* in Salt Lake City all carried stories on the meeting in their Sunday editions on January 11. Anxious police throughout the area responded with calls to Chief Marshal Sam Roundy to offer assistance in case there was a riot. Warren sniffed at such intrusive attention by the media and the law, since he considered the political massacre to be just an internal "setting in order of the people." He had dealt with the master deceivers and everything would now be able to return to normal.

That was not to be, for an insignificant Short Creek resident named Ross Chatwin had stormed into the mix. Chatwin had already been expelled for trying to take a second wife without permission, but Warren now learned that Chatwin, instead of being obedient, was fighting back. He had sent out hundreds of letters claiming that Louis Barlow was the rightful prophet of the FLDS. This brand-new enemy had come out of nowhere, and on January 14, the impertinent man held a news conference in which he denounced Warren as a tyrant. Short Creek was invaded by the gentiles—cops and the media—and all of Warren's hard work to put things in order there seemed to be coming apart at the seams.

Warren told his scribe, "We have no friends on earth." He canceled a plan to return to Short Creek, using the excuse that people were waiting there to kill him. Instead, he would take a road trip.

Despite the heightened tension, some needs remained constant, according to his Record, and Warren snatched two more children as brides: Gloria Ann Steed and Veda Keate, both only thirteen years old. They were happily given to Warren by their fathers and mothers. And as the storm broke, he married two more—Loretta Jane Barlow, also thirteen, and Permelia Johnson, fifteen. In his own words in the Priesthood Record, Jeffs admitted to marrying four underage girls within a few days. He simply took them. No little girl in the faith was safe if the prophet wanted her.

Accompanied by his wife-scribe Naomi, and with his brother Leroy Jeffs and moneyman John Wayman, Jeffs took off from Mancos on Tuesday, January 27, 2004, in a two-vehicle convoy, a spacious Ford Excursion and a Ford Navigator. He claimed to be on another mission ordered by God, but in retrospect it looks more like a holiday from his troubles. The little group had only traveled across the rest of Colorado and part of Kansas before Warren started making horrendous pronouncements concerning God's "judgments." Naomi recorded them: "There is such a dark spirit everywhere of great wickedness. The people on this land are only worthy to be swept off."

In the cold of winter, Jeffs tracked back to the very roots of Mormonism. Upon reaching the environs of Independence, Missouri, he stepped through a carpet of light snow in fifteen-degree weather to explore the place that once had been set apart as the site for a future temple by the early Mormons, although none was ever built there. Jeffs had first seen it during a three-month coast-to-coast trip the previous year, when he was out sizing up possible places of refuge. The site holds significance to the mainstream Mormon Church, but Warren wanted to rededicate it in behalf of the FLDS. He stood tall with both his arms held out on the square and prayed for the Almighty to strip the land of its current population of hundreds of thousands of people, so Jeffs could build "the New Jerusalem and the temple in Jackson County, Missouri."

It showed an evolution in his thinking. The FLDS had always clung to the idea that they were far beyond needing anything like a real temple, because they had lost the right to enter Mormon temples when they were excommunicated a century earlier. In the recent decades, however, prophets had made reference to the FLDS still not needing any temple, at least until after the end of the world, when everyone else had perished. Warren was now seriously thinking about that.

While on their trip, they also visited the Carthage Jail in Carthage, Illinois, where LDS Church founder Joseph Smith had been murdered by a mob on June 27, 1844. Warren repeatedly compared himself to Joseph, even claiming that he, too, would one day be called upon to reveal ancient texts that would become canonized into scripture. He surveyed the room in which Smith had been assassinated, saw the bullet hole in the door, and examined the window from which Smith had fallen. What image did he take away from that historic scene? "The room was quite small," he noted in what would become a persistent, peculiar refrain.

Early on the final day of January 2004, a Saturday, the little caravan crossed the Mississippi River and hurried to Nauvoo, Illinois. The early Mormons, when driven from their homes in western Missouri, had reclaimed this once swampy land and built a thriving city on it. Then it was on to Ohio, where Warren's troop did some laundry before heading to Palmyra, New York, and the Hill Cumorah, where a large statue of the angel Moroni marks the spot where Joseph Smith retrieved the golden plates bearing the runes that created Mormonism.

But Warren was at a loss as to why God had sent him on this particular trip in the middle of winter. Something continued to gnaw at him: Why did God and the angels and saints appear in humble surroundings? In a fit of clairvoyance and characteristic hubris, he proclaimed in the Record that while God and His messengers sometimes did drop into modest places, the Lord really wanted "a temple where He can appear in honor and glory to His faithful people."

After that declaration of God's true wishes, twisted to fit his own dream, Warren headed back west. The breakaway religion that had prided itself on never needing a temple was about to get a monumental one.

CHAPTER 19

There to Stay

The FLDS quest for secrecy in Texas would fail. Residents in and around Eldorado had not yet discovered the truth of what was unfolding with their reclusive new neighbors, but they did not like the rumors they were hearing.

They began asking questions of Schleicher County sheriff David Doran, an affable man of medium build with a mustache, and dark hair that is usually hidden beneath a cowboy hat. He was in his third term, knew his county well, and had been carefully watching the dramatic changes at the old ranch. Among those asking were his old friends Randy and Kathy Mankin, the publishers of the weekly *Eldorado Success* newspaper. Few outsiders knew more about the odd goings-on out at the ranch than the unflappable Mankins.

Randy was a hometown boy who had spent his younger years as a Texas oil wildcatter, a job that had taken him away from his roots. When he had had enough of the oil fields, he and Kathy had bought the newspaper and settled into what they had anticipated to be life in a sleepy small town. Then came the FLDS, and everything changed. The *Success* office was only a few miles from the front gate. In the months to come, Randy and Kathy would be reporting breaking news on the hottest story going. The little newspaper with about 1,100 subscribers would regularly scoop the bigger media.

The presence in town of the inquisitive newspaper ensured that there would be publicity when the mysteries of Eldorado started to unravel, which happened only two days before the end of February 2004. On that day, Ben Johnson, one of Warren's drivers and bodyguards, was stopped by a highway patrolman because the license plate on his vehicle was obscured. When a bloodied arrow was discovered, Johnson said he had been out hunting, and the patrolman summoned game wardens, who insisted on seeing the dead deer. Johnson had to take them onto the Zion property, where the visitors were surprised by the scope of the construction that was under way. Three multistory wooden buildings were going up among the scrub trees, and cargo storage containers littered the area.

Warren instructed presiding elder Ernest Jessop, who was in charge of the compound at the time, to lie and stick with the fabricated cover story. Jessop told the authorities that the workers there were merely an out-of-state construction crew building a private corporate hunting retreat. The materials in the big storehouse where the deer had been taken held food and other supplies for the crews and their families, he said. The game wardens took Ben Johnson, the archer, to court, where a two-hundred-dollar fine for poaching was levied by Justice of the Peace Jimmy Doyle.

The fine became a minor issue when Doyle declared that he was very familiar with the property; he was the pilot of a Piper Cherokee 180 airplane that frequently flew overhead, keeping a distant eye on them. Doyle had dug up information about unlicensed refrigeration and freezer rooms. Johnson quickly obtained the needed permits and headed back to the ranch to report. The "private hunting lodge" was not going over with the locals, and before long, Warren told his scribe, "The government officials of that county, Schleicher County, know of us."

Early in 2004, the prophet and I were finally starting to cross paths. While Jeffs was planning Zion, I had just started working for Ross Chatwin, hoping to help him keep his house in Short Creek. Within a few more months, I would be deeply involved with the Lost Boys case and the rape case involving Brent Jeffs and his brothers. By the end of the year, Warren and I would be in each other's cross-hairs.

One evening during that time, as he was picking at dinner with some members of his large family, a wife approached and whispered into his ear. The prophet, looking angry, stopped eating. Another concerned wife at the table, hoping to console him, asked what the trouble was. "It's that gentile investigator Sam Brower—he keeps popping up where he's not wanted!" responded the prophet.

Unfortunately, I learned a hard lesson during that first year that Warren Jeffs and his FLDS had remained all but invisible to outsiders. It was difficult to overstate what was going on in Short Creek, and it was equally impossible for anyone who had not been there to understand it. One result was that even the various investigations into Warren Jeffs and his FLDS were fragmented. Somehow, part of my task became building bridges between law enforcement and child protection agencies in several states, and between the locals and the federal authorities. That was a far cry from what I had originally signed on to do, but the farther along I went, the less choice I had.

One of the capable investigators involved in this uncoordinated effort was Ron Barton, from the office of Utah attorney general Mark Shurtleff. Barton had been doing a lot of digging, but he was hamstrung by orders to gather information without making waves. Nevertheless, he managed to pull together a lot of evidence of FLDS illegal practices, especially within the police department. But there seemed to be a lot of tension between Shurtleff and Barton, who left about the time I came on board.

I originally had entertained high hopes for Shurtleff, who had an impressive record as a prosecutor before winning the attorney general position in 2001. Shurtleff is quick on his feet and had a strong law-and-order stance. Here was someone with the clout to get to the bottom of what was going on in the Crick. But when it came time to prosecute on Barton's hard work, the AG didn't follow through, which frustrated Barton into resigning.

Barton was replaced by another state investigator, Jim Hill, who repeated the basic investigative exercise. Hill was in the middle of assembling more information when he, too, was reassigned off the FLDS case. He shortly thereafter quit the AG's office.

I liked Shurtleff; he is one of those guys that is hard to get mad at. But as the months progressed, I heard a lot more from the attorney general in the press than I actually saw him doing. I eventually came to the

realization that Shurtleff was no different from any other politician, trying to back his own agenda. When we needed AG help the most, he
seemed to pull back from the sticky situation.

No longer having a permanent home of his own, the prophet was wearing ruts in the highways of the West with his secretive travels, living in
motel rooms when on the road and not near a hideout. He had found a
new place of refuge, which he code-named R-23, in a forest some 4,600
feet above sea level in the Black Hills of South Dakota, and added it to
his temporary nests.

No matter where he was, Warren was constantly working: editing and
recording his Priesthood Record dictations to his trusted Naomi, preach-
ing back to the meeting house by telephone, undoing some marriages,
performing new ones, judging letters of contrition, collecting money, and
micromanaging decisions on the smallest day-to-day details of his flock
and the various construction projects. Women chosen for the refuges were
instructed to stay close to their buildings and not to shop in surrounding
towns, even if that required making trips over hundreds of miles to distant
stores.

He always returned to Texas, where his masterpiece was being built.
He traveled all over the ranchland and listened as the Lord filled in the
temple's details for him. There would be four levels. A baptismal font
would be placed in the basement, and the "telestial" floor on ground
level would have light green flooring and seats. The carpet and chairs in
the light blue second-floor "terrestrial" floor would be linked by a staircase of white carpet to the all-white "celestial" top floor, with rooms for
a "School of the Prophets." Warren secretly turned to the Internet to find
out how the mainstream LDS church had designed its temples, and then
he copied the results, saying they were God's special instructions to him.
As the weeks passed, there were satisfying moments, such as when God
decided on the kitchen tiles; there were also setbacks, as when Warren
reported that the Lord rejected the materials for the drapes and sheer cur-
tains upstairs. Apparently, no detail was too minor for divine scrutiny.

The most shocking order came when Warren directed the building
of a special bed to be used in temple rituals. He said that God revealed to
him during one of his heavenly sessions that it would be a special table

of strong hardwood that would be placed in the most sacred area of the temple—the Holy of Holies. His specific instructions, entered in his record, called for a ". . . table on wheels that could be converted into a sturdy bed when the top was removed. On the right would be a cushioned prayer bench that could be folded away and hidden when not in use . . . The bed will be a size big enough for me to lay on it . . . It will be covered with a sheet, but it will have a plastic cover to protect the mattress from what will happen on it—and ropes." A dozen chairs would surround it and a podium would overlook it.

"Something is going to happen in that room," he predicted in his journal, then repeated it: "Something is going to happen in that room."

On the second day of March 2004, Warren picked out still two more children to become his wives: Mildred "Millie" Marlene Blackmore, age thirteen, and Annie LaRee Jessop, who would not turn fifteen for another week. Their fathers were Merril Jessop, now a rising power in the FLDS, and Brandon Blackmore, one of the Canadians. The men, probably, had no objections, since they were not expelled from the church, thus committing various felonies with their silence in handing their little girls over to the pedophile prophet.

That night, Warren confessed to his scribe one reason for his compulsion to take immature brides. "These young girls have been given to me to be taught and trained how to come into the presence of God and help redeem Zion from their youngest years before they go through teenage doubting and boy troubles. I will be their boy trouble and guide them right." In other words, he could brainwash, mold, and molest them to his liking. Naomi was usually assigned the task of training the new girls on how a "heavenly comfort wife" should behave. Using language that a child could understand, she told them not to be afraid, and to stand back in silence when their new husband went into a "heavenly session"—or more accurately, a revelation fit, which might consist of falling down and writhing on the floor or might evolve into a sexual encounter with one or more of his *heavenly comfort wives.*

At the end of March 2004, activist and child abuse opponent Flora Jessop telephoned *Eldorado Success* editor Randy Mankin and asked, "Hey, do you know about that place being built in your area?" The editor replied that he did, and asked what she had heard. The conversation ended with Flora announcing that she was coming down to Texas to hold a news conference and reveal that Warren Jeffs and his Fundamentalist Church of Jesus Christ of Latter-Day Saints were going to be the new occupants on that spread outside of town, the area's biggest construction project. Mankin ran a front-page story headlined, COMMUNITY SEEKS ANSWERS TO QUESTIONS ABOUT NEW NEIGHBORS.

Nevertheless, David Allred, the official purchaser of the ranch property, stuck with the lie. He met with Sheriff Doran and a new face in the game, Texas Ranger Brooks Long, in the middle of April to assure them that it was indeed a corporate hunting retreat. But the busy editor Mankin tracked down longtime FLDS lawyer Rod Parker, who admitted that the compound was "connected" to the religion. As the story spread, the national media swarmed into tiny Eldorado.

That spurred government agencies to demand inspections on what was obviously developing into a huge project. Warren thought it was outrageous that others might consider the impact beyond the fence lines, because he had set a deadline of June 27 for completion of a new building that would become an interim meeting house. He believed that once the FLDS was forced to get official permission for everything, the timetable would be out of God's hands. Still, a host of issues needed to be addressed, from tax assessment to the sewer system and a planned cement batch plant, and despite the lack of building codes, Texas is very picky about the possibility of sewage or chemical contaminants polluting the water table and spreading downstream. Sheriff Doran, Ranger Long, deputies, tax assessors, environmental protection agents, and other public officials were calling for a visit. Warren blamed his flock for the situation, complaining, "We don't even have the faith to keep them away."

Finally, a party of government officials arrived and were allowed to see the orchard and the wheat field and the garden, the well, and trailer homes—everything but people. The sheriff asked where everyone was and was told that not many were around that day. Actually, dozens of Warren's children and wives were on site at the time, separated and hiding in upstairs rooms under firm orders to stay quiet.

While traveling between Colorado and Texas on Saturday, April 24, the prophet was given an update on the government visit, and he recognized that the ruse was over. There was no way to hide the obvious any longer. He hotly instructed his front men to lay it out and let the Texans know "we are there to stay."

Four days later, Allred met with Sheriff Doran and Justice of the Peace Doyle and admitted that the hunting lodge story had been false from the start. It had been needed, he said, to avoid media attention. The compound would only have about two hundred residents, he promised. That was a lie, too.

CHAPTER 20

On the Run

Warren Jeffs's paranoia spiked sharply after the discovery of his hoax in Texas, and it wound him even tighter. He was convinced that hired assassins were out to kill him.

The pressure was relentless. Things had not gone well with building the refuges during the severe bad weather in the winter of 2004, as ice and snow and hard winds delayed both work and travel. It had cost hundreds of thousands of dollars a month to maintain the workers and their families. Legal bills in excess of $100,000 had been incurred on matters ranging from property issues to court hearings to setting up holding companies. The prophet was feeling a financial pinch, with a lot more work yet to be done. Although some of his closest allies already carried debts of several hundred thousand dollars, Jeffs instructed every adult male FLDS member to cough up a "consecration"—donation—of one thousand dollars per month, a staggering sum for people who had little money. He also ordered each family to halt construction on their own homes and give the church any future funds they would otherwise spend on their own place. All of that came on top of the minimum 10 percent of each member's gross income that they were expected to hand over as a tithe each month. Also, Warren had banned Sunday meetings because the people were too slothful and no longer deserved the blessings of the sacrament, and there were not going to be any more Saturday work projects on individual homes, so the people were ordered to work weekends and take those extra earnings and consecrate them to the church as well.

This produced an immediate improvement in the cash flow, but soon he also would be trying to sell off hundreds of acres of FLDS-owned lands elsewhere and shuffling those funds into paying the bills for his refuges.

Worse, to him, was that everything and everyone was falling short of the Lord's schedule. He became even more demanding, ordering the builders at all of the refuge sites to "work twenty hours a day, and pray for the strength to work twenty-four." Men and women should not mingle. All of them were placed under divine condemnation for their laziness and lack of faith. He carefully chose who was good enough to work on the projects, picking from among the best-qualified in Short Creek. Not everyone was going to make it to Zion, and he moaned that the cut would be deep.

Even the children in Texas were not measuring up to his standards. "We have brought Babylon here in the form of toys, selfish toys, where children . . . they live to please themselves. The dolls, the trucks . . . all these are idols," he said. Every family had to search out all toys, then either discard or burn them. "Instead of a doll, a child can learn how to hold a real baby," he concluded.

Warren had what he considered an important dream on a Sunday morning in April 2004. He saw a navy admiral tempting his people with trinkets and dolls and goods from all over the world. His "ladies" decorated themselves, and tried to lure him into socializing. In his dream, Warren just wanted to leave that dreadful place.

"All I could find was a little scooter, a little motorcycle. I got on it and started driving away," the Record states. But he was stopped in his dream by a policewoman "over the simple excuse that I didn't have a taillight on my motorcycle, my little scooter." Warren read the episode as heavenly guidance to make certain that all vehicles were in perfect order so he would not be stopped for some minor infraction.

After that, he tightened his road security, traveling with a lead car a mile ahead of him, and often with a trail car, the vehicles staying in contact by radio. They did not exceed the speed limit. The goal was to not be stopped, but if they were, the drivers could not identify themselves as being a "Jeffs" or an "Allred." The little things could be dangerous.

His entourage of Naomi, the drivers, and the bodyguards would therefore wear "disguises" of normal gentile clothing, which would allow them to "mix among the people of the world" when they traveled. Naomi still wore a prairie dress over her jeans if they were in an FLDS community or refuge, but she took it off once they were on the road. If other wives came on a trip, they also would be disguised.

Having established these rules of the road, Warren Jeffs plunged even deeper into hiding.

As the summer of 2004 arrived, the prophet decided to have a reunion with forty of his wives who still remained in Short Creek and all of their children. Since the Lord had told him that the "dying community" was no longer safe for him to visit for any length of time, he arranged a rendezvous in a secluded campground of the Kaibab National Forest, on the edge of the North Rim of the Grand Canyon in Arizona. The geography made secrecy easy, but the family gathering backfired.

Individual wives and kids who had not seen their husband and father for so long competed for the opportunity to get some personal time with him, to go for private walks in the pine forests and confide their feelings to him. It made Warren uncomfortable. According to his dictations the hugs and kisses and private notes and photographs were somehow distasteful, and his approval went out only to a few who stayed apart, praying in heavenly light, instead of pestering him with selfish desires. When the outdoor get-together was finished, he fell into a dour mood. He felt few in his family were "prepared."

Afterward, it was back to the despair of Short Creek for the family members. For Warren, it was time for another road trip.

He was off on a warm-weather journey back to Jackson County, Missouri, to once again visit the early Mormon sites, this time without being hampered by snow and freezing temperatures. He considered the area to be not only a sacred site, but one that had been promised to him by God; he prophesied that after God's judgments devoured the land and the wicked, the righteous FLDS members who remained would resettle there to construct his ultimate project, the final temple.

The ranch that was blooming in Texas was merely a step toward that dream, an interim place where his people could learn to build a proper temple. Its official name would reflect that unfinished step, and it became the Yearning for Zion Ranch.

One of the sites Jeffs visited on his trip was the domed state capitol building in Jefferson City, where he strolled through the office of the governor and both chambers of the general assembly. As he gazed at the statues of Thomas Jefferson, Meriwether Lewis, and William Clark, he could not contain his inner fury at such brazen "idols." He found an unoccupied room, went in, and performed a ritualistic curse he termed "kicking the dust" from his feet, calling for the lawmakers and all of the citizens of Missouri to be swept from the face of the earth. His new Zion would need the space.

Waco was on everybody's mind when I made my initial visit to Texas in September. In that infamous 1993 bloody standoff between the federal government and the Branch Davidian religious cult, fifty-four adults and twenty-one children had died. Waco was only a two-hour drive to the east from Eldorado, and the shadow of Branch Davidian's maniacal prophet, David Koresh, easily stretched to the YFZ Ranch, where another prophet was gathering a fervent band of followers of his own.

I had been monitoring and trying to make sense of Warren's hideout scheme, and the rumor was that he was in Texas, so after the Brent Jeffs rape case was filed on August 5, I decided to see for myself. I flew into nearby San Angelo on September 4, got a hotel room, then drove directly over to Eldorado and started digging for information and meeting people who I hoped would be beneficial to our cases in the months to come.

My first stop was the office of the *Eldorado Success* newspaper, where I found editor Randy Mankin eager to share information. We enjoyed a steak dinner, then got into his truck and drove out to the site. Night had fallen, a wide canopied western blackness, but a bubble of distant lights marked the ranch. They were working around the clock. Randy pulled up beside the wire fence that surrounded the property, and I got out. Although the work was too far off the road to be seen, I could feel the ground quaking from the movement of heavy equipment at the site. "It's like this every night," Mankin said. "The only way to really see the place is to fly over it."

The following morning, I contacted Sheriff David Doran and told him that I had papers to serve on Warren Jeffs. I found him to be someone who liked to stay on top of what was going on in his county, and if someone new rolled into town, he would want to know about it. He agreed to help, and we drove back out to the ranch in his truck. There was not much more to see in the daylight than there had been at night. Everything was far away, but I could still hear construction going on. Doran dialed a number and soon the new head man at the ranch, Bishop Merril Jessop, came out to the old cattle fence beside the road. He was buttoned up and wore an old-fashioned brown straw hat.

I stayed in the truck and let Doran talk to him first. The sheriff had been working hard to establish a cordial relationship with the secretive religious group that had turned up on his doorstep, and he felt it important to try and keep the lines of communication open as much as possible. He had visited Short Creek back in May and had come away with the clear understanding the FLDS was not going to compromise, and Doran was still trying to figure out what kind of trouble that might cause. The sheriff had no proof of any wrongdoing at the ranch.

Finally, Doran called me over. We went through the subpoena delivery routine that had become so familiar to me by now. I asked if Warren was there. Jessop lied, saying no, Warren wasn't there and hadn't been seen or heard from for months. Then I handed him the papers, and the bishop said he could not take them. The sheriff interjected that under Texas law, he had to accept service. Jessop reluctantly did so, insisting that he wouldn't be seeing Warren Jeffs any time soon, so that it would be impossible to get the papers to him. Still, it was an important first step. It was necessary to show that all reasonable attempts had been made to serve Jeffs so that the court could proceed with the lawsuit, with or without the prophet's cooperation. Those papers gave Warren Jeffs only twenty days to answer them.

I still had not seen beyond the wire fence, so my next contact was with Justice of the Peace Jimmy Doyle, who regularly flew over the ranch. He invited me up in his four-seat airplane. The ranch was landlocked, and it was outlined by a five-foot-high wire field fence. I readied my camera as we approached, and the actual construction site came into view; it was a lot larger than I had expected, although still unfinished and with plenty of room to expand. A tiny guard shack was at the bend in the road leading to the main entrance, and beyond it, a network of good roads snaked out to various parts of the property. The biggest operation was a cement plant, with a silo sticking up like a rocket from the flatland, and atop it sat a doghouse-like guard post. As I flew over taking photos of their se-

Warren Jeffs with his twelve-year-old bride Merrianne Jessop, daughter of the bishop of the Yearning for Zion Ranch, Merril Jessop. Merril gave at least nineteen of his daughters and granddaughters in marriage to FLDS prophet Warren Jeffs.

Merrianne Jessop on her wedding day, just over a month before her new husband, Warren Jeffs, was captured.

A recently married and newly pregnant Veda Keate, the thirteen-year-old daughter of convicted child molester Allen Keate. Shortly after Allen gave Veda in marriage to Warren, he took an underage bride of his own. He is serving thirty-three years in Huntsville State Prison in Texas.

Ora Bonnie Steed posing with underage sister wife Veda Keate. Warren wrote that both conceived their babies during the same "heavenly session" with him. Veda also appeared in a photo in a *National Geographic* cover story on the FLDS, along with her daughter Serena. The caption in the magazine identified them only as two of the children taken in the raid on the YFZ Ranch.

Warren and Loretta

First Anniversary

January 26, 2005

Fourteen-year-old Loretta Jane Barlow and Warren Jeffs. Loretta is one of Bishop Merril Jessop's granddaughters, and the daughter of Rulon Barlow, who was excommunicated for asking Warren Jeffs to hand him some nails while working on the temple.

Fifty of Warren Jeffs's eighty-plus wives, including underage brides Merrianne Jessop, Veda Keate, Brenda Fischer, and Loretta Barlow, posing beneath a photo of their husband and prophet at the YFZ Ranch compound in Eldorado, Texas.

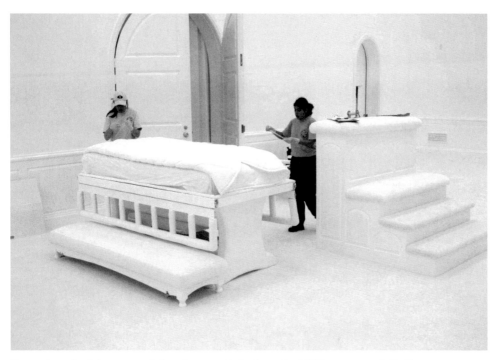

Forensic technicians examining the temple bed on the YFZ compound. Jeffs consummated many of his marriages to underage brides in bizarre group sex rituals on this specially made bed.

Temple at the YFZ Ranch. Also depicted are the temple annex and a couple of the typical H-homes common in FLDS compounds. (Photo by Kathy and Randy Mankin.)

El Cap section of the Vermillion Cliffs, as seen from Maxwell Park, Short Creek, Utah. (Photo by Sam Brower.)

The real Short Creek, where chickens peck on dirt roads roamed by large plyg-rigs and most people live in squalor. (Photo by Sam Brower.)

Ross and Lori Chatwin with three of their children at a family reunion in Cottonwood Park, Hildale, Utah. (By permission of Ross Chatwin.)

Giant cottonwoods in Cottonwood Park, Hildale, Utah. (Photo by Sam Brower.)

Like father, like son. Warren Jeffs and his father, Rulon T. Jeffs, enjoy a double wedding. Warren would later take his widowed stepmother (sitting on his father's lap) as his own bride.

After the death of Parley Harker, Warren Jeffs (left) usurped the position of first counselor to his father, the prophet Rulon T. Jeffs (center). Second Counselor Fred Jessop (right).

Author Sam Brower (left) with Schleicher County Sheriff David Doran, attempting to serve a subpoena on Warren Jeffs at the front gate of the YFZ Ranch. Bishop of the YFZ Ranch, Merril Jessop (right), is stonewalling, insisting that Warren Jeffs had not been seen in months. (Photo by Randy Mankin.)

Candi Shapley (second from left), leaving the Mohave County Courthouse after refusing to testify against Randy Barlow. Candi had previously testified under oath at a grand jury proceeding that Barlow had raped her repeatedly. (Photo by Sam Brower.)

Front entrance to the Hildale medical clinic and bishops' residence where Sam Brower had just served papers for Will (Timpson) Jessop. (Left to right) Deputy Town Marshall Sam Johnson (picking up papers and attempting to return them to Brower), Hildale deputy marshall Helaman Barlow, Washington County deputy Matt Fischer, and author Sam Brower.

Press conference at the home of Winston Blackmore in Bountiful, British Columbia, Canada. Winston Blackmore (center) and his wives (left to right) Leah, Ruth, Edith, Marsha, and Zelpha. (Photo by Sam Brower.)

A guard tower that overlooks the FLDS "place of refuge," code-named R-23, near the town of Pringle, South Dakota. (Photo by Cookie Hickstein.)

Town cemetery, Colorado City, Arizona. Note the mounds of red earth stacked on the graves, an FLDS tradition dating back to the original settlers in the early twentieth century. (Photo by Sam Brower.)

Warren Jeffs renounces his position of prophet in open court: "I'm not the prophet . . ."

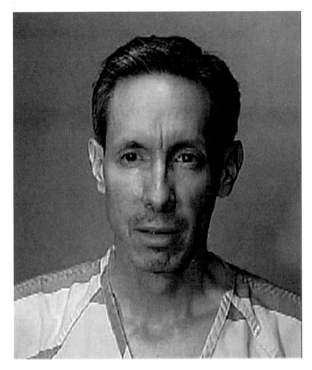

Warren Steed Jeffs's booking photo at Mohave County Jail, Kingman, Arizona, February 2008.

Author Sam Brower (left) with Brent Jeffs, nephew of Warren Jeffs, who sued his uncle Warren for raping him from the ages of five to seven. Photo taken in front of the courthouse in San Angelo, Texas, during the hearings following the raid of the YFZ Ranch. (Photo by Trent Nelson/*Salt Lake Tribune*.)

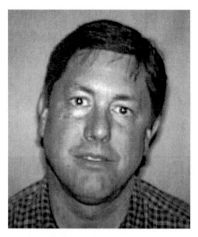

Lyle S. Jeffs, younger brother of Warren Jeffs and the new "prophet's mouthpiece" during Jeffs's incarceration.

Raymond Jessop (left) and his brother Leroy Jessop (right), leaving the court in San Angelo, Texas. Only a few months later both would be found guilty of child abuse for their roles in a bizarre triple wedding ceremony with Warren Jeffs involving three underage girls as young as twelve. (Photo by Sam Brower.)

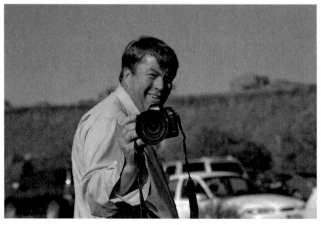

Willie Jessop stalking Sam Brower as the author leaves an appointment with his cardiac surgeon prior to open heart surgery. (Photo by Sam Brower.)

Room 15, the marriage suite at the Caliente Hot Springs Motel, Caliente, Nevada. (Photo by Sam Brower.)

The interior of Room 15. Rulon and Warren Jeffs performed scores of underage marriages here. (Photo by Sam Brower.)

Front gate of the YFZ Ranch after the rescue attempt. Security cameras are visible, as are the guard tower and temple in the distance. (Photo by Sam Brower.)

curity setup, I peered through the camera at some guy perched on the landing of the silo staring back at me through a pair of binoculars. Some large living quarters were well under way, and some industrial-style buildings were complete. Work had also begun on a large meeting house on the center of the property. Doyle pointed out one construction site as a commissary, which I knew would be the bishop's storehouse. There was no sign of any temple. The only greenery was the heat-loving mesquite and scrub brush, and much of that was being cleared for future building sites.

Machinery and building materials were down there, but where were the people? I would learn later that at the first sound of an aircraft, they would scatter inside or hide under the porch overhangs on the houses.

That evening, I went back out to the compound on my own. I had seen some wires leading from the exterior fence and wanted to determine if they had installed cameras for extra security—and if so, were they to keep people out or to keep people in? When darkness fell, I shined the infrared light from my own camera on the wires and followed them to the power source, a car battery. As far as I could tell, the FLDS had cameras watching every foot of their ranch. Perhaps they were able to see me, but there was no reaction.

On the way back to Utah, I mulled over what I had found out. A large and isolated hideout, tight security, dodging the law—it all brought to mind what other fanatics like Jim Jones and David Koresh had done. In fact, Warren Jeffs had more followers and more money than either Jones or Koresh. His followers did not cling to him just because of personal charisma; they had been born and bred into the FLDS and had little understanding of the outside world. They would do whatever was required to defend their God, his prophet Warren, and their way of life. I feared things were headed in a bad direction.

Just after I got back from Texas, the Chatwin family feud erupted again. Ross Chatwin had grown weary of his brother Steven living upstairs and had asked my advice on how to get rid of his unwanted tenant and relative, who had been installed in his home by the FLDS. There was no question that the house was Ross's; the "life estate" decision specified the entire house belonged to him for his lifetime. But the prophet remained angry about it and had been hounding the United Effort Plan lawyers to find a loophole.

In desperation, the UEP flipped the "unjust enrichment" argument that had given Ross the victory, and now claimed that Ross could not take possession of the second floor without first paying Steven some $23,000 for improvements that Steven had made on the small and blocky blue-gray house. The claim was bogus. It was the church's work crew, and not Steven, who had made those unwanted, unauthorized, and illegal changes, and they had been made under protest of the home's true legal occupant.

Instead of obeying the law, the FLDS had relaunched the matter as a new civil case. It had become rather silly. The original tenant of the UEP-owned property, the Chatwins' mutual brother David, had gone away and was now following Winston Blackmore in Canada, a situation that further fueled Warren's ire. Any friend of Winston's would be considered an enemy by Warren. I advised Ross to talk to a lawyer before doing anything, and a strategy was put together in which Ross posted eviction notices on the upstairs door for several weeks. Those warnings were ignored and torn down.

So on September 7, when Steven left the house, Ross slithered through an upstairs window and changed the locks. Steven, unable to open the doors, called the Short Creek police, and officers Helaman Barlow and Fred Barlow showed up asking to see the court documents. Having already been through a similar exercise back when Chief Sam Roundy had simply ignored the documents, Ross demanded that his attorney be present before handing anything over. When he refused to change back the locks, the officers charged him with criminal trespass, cuffed him, and hauled him to jail. Steven Chatwin then climbed through the same window that Ross had used and reinstalled the old locks.

Lori Chatwin had recorded the entire episode on a video camera, and she called me while I was in the middle of a dinner meeting at the home of attorney Pat Shea in Salt Lake City. I could not break away, but I told her the audacious arrest would not stand. The following day, Mohave County authorities read the life estate ruling of Judge Chavez and dismissed the criminal charge. Ross was once again a free man.

Steven begged the prophet to let him move out of the house and get away from his apostate brother. He said when he was listening to Warren's recorded sermons upstairs on Saturday mornings, Ross would turn up his television set downstairs so loudly while his kids watched cartoons that Steven felt his family was being corrupted by Ross's evil ways.

When one of Ross's grandmothers died, he tried to attend her funeral at the meeting house. But Willie Jessop and other church security men were posted at the door to make sure no apostates were allowed inside to defile the service. Ross and his family were turned away.

He decided he would at least attend the graveside services to pay his last respects, and he took along his video camera to record the event for other family members. Willie Jessop was on guard there, too. He walked up to Ross and snatched the camera, shoving Ross away. But Ross was becoming adept at sticking up for himself, so he not only called the local police, who he knew would do absolutely nothing, but he also called the Mohave County sheriff's office and filed a theft charge regarding the camera. Within an hour, Willie was knocking at Ross's door, camera in hand, red-faced in embarrassment and too mad to talk. Willie handed the camera over and left without a word.

Several months later, in April 2005, Steven and his family were allowed to move out, and Ross Chatwin's house finally became his own.

CHAPTER 21

Mancos

As the fall of 2004 approached, I was trying to pick up the scent of the runaway prophet. It was laborious and painstaking work, but I had polished my investigative teeth as a bounty hunter. There are times to sit behind a desk and times to hit the pavement. This was desk time, and I spent hours combing through special computer databases available only to investigators and law enforcement. I would feed in names of the FLDS hierarchy and dates and license plates and other scraps of information and see what came back. Hundreds, even thousands, of hits might pour in, leaving me with the mundane task of eliminating useless data. It is not exciting work, but it is effective. The piece of information that can't be discarded is usually the piece that fits the puzzle.

Such was the case when I ran the name of David Allred, the original buyer of the property in Texas. An avalanche of hits came back. There were a lot of David Allreds out there in cyberspace, most of them having nothing to do with the FLDS, but as I began chipping away at it over the next couple of days, the stack became more manageable, and late one night an interesting connection popped up. Allred had a company called Sherwood Management, which had been incorporated in Nevada—a state notorious for allowing corporations anchored there to hide their officers and shield assets from prying eyes. Sherwood was cross-indexed to a piece of property that had been bought six miles north of the isolated little mountain village called Mancos, located in the sparsely populated Four Corners area of southwestern Colorado. I considered the equation. David Steed Allred, a confirmed FLDS moneyman, had been the one to establish the "hunting lodge" foothold in Texas. Allred and Sherwood were tied to the purchase of a pair of sixty-acre lots near Mancos for $1,394,000. It was time to get out from behind the desk and hit the road.

I gassed up and headed east. I had a feeling that I might need some backup on this trip, so I called Jon Krakauer at his home in Colorado. We had made telephone contact several months earlier, and I had grown comfortable talking with him. His book, *Under the Banner of Heaven*, had already been published and he had no intention of writing anything more about the FLDS, but his disdain for some of the group's despicable practices had remained, and he was fierce about wanting to help. He, too, wanted some answers, and he did not hesitate when I invited him to join me in Mancos.

We arrived at a hotel in nearby Cortez simultaneously, and actually met for the first time in a hallway while walking to our rooms. Jon has piercing eyes and is of medium build, and he is physically fit from a lifetime of mountaineering and other hard exercise. It would be useful to have someone who knew so much about the case, who could also watch my back. Over dinner, we joked that if the FLDS were to come upon us prowling around the Mancos compound, we might find ourselves under the next foundation they poured in Texas.

Before doing anything, we had to deal with a media leak that could jeopardize our plans. Flora Jessop had happened to call during one of my late-night research sessions on Allred, and I had made an offhand comment to her about the interesting data coming back concerning a little Colorado town. While trying to develop more information on her own, she had passed the discovery to a reporter in Phoenix. I am particularly wary about allowing the media into my investigations. Reporters are not paid to keep secrets. Some journalists had earned my trust; others had not. I had never met the guy Flora had contacted, so he was in the latter category.

He planned to broadcast a story right away, which could have torpedoed our whole plan, so Jon tried to make a deal with him. If he would hold off for forty-eight hours, we would give him exclusive access to everything we had discovered, and Krakauer, who rarely gives media interviews, would sit down and talk to him on camera. Just give us time to get there and look around, we asked, and perhaps serve papers on Warren Jeffs. Then the reporter would be able to break the even bigger story, with a famous author on the subject answering all questions. It was more than fair. In fact, it was a no-brainer. The reporter said he would talk to his producer. When he got back to us, he said a huge storm front was coming in and his producer wanted him to cover that instead. With the deal made, we could exhale and get a well-needed night's rest.

Jon and I were up early the following day to scout the property, only to find out the reporter and his crew had already been out there and filed a story at dawn from the front of the FLDS compound. It would air that night and his presence had tipped off the FLDS that their secret compound had been found. I was ready to chew nails at being double-crossed, and Krakauer telephoned the reporter to verbally whip his butt for lying to us. Unwilling to let him enjoy his exclusive, I called *Eldorado Success* editor Randy Mankin down in Texas, who also had been brought into the loop about the Mancos development with the understanding that he would not publish anything until I checked it out. Now, I gave him the green light to post the news on his Web site, www.myeldorado.net, and he scooped the TV show by hours.

Jon and I headed to the compound for some daytime surveillance. The only way to get a look at the property without being noticed was to skirt around about a mile to the north and go in through the woods. It had been quite a while since I had done any hiking, and I had a tough time trying to keep up with Jon, but—I kept reminding myself—he'd climbed Mount Everest.

When we finally reached a vantage point where I could catch my breath, I said, "Okay, Jon, if anything happens I've got my .22 pocket pistol and a .45 Colt with me. I'm going to toss you the .22, and you run for help and I'll stay here and shoot it out!" I was only half-kidding. The truth was that Krakauer could have been out of the woods and back with a posse and a cup of coffee before I had made it halfway back to the car.

We were able to get the lay of the land without being noticed. We spotted several parked vehicles around the area, but they were too far away to get their plate numbers. The fences were down around most of the heavily wooded property and it was hard to tell where National Forest started and the compound property began. We decided to return that night to see if we could get a little closer, then went back to town and enjoyed a pleasant dinner at a little restaurant that featured a big sign: WELCOME DEER HUNTERS. The season had begun in Colorado.

We returned to the forest when it was pitch black. Earlier in the day, we had heard generators purring in the distance, and the coughing of a tractor, but it was dead silent now, and there were no lights burning anywhere. Apparently the news had gotten back to them about the discovery, and a total blackout had been imposed. Jon was clearly in his outdoorsy element, clipping along in the darkness almost as if he knew the GPS location of each tree. He was my navigator, so I stayed close enough to make out his shape and listened to his footsteps in the darkness.

I was counting on him to get us close to some of those cars so that we could get a visual on the license plates in the hope that they might lead us to Jeffs.

Suddenly I heard the crunch of someone else's footsteps, coming from the opposite direction. I switched off my night-vision goggles to prevent anyone from spotting their faint glow. Jon was about ten feet ahead, too far for me to call out a warning without giving up our location.

The newcomer was within about four feet of me when he realized he was not alone. He snapped on his flashlight, shining it directly in my face. So I turned on my flashlight and put it directly in his face.

"Whoa! Who are you?" he asked, totally surprised.

Think fast, Brower. All the talk about the violent history of radical fundamentalists came flooding back to me. Jon was far enough ahead that he hadn't even heard the guy until he spoke. Ignoring my earlier advice of going to get help, Jon returned to back me up.

The best defense is always a good offense. "Who are you? What are you doing out here?" I snapped back at the guard with whom I was having the flashlight duel.

"Take that light out of my face," he said.

"Okay, take yours out of mine," I commanded back, unwilling to give up any ground.

"This is our property!" He was a big dude, at least my size, a little heavier and at least twenty years younger. His comment confirmed he was an FLDS guard.

I needed to keep him talking, so I protested, "No, it's not. This is National Forest Service land!"

A little unsure by now, he admitted that the fences were down in some areas, and that maybe we had stumbled through one of those gaps. His tone changed. "Why are you here?"

For some reason, the welcome sign from that little restaurant blinked in my mind. "We're deer hunters," I responded. I saw Jon's jaw drop when I said it.

The guard looked us over. "Well, how come you don't have any rifles?"

"You can't shoot deer at night," I argued, sounding frustrated. "That would be illegal. You even get caught with a rifle at night you'll get fined."

I explained that we had spotted some deer bedded down in the meadows earlier in the day and were trying to find where they might be feeding so we could come back at daybreak and fill our tag. The guard eased up a little. I asked if he had seen any deer around. He told me that there were a lot of them out in the woods and that he had seen some big bucks. By now, he was relaxed, so we had a little conversation about hunting, exchanged some pleasantries, then said good night and walked away.

When we had gone about a hundred yards, Jon looked at me and said, "How the fuck did you do that?" Bounty hunting had taught me to think fast, but this meeting was not quite over. When I had shut off my night-vision scope, I had stuck it in my jacket pocket, but apparently not all the way. It was no longer there and was too expensive to lose.

I told Jon that I needed to go back and get it. We both felt we had just dodged a bullet, but I didn't want to leave without my night vision. Jon pleaded with me to forget it, but I was stubborn and turned round and yelled back in the direction of the guard that I had lost my scope and wondered if he had found it.

The voice came back from the darkness. "Does it look sort of like a flashlight?"

As Jon and I approached, the guard had the scope to his eye, trying to figure it out. I told him I was using it to try and track the deer and gave him a lesson on how it worked. He was so interested that he asked how much the scope cost and where he could get one. We talked a bit longer, then excused ourselves once again and left, this time for good.

When we got back to the car, our nerves were still jangling. Then we laughed and the tension drained away.

By mid-morning the next day, I was once again at the fence line. Krakauer had had to return home. After the previous night's experience with the guard, I wasn't all that eager to poke around out there alone, but I still had work to do; I was walking the perimeter of the property with my camera and video-recorder when an all-terrain four-wheeler came grumbling through the trees. Opportunity or threat? The driver rolled to a stop and sat on the stuttering machine, staring at me.

"Hey!" I called out, as cheerful as could be. "Come over here and talk to me!"

He shook his head and stayed put on the John Deere machine. "You'll start taking pictures of me," he countered.

"It's too late for that, pal," I said with a smile. I put my cameras on the ground and walked over to the fence some twenty yards away, hands empty. "Come on. What? Are you afraid to talk?"

The slender man was not flustered by my goading. "No, I'm not afraid to talk." He wore a nice forest-green jacket and a baseball cap. I could almost see his mind weighing the situation.

"Then what's the big deal? You're not going to get in any trouble, are you?" I tried needling him into action.

He turned off the engine and quiet enveloped the area. "We had some intruders out here last night," he said.

"Really?" I kept my face straight.

"Yeah. We found some boot prints and I was out looking around." He dismounted and walked over to the fence.

Introductions were in order. "I'm Sam Brower."

"David Allred," he said, and we shook hands.

He said he had heard of me. By that time, a lot of FLDS people had the idea that I was the devil incarnate. I believe both Allred and I thought that we had each made a huge find, and began fishing for information. The Mancos trip was not going to be a dry hole after all.

He was cordial when he got to talking, telling me stories about the natural beauty of the area, with which I agreed. He said he had enjoyed the winter weather, which indicated that he had been at the Mancos hide-out for at least part of the winter months. When he said that only his family was living there and he was doing some remodeling, I knew he was blowing a smokescreen. You don't post guards at night for a little family get-together. And by this time, I had photographed the license plates of a number of cars in the area, some of which I would find were registered to FLDS members.

It turned out that they had become pretty curious about me, too. Allred and I played each other for intelligence for a while, but I knew he was too sharp to tip me off that Warren might be there. Had he done so, I had a subpoena folded up in my jacket, ready to hand over. Nevertheless, I had made a good contact, and I wanted to keep him on the line. I gave him my business card and said if he ever had any questions or wanted to know the truth about what was going on, just give me a call and I would tell him whatever I was at liberty to discuss.

That seemed to open him up a bit, and we agreed that it was a good idea to keep a back channel open, so he gave me his office number. It was a smart move on his part, because if I called, he might find out something useful.

I had gone into Mancos to verify a hunch and had come out on speaking terms with one of the top men in the FLDS. Sometimes you make your own luck. I would call Allred twice later during the investigation, and we chatted, but after that, he shut down contact.

"R-1 was discovered by our enemies," Warren wrote soon after in the Priesthood Record. "A certain private investigator [is] searching for me."

I had come very close to my quarry. According to his journal, both the prophet and Uncle Fred were at the Mancos compound when Jon and I were in the surrounding forest. The prophet later claimed that he had been having weird dreams that "the devil himself was on the land."

My unexpected appearance at his place of refuge knocked Jeffs further off balance. He quickly started to move most of the Mancos residents down to Texas, whether or not they had yet been deemed worthy to go there.

CHAPTER 22

Janetta

"I can't take it anymore! I have to get out!" The trembling voice of seventeen-year-old Janetta Jessop was a terrified whisper when she telephoned her older sister, Suzanne Jessop Johnson, on November 5, 2004. "Can you please help me?" Suzanne had not seen or heard from Janetta for more than a year, ever since Suzanne had taken a plate of cookies over to the family home in Colorado City to congratulate Janetta on her sixteenth birthday. But the birthday girl had not been there. Neither had her belongings. "All of a sudden it was like Janetta had never existed," Suzanne told me later.

There was open strife between Suzanne and her parents, because she had abandoned the FLDS and did not recognize Warren Jeffs as a prophet. She was the only wife of Lester Johnson, who had also parted ways with Warren's madness and had become a follower of Winston Blackmore in Canada, although they both continued to live in Short Creek. Suzanne had asked her mother about Janetta's whereabouts and received only a stare and a bland, "Well, I don't know." After some prodding, her mother finally said that Janetta was on a special mission and was happy and well.

For Suzanne, it was no real mystery. She just hoped what she suspected was not true. Two of her other sisters, Kate and Velvet, had been married to old Uncle Rulon and were among those wives later taken by Warren. Suzanne believed that pretty, blonde Janetta also had become a new bride for the prophet and was stashed away in some secret place against her will, struggling to make a run for it. I would later discover a photograph showing Warren Jeffs and Janetta, their arms entwined, drinking from silver goblets on their wedding day, after she had just turned sixteen.

The surprise telephone call from Janetta on Friday, November 5, made Suzanne afraid for her sister. "The first thing that crossed my mind was that Warren or somebody was doing something bad to her, or making her do things she didn't want to do, and it was scaring her." Suzanne tried to calm her little sister and promised to help. Janetta quickly said she would pack some things and call right back to arrange a rendezvous.

That was the last that Suzanne heard from her. The following day, their mother came to Suzanne's place in Hildale to deliver a message: "I don't know what's going on, but Janetta told me to tell you, 'Never mind.'" Suzanne asked why her sister had not called her directly, and the mother shrugged. "Well, you know Uncle Warren has to be in hiding right now. It just has to be this way for a while."

Knowing that calling the Short Creek police would be a useless exercise, and desperate to help Janetta, Suzanne and Lester instead phoned Winston Blackmore. He called me, and I felt a surge of adrenaline rushing through my veins. I was furious about this little girl being handed over to the prophet on her sixteenth birthday by her proud parents. That would make three of their daughters in the prophet's household, quite a coup for Frank Jessop, as valuable as a truckload of gold in that cult. Janetta was in trouble, and we had to find her.

The situation was the sort of opportunity for which I had been waiting. It is a felony in Utah for a man to marry an underage girl who is ten or more years younger than himself. Warren was about fifty at the time, and Janetta sixteen. If we could persuade her to tell authorities what had happened to her, confirm the sham marriage on the record, there would not only be civil matters pending and under investigation, but possible criminal charges, too. Every cop in the land, except those around Short Creek, would be looking for Warren Jeffs. Taking it one step farther, if she would testify, it would also help focus some much-needed national attention on the plight of young girls in Short Creek.

It could not have happened at a better time. I had some dependable law enforcement help. Riding in from the West, as the storybooks say, came Gary Engels, a no-nonsense former homicide investigator hired by

Mohave County, Arizona, specifically to monitor what was happening in Short Creek. Gary had been wounded in the line of duty, he was fearless, and he would never back down from any church goons. It would not be long before the entire town hated him as he dug into the FLDS criminal organization.

We would become close friends during the coming months, and we were happy to have each other as backup. Often, as we drove around Short Creek together, it seemed that we were the only two sane people on an otherwise screwball planet. In many such moments, we would adjourn to Gary's office, a double-wide modular trailer that had been set up on the edge of town on a rented rare piece of land that was not owned or controlled by the FLDS church. We dubbed it "Fort Apache," and it became our only sanctuary in an area where we felt surrounded by hostiles.

We made a good pair and, at the time, we were the only two investigators in the trenches actively working cases involving the FLDS. If a possible crime was involved, I always made Gary aware of it.

Gary was still brand new to the job when Janetta Jessop telephoned her sister for help. The case was his baptism by fire, and he went after it hard, as was his style. Janetta's family lived on the Arizona side of Short Creek, within his jurisdiction, which gave him the authority to open an investigation. But Suzanne Johnson, who had received the distress call, lived on the Utah side. That invisible border had bedeviled real law enforcement for decades.

The FLDS can run back and forth across it as they will, but a police officer with the wrong badge may end up hamstrung. Because of the jurisdictional mess, the first thing I advised Suzie Johnson to do was file a missing persons report with the Washington County sheriff's office on the Utah side. They are the closest legitimate law enforcement agency, although Sheriff Kirk Smith was never pleased to have a Short Creek case dumped in his lap.

A Washington County deputy was instructed to telephone Janetta's parents, who naturally said that she was safe and sound at home. That was "case closed" as far as the sheriff's office was concerned. I couldn't believe they would have made such a careless phone call, which tipped off the parents that the authorities were now looking for their daughter. That meant that any opportunity of finding her without alerting Warren had evaporated.

Suzie and Lester raised such a fuss about this that the sheriff agreed to send someone to verify whether Janetta was really at the house.

A county detective knocked on the door of Frank Jessop. He had not been provided with a current photo of the girl for whom he was allegedly searching. The detective saw two girls wearing long dresses and the swept-up plyg-do hairstyle, but neither showed identification and the detective was not allowed to talk to them. When the parents assured him that one of girls was the missing Janetta, the detective said, "Okay," and left. The sheriff's office in Utah had done what it had to do, and no more.

I was frustrated and concerned at the seeming apathy I was encountering in some of the law enforcement agencies. They had ignored Short Creek for so long, allowing the community itself to handle any problems within the little theocracy, that I felt they needed a push to start treating the Crick like the rest of the country.

Jon Krakauer, untroubled by borders, stepped forward and wrote a detailed news release about the missing girl on November 12, 2004. It carried the boldface headline, UTAH SHERIFF WON'T INVESTIGATE CALL FOR HELP FROM UNDERAGE BRIDE OF POLYGAMIST LEADER WARREN JEFFS. If the media picked up the story, the Utah sheriff's office might finally feel compelled to actively get involved.

The news release worked. It led to appearances by Sheriff Kirk Smith and me on the nationally televised news show *Deborah Norville Live*, where we discussed the case in separate interviews. Smith defended his department's actions in public. The undersheriff was so steamed about me pressuring them to do their job that he called me and threatened to arrest me for filing a false police report. That was ridiculous: The missing person report was not false, and I hadn't filed it; Suzie Johnson had.

Gary Engels also had been fuming about the inaction on the Utah side. He was not used to walking away from a challenge, and he made plans of his own to try to get a one-on-one with the girl, away from her parents. They lived on the Arizona side, which was his turf. He ignored the locals in Short Creek and launched his own investigation, bypassing the sheriff's office in Washington County. He arranged for some Arizona Child Protective Services workers to go to the house for a surprise visit, backed up by Arizona deputies. I followed with Suzanne in my car.

A deputy knocked on the door, but there was no answer. We weren't surprised. My sources had warned me long ago that all FLDS residents in Short Creek had instructions from church leaders not to answer the knock of anyone who does not first call ahead. We were about to leave when Suzanne spotted her mother's car coming down the street, with Janetta in the passenger seat. When she saw that we were at the house, Mrs. Jessop kept driving right past the driveway. I pointed and yelled, "There they go!"

The deputies pulled her over a short distance away as I drove up along with the CPS people. Janetta and Suzanne fell into a tearful embrace as their mother went into a tirade, shouting the automatic FLDS response about how government could not take away her child.

The Short Creek police arrived and demanded to know why they had not been consulted. Gary responded in his usual professional manner, although I could tell he was tempted to laugh in the faces of the local cops for asking such an absurd question. Janetta was ferried to neutral territory at a children's justice center in nearby St. George, Utah, for an interview.

Our hopes for a big break now lay on the frail shoulders of young Janetta, who was overwhelmed by what was happening. The CPS workers spent four hours with her and determined that her shaky physical and mental states were in part due to large amounts of drugs such as Xanax and Prozac. She appeared to be near to the point of incoherence.

Janetta had spent time with some of Warren's other concubines at the R-1 compound in Mancos, Colorado, where she had been moved after Warren took her into his fold on her sixteenth birthday. Once again, since it was not a legal marriage but an FLDS imitation, no laws had been broken. She was to complete her training there to become a "heavenly comfort wife" and learn the importance of keeping sacred things secret. She would get out of bed at four in the morning, say her prayers, then feed the birds in the chicken coop. Such superficial descriptions of her daily life were a start, but not really helpful.

She would not elaborate on where she had been for the past year and would not discuss her relationship to Warren Jeffs. Once again it appeared that the guilt and brainwashing that had been instilled in her, and her fear that she might be putting her salvation in jeopardy, stopped her from speaking out against the prophet. The family and church had gotten to her before we intervened. Janetta's most frequent answer, repeated over and over, was, "I don't want to talk about it."

My hope of finding someone willing to come forth and tell the whole story of what had happened to her was dashed, but by this point in my investigation, I had learned not to expect much; nothing was easy in dealing with an entire culture that was so completely dysfunctional. I had to be patient and thorough.

Only later did I piece together what Warren claimed had happened to Janetta. In one of his "heavenly sessions" recorded in his journal, Warren justified what he did by making the ridiculous assertion that "evil powers" had made Janetta tiptoe in the night to the room of Warren's own son, Mosiah, with the desire to have sex with him. According to Warren, Mosiah later confessed an attraction to her, so despite the fact that nothing had taken place between them, and that Janetta had never even entered the room, they both complied with the prophet's insistence that they confess the sins of their hearts. Warren then banished them from R-1 and sent Janetta further into hiding in Nevada.

Putting together the interviews I had with her sister over time, plus the prophet's record, the story emerged that when the supposedly errant young wife got caught phoning her sister and planning to escape, and word came that police were involved, Janetta was sent back to her family in Short Creek to avoid further scrutiny by the law. Her father was given the responsibility of bringing her back under control, so that she might one day again prove herself to be a worthy wife of the prophet.

As disappointed as I was that Janetta would not talk, I was more surprised at the effect that her story had on me. It had very little shock value. Crimes had been committed against this young girl and only a handful of people cared enough to even try to rescue her. It was maddening, but as the case had gone on, I found myself growing more matter-of-fact about the sick, hidden sins of Short Creek.

The truth is that an investigator cannot survive and be effective if he walks around in a constant state of shock. You have to put the outrage aside and do your job.

Poor Janetta was another young girl abused by the FLDS—one among so many. As usual, I would stay in touch with her sister in case something else developed, but I had to move on and think of the thousands of other children who still might be helped.

Christmas does not exist in Short Creek. Warren had declared all holidays to be a distraction for the people and proclaimed Christmas in particular to be evil and idolatrous. He weighed this as another chance to test how far the people would go in obeying his seemingly irrational commandments. There was little resistance about the ban on the Christmas holidays. With no bright lights or outdoor decorations, no toys, no trees with ornaments, and no joy, Short Creek seemed even more dreary than usual as 2004 wound to a close.

That did not mean the fundamentalists were idle.

Aerial photos of the ranch outside of Eldorado, Texas, had been gathering on my desk, and they showed the progression of a large, new project down there. A wide, flat area had been cleared and the latest photos showed that a huge foundation was being laid, with footings approximately eight feet wide by six feet thick. Whatever was going in there would be enormous.

Rumors were circulating that it was to be a temple. To most untrained observers, it was just another manifestation of Warren's eccentricities; but to me, it was evidence that Warren was taking his revelations of doom to the next level. Previous FLDS leaders had always been very vocal about not needing a temple, at least until the end of the world. I considered the sudden emergence of a temple to be significant, and worrisome.

Nothing happened over Christmas in 2004, but Jon Krakauer and I couldn't shake the eerie feeling that something was up. We devised a plan to split the New Year's duty and try to cover all of the bases. Gary Engels and I could keep an eye on Short Creek because we were invited to a New Year's Eve party there at the home of Marvin Wyler, the father of Ross Chatwin. Marvin also had been tossed out of the church but, like a handful of others who had been excommunicated, he refused to leave Short Creek. Jon volunteered to travel to Eldorado and check out the Texas compound.

The party was a rare opportunity for Gary and me to meet some more of the increasing number of FLDS refugees in a social setting as opposed to formal interviews. No longer having to abide by the onerous rules laid down by Warren Jeffs, they could celebrate the holidays as they pleased. We were surprised to find that the gathering had grown into a large event. About sixty people—representing most of the excommunicated and isolated families in the area—dropped by Marvin's well-worn house on the Arizona side that night.

Gary and I had grown accustomed to being vilified in this town, and it was pleasant to be able to just relax a little with people who knew that we were on their side. Presents were exchanged, and at midnight, the kids shot off fireworks. Some people in Short Creek were actually having a good time! That scared the heck out of the cops. Police cars circled the house seventeen times in the space of one hour, looking for a reason to stop the party, but no laws, not even their made-up kind, were being broken. Fireworks were not illegal in the state and the streaks of sparks in the night and the firecracker pops made the house seem like a little oasis of merriment as the rest of the town hunkered down, dark and fearful. I was given a thick glass drinking mug decorated with ribbon and filled with home-made candy.

We stood out as oddities, of course, but everyone wanted to shake our hands and ask what was going on with the legal side of things. They were curious about the missing prophet. Those at the party didn't know where he was either.

Jon Krakauer awoke before dawn on the first day of 2005 and a short time later was strapped into the passenger seat of Jimmy Doyle's small airplane, flying out to the Texas site. As they approached, they saw activity down below at the ranch, but they were too high to make out details. As Doyle swooped the plane down for a closer look, Krakauer grabbed his camera and began snapping pictures.

On the ground, panic ensued. People scattered, jumping into cars or heading for the tree line. A large black Suburban sped off. In moments, the place was clear, except for the big foundation footings that had drawn our attention in the first place.

Later that same day, Jon downloaded the images onto his computer and studied the details. We had guessed right; the FLDS had picked a major holiday on which to dedicate the new foundation, betting that no curious outsiders would be around. They had gathered in a prayer circle, and in clear view, standing right in the middle, was a long, lanky figure: Warren Jeffs. It was Warren who had piled into the SUV at the approach of the aircraft. He later expressed his displeasure at being caught in the middle of the prayer circle and blamed the interruption on workers who had not removed some concrete forms, and were thus responsible for delaying the dedication on the Lord's scheduled time. Warren noted that he had intended to depart the site by 6:30 A.M. Jon had caught him by only a few minutes. Uncle Fred, wheezing and on oxygen, was also there.

It was a great way to start 2005. This was the first Warren sighting in many months, and it meant that he had not fled to Canada or Mexico as rumored. He was around, close enough to participate in activities at the compound. FLDS ranch spokesman Merril Jessop had been lying when he had said that Warren never went there. In fact, according to the journal, once the plane had departed and the morning sky was again safe, Jeffs and his followers returned to the site and finished blessing the foundation before he sped off on his next road trip.

CHAPTER 23

Wicked

Heavy framework started going up at the Texas temple site a few days after the hide-and-seek dedication ceremony. Only then did I start to get a feel for the size of the new building. As temple workers laid sheets of plywood for the first floor, I began making estimates of the size of the structure. It was going to be at least 17,000 square feet on each of three floors, and they were sparing no expense on the quality of building materials. Millions of dollars worth of mining, rock cutting, and construction equipment was brought in to extract the low-grade limestone from the ground.

Under Warren's alternating whips of blessing and condemnation, construction went with lightning speed. Nobody can build faster than a troop of motivated FLDS builders who are convinced they are working for their very lives and the prophet.

Jeffs's journal would show that he constantly babbled directions: precise dimensions for a thirty-foot-tall tapered tower to go atop the three-story building, double insulation in the walls, darkly tinted windows. He had a mental vision for every inch of the building. But Warren was not one of those sweat-stained kids that the FLDS consigned to learn the building trades instead of going to school. He had none of their construction skills, nor did he possess the necessary architectural training. His design plan came through his fevered revelations, which meant some of it was impossible to carry out. That did not stop him from giving orders.

When some irregularly shaped walls that he had dreamed up did not turn out as envisioned, he ordered Rulon Barlow, who was in charge of the framing, to double his crew and make it right.

Barlow, an experienced hand, explained that they were in the middle of putting up windows, but Warren again firmly ordered him to fix the walls instead. "I started helping them, carrying the sheeting that covers the outside of the wall," Jeffs would recall. He wanted to see to it that the job would get done.

Then Barlow, holding his nail gun and standing next to Warren, made the terrible mistake of asking the prophet, "Will you get me my nails in that box right there?" Jeffs stiffened, but handed him the few remaining nails.

Rulon Barlow might have thought he could get away with such a liberty because the two men were related through the barter system. Barlow had gotten the prestigious foreman position among the temple builders at the ranch, while Warren had been given the Barlows' thirteen-year-old daughter as a bride. Within a year, she was pregnant. Therefore, Rulon Barlow was one of Warren's many fathers-in-law, although he was a decade younger than the prophet. Technically, he deserved some respect. He got just the opposite. "I detected through the spirit of God that this man delighted in directing me," Warren complained in his journal.

That night, Jeffs had a vision that Barlow no longer held priesthood and would have to be expelled from Short Creek, along with his family.

Asking for a handful of nails had cost Rulon Barlow everything.

Warren was laying plans for more than just routine construction. One of the last men the church had allowed to go off to be educated by outsiders had obtained a degree in electrical engineering before returning to the fold. He gradually was elevated into higher positions within the secret confederation of men and women found worthy of being "temple builders." That required an oath of secrecy that read in part, "For and in behalf of the Lord and Our Prophet; I do willingly enter into this covenant with the Lord to keep sacred things secret and not reveal what I hear in this training to anyone except by the Prophet's immediate direction."

He was instructed to build a high-tech thermostat that could take an incinerator up to an astonishing 2700 degrees Fahrenheit. As he worked, the engineer grew concerned about the ultimate use of the device, because that temperature was much higher than needed for almost any commercial application. He knew that even a crematorium operates at between 1600 and 1800 degrees to completely consume human bodies.

When the leaders would not tell him the purpose, the engineer quit, and he was soon expelled from the church.

Sheriff David Doran would eventually question Bishop Merril Jessop about the super-furnace, and he was first told that it was to be used to make some gold fixtures for the temple. But the melting point of gold is just 1900 degrees, so Jessop changed his story; they were developing a powder-coating operation, although that could be done at about only 700 degrees. The third time around, Jessop said he was not sure why the powerful furnace had been built, but that probably it would just be used to burn trash.

Although no one can say for certain, in my opinion, the existence of a high-tech extreme-temperature furnace operation in the hands of a man with the mental and emotional instability of Warren Jeffs, who talked of blood atonement and made end-of-the-world proclamations, could be a dangerous thing. The idea of using it just to burn garbage seems ridiculous.

I was unable to come up with a rational answer to the question of why Warren was secretly building such a futuristic piece of equipment. Was there some kind of evidence that could only be destroyed at very high temperatures? If so, what could it be? That Merril Jessop could not come up with a plausible explanation bothered me. The question has never been satisfactorily answered.

"What do we do about the Walter Steed case?" the prophet asked of his counselors in February 2005. Still another attack had come at them, this one launched in a complaint to the Utah Judicial Conduct Commission against Hildale Justice Court's Judge Steed by an antipolygamist group known as Tapestry Against Polygamy. As implied by its name, Tapestry had been formed by a coming-together of other groups to battle the polygamist lifestyle and help those wanting to escape. It operated independently, another example of how diffuse the overall effort against the FLDS remained.

When I made a call to the commission to see what action might be taken about Judge Steed, who had steadily punished our clients with his own brand of heavy church justice, I learned that Tapestry was already in the process of filing a similar complaint, so we supported them and I gave the commission a briefing on what our clients felt were some of the judge's abuses of power.

With their automatic immunity from prosecution, judges are hard targets, but the stubborn Judge Steed was his own worst enemy. The part-time judge had been on the bench since 1980, hearing cases primarily on Saturdays so as not to interfere with his job as a truck driver. He was just another cog in the FLDS machine. Steed provided a legal shield for kicking young males out of town, or he would team up with the cops and frustrate the young men long enough that they would leave on their own. Some of our clients in the Lost Boys matter told of being picked up by the police on some absurd charge and taken directly before the judge, who sentenced them to perform community service without even being granted a hearing. Some boys literally had thousands of hours of community service stacked against them, for charges such as being out past curfew or "running away," the court's term for leaving the house without parental permission.

Steed also provided revenue through court fines such as traffic tickets on unsuspecting travelers, and he generally settled disputes however church leaders wanted. He belonged to them.

Judge Steed was an unrepentant polygamist. So the easiest way to expose his unworthiness for the bench was not a stack of examples of bias and misconduct, but the underlining of how he had violated his oath of office. He had sworn to uphold the law, and polygamy was against the law. The judge was married to three women and had thirty-two children.

Warren Jeffs certainly was not going to emerge from hiding to speak on his behalf. Answering his own question about what to do in the Steed case, Warren said, "The Lord showed me through the night that I must answer them nothing. So I answer nothing." Judge Steed was thrown under the bus. It took more than a year, but in 2006, the Utah Supreme Court finally kicked Walter Steed off the bench, ruling that his personal religious beliefs could not trump the law.

In February 2005, the Lord told Jeffs to take another road trip, this time to the last place I would have suspected. "He will have me witness one of the most immoral parties that this nation allows," he stated, and with ten thousand dollars in his pocket, he led his little cadre of Naomi and their driver-helpers Isaac Jeffs and Ben Johnson to New Orleans. He had been there the previous year and witnessed the evils of a New Orleans Saints professional football game. This time, there was an even bigger attraction: Mardi Gras.

They arrived in the Big Easy at eleven o'clock on Sunday morning, February 6, and Naomi and Warren were dropped off at Bourbon Street to stroll the French Quarter while Isaac and Ben hunted up hotel rooms. Soon, partiers were massing in what the prophet called "one great ugly, dark immorality." It was everything he had dreamed about.

The parades began, and outrageously costumed and masked women and men aboard carnival floats pulled by little tractors hurled beads and necklaces into the cheering throng. Everyone seemed to be drinking. Girls were having their faces painted. Funny hats were everywhere. Wild music rolled out of bars. It was not yet three o'clock in the afternoon, and the prophet and his team retreated to their hotel rooms about a mile from the action. Isaac and Ben were dispatched back into the party zone on a scouting mission.

While Warren and Naomi rested, the two appalled elders reported by cell phone at five o'clock that things were getting wild. Men were hollering to women to bare their breasts in exchange for strands of beads, and the women were doing it! Ornate balconies around hotels in the Quarter were thick with people flinging down beads and flashing their bodies while motioning for women to take off their clothes, too.

The shocked FLDS men came back to the rooms, so that Warren could join them for a nighttime foray after sending a message back to the faithful to pray for him because he was in "great danger." He decided that he could not allow Naomi to witness the shocking goings-on, so he gave her a cell phone and ordered her to stay in the hotel room and push the sofa against the door.

Naomi probably would not have been very pleased about being left out of the party. The woman was no fragile flower and was more than capable of taking care of herself. While most of his followers had not seen Warren Jeffs for more than a year, since August 10, 2003, Naomi had been constantly at his side as his most trusted and favored wife, friend, scribe, and lover.

"Howdy, Naomi's gorgeous!" he happily declared to start one entry in his Record. "Nomes" was pretty in her long FLDS dresses with her flowing auburn hair wound up in a plyg-do, and she was even more delightful to Warren in the gentile clothes she wore on the road. One might think that she was really just another of Warren's many wives, a cowed adjunct to his massive ego. That would be a misconception. Anyone who challenged the queen bee would later regret it. Naomi was a player, and she had the prophet's ear.

It seemed that she had been conniving her way to the top forever. As a daughter of Merril Jessop, who was among the FLDS elite, she had been treated gently by others as a child and had quickly grown to understand the benefits of power. When she was only eleven years old, Naomi had created a sensation by kidnapping a girl of about eight or nine that she did not like and taking her down to the overgrown waterway from which the town of Short Creek drew its name, where she tormented her adversary and held her captive for an entire day. The whole town turned out to search for the missing girl, only to discover the perpetrator of the crime was off-limits to discipline. Instead of punishing her or getting her professional mental-health treatment, the community hushed up the event and handled it in-house.

Only six years later, on July 18, 1993, the seventeen-year-old Naomi had the honor of becoming a wife for the aging prophet Rulon Jeffs, who was eighty-three at the time. That catapulted her into an even more prominent role. The teenager matured into a shrewd young woman and became a favored wife of her elderly husband, although rumors swirled about her simultaneous closeness to his son Warren. When Rulon died, Naomi quickly switched her allegiance and became Warren's first new transfer bride. She had no children by either of them, so there was no competition for her attention. Naomi got close to Warren and stayed there, a woman who knew all of the secrets of a religion run strictly by men. She appeared to be as adept at manipulating Warren as she had been in handling the old man, and by letting her transcribe the Priesthood Record, Jeffs gave her immense power. She was always at hand, or at least nearby, and in his description, she heard "the [heavenly] whisperings."

She was very careful and knew exactly how the game was played. Warren might issue some vague warning, such as, "The Lord is watching you closely, Naomi, beware lest you fall." That would spell doom for most FLDS members, but Naomi knew how to respond. "I rejoice in you, Sweetheart. I humbly acknowledge the error I am in, in questioning through a lack of reaching." The problem was solved, the doubt crushed, and Warren's ego stroked.

Her power lay not only in assembling his thoughts and sermons while he was awake, but in doing so even while he slept. Nomes was the eternal sentinel, always there, and Priesthood Record sections frequently opened with the phrase "Naomi's Testimony of What Happened Through the Night." She would spill forth some of the most dramatic scenes to be found in the thousands of pages of the Record. She would bear witness that Warren would fall unconscious and be surrounded by circles of flame, be thrown about and twisted on the bed, at times actually levitating above the mattress. Mysterious pillars of light would pulse at the bedside while heavenly bodies communed with the incoherent prophet. Naomi would claim that a veil would cover her eyes and Warren would be gone from the room. She would hear soft voices as flames danced and the prophet would be returned to his bed, drained from visiting with heavenly beings.

Even the prophet was impressed with what she said went on during his sleep. The revelations must all be true, because Nomes was a singular witness, right there watching, listening, and writing it down, night after night. She was the portal through which Warren was seen as a god, and he knew it. It was in his best interests to keep her happy, and so Naomi reaped the rewards of her transcriptions, be they fact or fiction. It was a win-win deal.

Darkness amplified the hedonistic partying in New Orleans, almost overwhelming the three FLDS explorers as they shouldered through the drunken crowd. Warren had led them all in prayer that they would not be "sickened" by what they were about to witness during this stern test by the Lord. Women kissed and touched in the streets. They stripped in shops that painted their entire bodies. Male and female nude dancers shimmied in bars. Restaurants overflowed with business. Some couples danced crazily with the women unzipping their partners and groping in public. People with cameras took pictures of every lewd act, and police wandered around almost aimlessly. Huge loudspeakers boomed deafening bass beats. Women fainted, drunks fell. As revolting as it was, God kept sending Warren and his two wide-eyed men back to be witnesses to the immorality of the world.

As Warren watched it all he appealed to God to "destroy this wicked generation," he would recall. He leaned against a wall, raised his arms to the square and delivered the revelers over to the judgments of God. When the three men eventually returned to the hotel, Naomi pulled the couch away from the door to let them in, and Warren got busy on the phones to set up the schedule for Sunday school back in Texas and Utah.

After obeying the Lord's command to witness some more sinful behavior on the room's television set, they tried to get some sleep, although a man and woman had a loud fight in the adjoining room at four o'clock in the morning. The Lord ordered Warren to stick around for another night so that he could actually witness more of the city's sins.

When Hurricane Katrina struck the Louisiana coast six months later, on August 29, devastating the city and leaving more than 1,800 people dead, the prophet was convinced that he had literally summoned down to this place of sin one of his oft-sought whirlwind judgments from God.

CHAPTER 24

Candi

The chill of winter still gripped the high desert and I was looking forward to taking some time off on a Saturday in April 2005, a foolish hope on my part. The phone rang and Gary Engels's name flashed on the caller ID. I always answered his calls. If some FLDS zealots had flipped out and were after him, I was the closest reliable help. He would do the same for me; it was an unspoken agreement.

"Hey Sam, guess what?" Gary sounded excited, rare for him.

"What?"

"You remember that girl, Candi, who was married to one of Joe Barlow's sons when she was sixteen?"

Vaguely. "Kind of. Why?"

"Well, I got her phone number. She's living over in St. George. We should probably give her a call and see if she'll talk to us. Her sister seems to think she will. I guess she really hates the guy she was married off to, and she is pretty pissed at Warren for forcing her into it."

We had heard so many of these stories that it was hard to keep track. "Who's the sister again?"

"Tammy Shapley. She's Joe Holm's girlfriend; Richard's nephew's girlfriend," said Gary. The names were tumbling into place, another strand of somebody related to somebody else, knowing still somebody else. "Do you think we should give Candi a try? She probably won't talk, but you never know."

I had learned to seize any opportunity when it came to the FLDS.

Drag our feet and a guilty conscience might kick in and prevent our potential lead from talking, or the Warrenites might find out and it could be over before it ever really began. "Yeah. Give her a call right now. If she agrees, I can be down there in forty-five minutes." We had no way of knowing that we were on the verge of our biggest breakthrough yet.

Gary and I had befriended an ex-FLDS businessman and former Colorado City councilman named Richard Holm, who hated the prophet so fiercely that he referred to Warren on national television as "a dirty, rotten bastard" and would refer to the Jeffs's compound in Short Creek as "that brothel up the street." Warren had kicked him out of the church in 2003 and reassigned his family to Richard's own brother, Edson. After several months, Richard went to see his children, who no longer referred to him as Father; they just called him Richard. The reassigned wife told him she was already pregnant with his brother's child. To say Holm was bitter would be an extreme understatement.

We had recently attended a small party for FLDS refugees at Richard's house, where we had met one of his nephews and the young man's girlfriend, Tammy Shapley. The conversation had veered to the subject of Tammy's sister, Candi, who Tammy said had been forced to marry "a real asshole" at the age of sixteen. Candi had run away, but her brothers had been dispatched by her father to find her and they had brought her back. She eventually ran away again and made it out for good by finding a boyfriend and having sex with him. Once tainted by "adultery," although there had been no legal wedding in the first place, she was considered sullied goods, her FLDS "husband" no longer wanted her, and she was drummed out of the fold, never to return. She was another refugee who preferred to stay in the area rather than go out into the real world.

When Tammy had told us that Candi might be willing to talk, Gary and I had exchanged glances. Was this a real lead or just another dead end? It deserved a try, however, and Tammy had soon forwarded the needed telephone number through Richard.

It worked. After our initial conversation, Gary phoned back to say the girl would see us. I hit the road from Cedar City to St. George and linked up with Gary.

Less than an hour later, we pulled up in front of Candi Shapley's town house, feeling a push of anticipation. She answered the door herself. I found her to be a personable and pretty young woman, still only nineteen, with bright red hair and a little overweight from recently having had twins. She had a bit of fire in her eyes, still angry that no one had listened to her when she claimed she had been raped and brutalized by her FLDS husband. Within minutes, she was telling her story. She had waited a long time to be heard.

Her tale could have been an FLDS primer. Candi grew up in a twenty-bedroom, sixteen-bathroom home with her father, his six wives, and most of her fifty-six siblings. She was taught to keep sweet and prepare to be a good wife and bring children of her own upon the earth.

Her trouble began when one of her sisters turned seventeen and told their father she was ready to be "turned in," the term for being placed with some worthy priesthood holder as a wife. Her father gave his approval and an appointment was made for the girl to be interviewed by the prophet, who would choose a suitable candidate. Candi, who had just turned sixteen, went along to keep her sister company. Warren took it upon himself to add Candi to the list of brides-in-waiting.

Soon, her father happily informed Candi that she would be married the very next day. He did not know anything about the groom other than that he was a member of the large Barlow clan. Candi's life was catapulted in an instant from her comfortable day-to-day routine into a supersonic ride into the unknown. She had not seen this coming, and she was scared.

Another friend and valuable resource would later fill in for me what happened next. Carolyn Jessop, who eventually left the cult and ripped the lid off many FLDS secrets with her bestselling book *Escape*, was managing the Caliente Hot Springs Motel in Nevada at the time. Her husband, the powerful FLDS functionary Merril Jessop, owned the motel on State Road 93, and it had become a favored hideout in which Warren Jeffs would perform multiple marriage ceremonies. Secrecy was paramount. No matter the age of the bride-to-be, crossing interstate boundaries for illegal sexual purposes is a serious crime covered by the federal Mann Act. Some underage brides were transported down from Canada, making it an international crime as well.

The routine Carolyn described was very cloak-and-daggerish. The day or night before a set of marriages was to take place, she would receive a call to set aside a number of rooms, and the reservation would be confirmed the following day. The tipoff for Carolyn was if Room 15 was among those to be reserved. Room 15 was a boxy little bungalow that sat alone near the office and was the place where the marriages were always performed.

Each designated new bride would be assigned one of the other rooms and would stay inside with her family until it was her turn. Her groom, the priesthood holder, might wait outside in his truck. Then both would be summoned to Room 15, which was decorated in pink, and the ceremony would be quickly conducted. The new couple would then usually drive off to their new lives while another couple would be called in for the next arranged marriage. Room 15 was a wedding assembly line for underage girls.

That was exactly what faced the bewildered sixteen-year-old Candi Shapley. Candi told us that she was taken to Room 15 and stood beside Randy Barlow and Randy's first wife, Valene, and his mother. Randy was twenty-eight-years old and had children by Valene, and although Candi had seen him around Short Creek, they had never spoken. Warren Jeffs performed the ceremony as Uncle Rulon Jeffs watched, and afterward Uncle Rulon croaked out a blessing.

I leaned back in my chair and quietly exhaled as she spoke, glancing over at Gary. This was huge. We were talking to someone who could personally testify that the prophet had married her off, knowing she was sixteen, to a man twelve years her senior. The fact that she had been shuttled to another state to avoid detection verified that a crime had probably been committed.

Candi said that as they drove away from Caliente Hot Springs, she was apprehensive and confused. She did not even understand why she had had to travel all the way to Nevada just to get married although her father had told her there was a law against plural marriage in their home state of Utah. The real reason was that the Caliente motel marriage factory drew no attention from outsiders, there were controls on who would attend, and it was a safe hideaway for the secretive prophet; Short Creek was too public. Her only comfort was that her father had also promised her she had the right to say no if she did not want to have sex with her new husband. Candi resisted for as long as she could because anything to do with sex was entirely foreign to her, and when Randy finally made his move, she refused.

The spurned husband bided his time and even met with Warren to complain that his young bride did not want to have children yet. The prophet instructed her husband to find a way. The next time, when she again resisted, she said Randy pinned her down and raped her. Later, she claimed he raped her again. Taking her problem to Warren did not help. The prophet told her the way to make things better was to become more obedient and have children. Feeling helpless, she submitted, but things only got worse. She would confide to me later that Randy was a brute who treated her like a slave and forced her to engage in group sex with him and another woman.

By the time we left the initial meeting with Candi, we could see potential criminal charges all over the place, as well as a possible witness in our civil racketeering case. Candi's testimony could send both Warren Jeffs and Randy Barlow to prison. In this case, the wedding was a sham not only because Candi was underage and Randy was already married, but also because Warren, who performed the sexual arrangement, had no lawful authority to marry anyone.

To be a witness in a sexual abuse case is difficult, and it takes a very brave woman to carry through to the end. But I headed home to Cedar City feeling optimistic. I liked Candi. Maybe we finally had found someone ready to take it all the way. Maybe not. I rated it fifty-fifty at best.

Fred Jessop, the genial Uncle Fred, had been missing for more than a year, ever since Warren had stripped away his position as bishop of Short Creek and forced him into hiding. At the age of ninety-three and in failing health, Fred had disappeared in the middle of the night, and he was said to have been sent on a special mission.

Information about what had happened was sparse. People who had been at the house the night Fred was shuttled off told me that a crew had been assigned to remove his belongings. Things he could use the most, such as clothes, were left behind, while items of value that he had amassed over his long lifetime disappeared. Will Timpson, the new bishop, moved into the house the day after Fred disappeared.

There are a lot of Jessops around, and the family tree is so strange that I did not find it unusual when I accompanied Joe C. Jessop Jr., who was the combination son, grandson, and nephew of Uncle Fred, to the

Washington County sheriff's office in the spring of 2005 so that he could file a report placing the former bishop into the National Criminal Identification Center's computerized federal database as a missing person. Other family members who were no longer in the FLDS were worried about him and feared he would not last long without appropriate medical care.

Uncle Fred, who had personally known five of the nine prophets, was very sick, totally dependent on others, and cowed in his old age by Warren. He had been turned into a perfect yes man, the ultimate loyalist, as his health failed.

"Uncle Warren is an Enoch. He is a Moses!" Fred had praised in a sermon. "He told us once he knew what Noah went through. He is a revelator like the Prophet Joseph, a colonizer like Brigham Young, one who lives in hiding like John Taylor . . . All of those Prophets are centered in Uncle Warren now." That was about the highest endorsement anyone could give. As the months passed, Fred slipped so completely off our radar that I didn't know if he was alive or dead. Very few people did.

Warren took a personal interest in the care of the ailing Uncle Fred, who was suffering from heart and kidney problems, was diabetic, and needed an oxygen tank to breathe. He insisted Fred's ladies were to give him only special bottled water, yarrow tea, and garlic drinks. Such instructions made it unclear to me whether Warren's intentions were meant to help or hurt the ailing old man.

In early March 2005, hidden away in Texas by Warren, Fred's health took a turn for the worse. Two wives who were nursing him alerted the leadership, but instead of being immediately moved into a hospital, the frail old counselor was ordered to be driven to another hideaway in distant Albuquerque, New Mexico, about nine grueling hours by car. The paranoid prophet wouldn't take the chance of that illness leading authorities back to Zion and ultimately to himself. According to Warren's journal an FLDS doctor secured some medicine from prescriptions he wrote for people in Short Creek, and he was assigned the task of escorting Fred, along with two other couriers, on the cross-country journey that would surely end in the old man's death.

Once they were settled in New Mexico, another wife pleaded that he be taken to a hospital immediately, and she was scolded for her lack of faith and for assuming to know more than the prophet, who was back in

Texas, praying and ordering them to sit tight and wait to see whether Fred improved.

Fred's inability to get medical attention was not unusual within the FLDS. It was never easy to get permission to go to a hospital, where a vulnerable patient would face questioning authorities and might inadvertently expose some sort of illegal activity back home. Permission had to come directly from Warren.

But Fred was not the only thing on Warren's plate. Fresh off their eastern swing, he told Naomi that he was feeling the call to go to some foreign country and wanted maps of England, France, and Germany.

While Fred was languishing in Albuquerque, Warren received another revelation and the old man was put on the road again, transported farther north, into Colorado, once again depriving the dying old man of much-needed medical attention. As the little convoy of two vehicles neared Denver, it seemed as if the venerable old church legend might die right there in the car. Permission finally was given to hospitalize him at the Sky Ridge Medical Center, about twenty miles from downtown Denver. He was placed in the intensive care unit, and the church's doctor, Lloyd Barlow, reported back to Warren periodically. (Lloyd Barlow was later indicted in Texas for failure to report child abuse.) The hospital staff was warned that Fred's only chance for survival was to have a stent surgically placed to stabilize his heart and then undergo arthroscopic surgery to repair a valve. About that time, Warren had another vision, which often happened when he needed to justify his actions. This one showed Uncle Fred getting into a car and going away to visit his family, but leaving Warren behind. The prophet was left with the impression that once Fred died and was on the other side of the veil, their work could continue faster than before. He instructed the doctors to make Fred as comfortable as possible but to take no other medical actions.

Warren decided to travel up from Texas to see Fred. At the hospital, he stood beside the dying man, who had a respirator down his throat. The doctors gave no hope without the surgery, which would have been performed at still another hospital and was dangerous in any case for a patient in such poor health and at such an advanced age. Warren decided that his vision about the car was a sign from God to let Fred go. He coldly did not express any remorse for making the stricken man, who had been a loyal friend and follower for many years, travel hundreds of miles before allowing him to receive medical care.

Once Uncle Fred passed away, the journal showed that Warren left in a hurry, because the Lord had shown him that if he stayed in Denver, he "would be accused of killing the old man" and that "as soon as [the] word [got] out, [he would] have the news media and also [his] enemies trying to trace the family."

Next came the charade of a funeral. Fred had served his terrestrial usefulness to Warren, but he could continue to be a means of validating Warren's power. Will Timpson, now Will Jessop, who had replaced Fred as the bishop, lied to hospital administrators by saying that he was Fred's actual son and had authority to take possession of the body. He was allowed to haul the corpse away in the rear of an SUV to a hidden location. Colorado authorities considered filing criminal charges for illegally taking possession of a dead body and falsifying records, but they eventually gave up when jurisdictional problems cropped up because the Utah border had been crossed. Warren held some private moments with some of Fred's family at a secret hideaway, where he also decided details of the funeral and burial details to take place in Short Creek.

The outlaw prophet then returned to the safety of Texas until the night before the funeral, when he jumped over to New Mexico; and a day later he and First Counselor Wendell Nielsen checked into an Albuquerque motel, which was as close as they would come to the funeral of their dear friend and Second Counselor Frederick Meade Jessop in Short Creek. They did not show up personally, nor did the program contain their names.

Even before the services started, the paranoid weirdness of the FLDS was on full display.

The central hall at the LeRoy S. Johnson Meeting House overflowed with the faithful on the balmy afternoon of Sunday, March 20, 2005. Technicians rigged transmissions to side rooms, to Albuquerque, into private homes, to Mancos, to the ranch in Texas, and all the way to Canada.

Apostates who had known Uncle Fred for many years filtered up to the meeting house, but the bullies were ready. MacRae Oler, a cocky young Canadian, was at the door to point out familiar faces from north of the Forty-ninth Parallel, and those visitors were physically denied entrance. Big Willie Jessop wrenched the arm of one of Fred's relatives behind his back and shoved him out the door. Chief Marshal Sam Roundy blocked others in what Winston Blackmore later derisively described as special "keep sweet" moments.

After the song "Dear Uncle Fred We Love you," Wendell Nielsen came on the speakerphone hookup and delivered an eleven-minute tribute from the motel in New Mexico. Then, like the voice of a disembodied god, the unmistakable drone of Warren Jeffs drifted in. For the first time in more than a year, his Short Creek followers were hearing his actual voice and not a recording. He spoke for thirty minutes.

In months to come, Jeffs would invoke the memory of the popular Uncle Fred to strengthen his hold, although his power was already complete. He was finally rid of the last real threat to his authority. Warren later would appoint an even stronger henchman, Merril Jessop, to fill the vacancy left by the departed Uncle Fred in the First Presidency. Adding up the tally later, it seems that the price Merril paid to become so influential was the placement of at least eleven daughters and two grand-daughters, some of whom were only underage children, to join Warren's long list of "heavenly comfort wives."

The only other truly important position in the FLDS church was that of patriarch, to which Warren had appointed one of his own brothers, Leroy Jeffs. Warren began looking at him with suspicion.

CHAPTER 25

Twelve Years Old

Although Warren Jeffs had finally allowed Steven Chatwin and his family to escape from the battleground home of his apostate brother, Ross Chatwin, I suspected that the church still wasn't ready to give in.

Ross had the building, but the court had said nothing about the utilities that served it, and the FLDS was always alert for an opening. The utilities were cut off, an intentionally cruel move since it was still bitterly cold in Short Creek. He had been heating the lower floor with a propane gas burner, but when Ross went to the city to change the water, gas, and electricity for the upper floor into his own name in March 2005, he was refused.

The Chatwins went without utilities for nearly a month before the Hildale City Council agreed to take up the matter in an emergency session. I drove down for the meeting and listened as Ross made a reasoned plea before the council members, all of whom were prominent FLDS members who detested him. I scribbled my name on a list of speakers to comment.

I was not happy to hear them belittle Ross and his family as "squatters" on church land. They spoke in a self-righteous tone, even as they were depriving a couple with six young children of water, heat, and electricity in harsh weather. The council's hypocrisy was highlighted when the cell phone of Richard Allred, the Colorado City mayor, suddenly chirped out its custom ring tone, the familiar Mormon hymn

"Love At Home." When my turn came to speak, I let them have it, lecturing them about religious persecution, civil rights violations, and the law.

Chief Marshal Roundy, one of his deputies, and the ever-present enforcer Willie Jessop were staring daggers and closed in on me, but I ignored them, stood my ground, and said my piece.

The previous day I had been out target shooting with my regular sidearm, and it wasn't until I arrived at the meeting that I realized I had left it at home to be cleaned. That was a careless mistake; I had learned that when dealing with the FLDS thugs, especially on their turf, it was prudent to be prepared for anything. The only weapon I had with me was my six-pound Desert Eagle .44 Magnum, which I had also taken to target practice the day before, and I had tucked that huge hog-leg pistol beneath my jacket. It was uncomfortable and hard to hide. The Short Creek god squad got close but ended up hanging back, perhaps recognizing the distinctive imprint of the huge pistol.

The council's rubber-stamp decision on behalf of the church was never in doubt. They voted unanimously to deny the utility hookups, just as Warren instructed.

The situation was tense. As I left, the three goons were huddled together on the sidewalk in front of the council chambers, bragging about how they were going to "take me down." Big Willie followed me out to the parking area and gave me his best death glare as I got into my car. He reminded me of a playground bully who had suddenly come face-to-face with someone who wasn't afraid of him. His juvenile tactics usually worked with the church members he was assigned to strong-arm but seemed comical to me.

I decided that there was still one more thing that I could try to do to help the Chatwins with their problem. Later that day I telephoned every media contact I had, and the reporters deluged the city offices and Mayor David Zitting with questions about why the church had terminated the needed city-run services to a desperate family of eight in their own home. With the court order in place, outside law enforcement agencies becoming curious, and the media breathing down his neck, Warren decided not to continue that particular fight. The utilities were turned back on before sunset.

It was a minor victory for us, but it felt good to put still another one in the win column.

Leroy Jeffs did not last another month as the patriarch of the church. Warren heard that some FLDS people were turning to his more approachable brother for counsel because they did not know how to access the prophet. A dream soon followed in which God revealed to Warren that Leroy was no longer worthy of priesthood. Warren telephoned his brother the very next morning and stripped him of his title, wives, children, and home, although Leroy was allowed to continue working as an accountant for the prophet and in the businesses of David Allred, the purchaser of the FLDS refuge lands.

Warren's thoughts were raging. He had a mountain of things to think about and decisions to make, and his word alone mattered. His thrashing dreams grew wilder. They could be about something as simple as detecting a lack of faith in an errant member, a routine piece of church business, or a decision to forbid FLDS kids from eating "gentile candy." But he also had apocalyptic visions, such as fleeing to Europe and leading "invading armies" back to America. After telling his scribe that they were about to face the greatest destruction that has ever been on this land or on the face of the earth," he would then easily slide right back to planning a landscape of roses and shade trees for the Texas compound, and the type of crown molding needed around the temple walls.

According to Naomi, just before dawn on Monday, April 11, 2005, Warren uttered an emphatic, "Wow. Whatever you say. Yes, sir." The Lord had just told him to collect a "pure, innocent girl" to add to his fold. A little later, he identified her as Brenda Fischer, the eldest daughter of Wayne Fischer, and, as Naomi recorded, the prophet asked and answered in his sleep, "How old is she? She is twelve."

Warren dispatched another of his brothers, Seth Jeffs, his most trusted courier, to Short Creek to fetch Wayne and his preteen daughter to Texas, along with some $200,000 in fresh greenbacks. Wayne Fischer apparently was less than enthusiastic that his child had been chosen at such a tender age, and he and his little girl had to endure Seth playing recordings of Warren's hypnotic "trainings" throughout the long drive to Texas. Warren kept in touch with Seth by telephone and told him to take an even longer route, so that Wayne and his daughter would have more time to listen to the mind-numbing lectures and read booklets of selected sermons. Warren required that both child and father sign agreements to keep the sacred nature of their journey secret.

"It is just marvelous," Warren told his scribe. "The Lord is choosing young girls who can be worked with and easily taught."

He personally drove the Fischers around the ranch for ninety minutes on Saturday afternoon, and he spent time alone with Wayne until the man finally gave in and wept his approval for his little girl to be handed over. The prophet married twelve-year-old Brenda at nine o'clock that night, only a few days after picking her out in a dream. The incident, recorded by Naomi in the journal in its troubling entirety, wiped out any doubt that FLDS men only married women who were consenting adults. It was child rape, over and over. And it took place across interstate boundaries in violation of the U.S. White Slave Traffic Act (the Mann Act) of 1910. I was starting to wonder why the Feds had made such a dismal showing on cases like this that were so obviously a slam dunk. I knew that they were aware of human trafficking within the FLDS, and yet, after showing interest, they would fade away, accomplishing nothing.

On April 13, I was in the Texas state capitol in Austin along with Jon Krakauer and others to testify before a legislative committee in support of a bill to raise the legal age of marriage, which at the time was only fourteen. That had been one reason the FLDS had zeroed in on Eldorado in the first place.

"By God, this is Texas and we do not tolerate child abuse in this state! Child abusers go to prison for a long time here," an old legislator barked at me, apparently thinking I had some sort of control over such matters. I was not the one he should have been attacking, but he was showing the right spirit.

Utah attorney general Mark Shurtleff also appeared as a witness, and he admitted that law enforcement in his state had dragged their feet in the prosecution of polygamists who had taken child brides. He pleaded with the Texas legislators not to make the same mistakes that had been made in Utah.

The Texas legislators not only raised the age of consent in their state to seventeen, but also strengthened penalties for child abuse and bigamy in the commission of other crimes. That squarely put the polygamists at the YFZ Ranch on notice that marrying a child could mean a long prison term. In the years to come, that legislation would pay huge dividends in the prosecution of FLDS members, including the prophet Warren Jeffs himself.

CHAPTER 26
Grand Jury

We hoped that the deep hatred Candi Shapley felt for her abusive ex-husband Randy Barlow would propel her forward to the witness stand despite some misgivings. Trust was key to getting her there. Although we kept everything very hush-hush to prevent her family and the church from finding out, no secret can hold indefinitely, so Candi was put on the fast track to lock in her testimony.

She was so fragile and unaccustomed to dealing with the outside world that she was having a problem responding to the brusque law-enforcement manner of Gary Engels. I altered my approach. While Gary pushed the case to the next level criminally in Arizona, I used a softer tone, sitting quietly for long spells while she showed me photographs of her wedding day and gradually opened up, revealing more details.

Finally, Gary had enough evidence to take to his boss, Matt Smith, the aggressive Mohave County prosecutor, who launched the procedure for a grand jury appearance in Kingman. Once again, the state lines got in the way.

Candi kept her focus, and by early June 2005, only about eight weeks after our initial conversation on April 2, everything was in place. I met with Candi and her sister Tammy to talk them through the process and provide a realistic understanding of what to expect. I knew it was going to be tough on Candi, and I wanted to minimize any surprises.

Since Candi had already been booted out of the FLDS, she had nothing to lose on that front, but she still had great concerns. One of her questions was, "Am I going to have to testify against Warren?" I knew that she might balk at that possibility, because it exposed her to being castigated by almost everyone she knew as a traitor who was trying to bring down the prophet. I replied honestly that she might have to do that at some point, and that plenty of people would be around to help when that time came. For now, I said, concentrate on Randy.

Candi had another major worry. One of her twin daughters had been born with serious birth defects and required virtually constant care, a challenge for anybody. There was a last-minute delay when her child was rushed to Primary Children's Hospital in Salt Lake for emergency treatment, and her testimony was postponed until the baby was stable. Finally, she and Tammy were comfortable to go, boarding a small plane sent to Salt Lake City by the Mohave County sheriff's office. Neither had been on an airplane before, and they were as excited as if it were an amusement-park ride.

They flew across the border from Utah and into Arizona, and on June 8 in Kingman, Candi Shapley delivered her testimony before the grand jury in a firm voice and without hesitation, not only responding to the questions, but expanding on her answers. She was articulate and accurate and knew exactly what she was doing, and was so convincing that the grand jury not only hit Barlow on charges of rape and unlawful sexual conduct, but also indicted Warren Jeffs on two sixth-degree felony counts of sexual conduct with a minor and one charge of conspiracy to commit sexual conduct with a minor.

Candi had come through. The prophet was now wanted not only on the civil charges, but on criminal charges that could mean several years in prison.

I slept a lot easier that night. This had been the game-changer I had sought for so long. It held out hope that in the future, other girls finding themselves in a similar predicament might understand that some sort of recourse was available. I was proud of Candi.

The secrecy of a grand jury room is supposed to be inviolable. Even I did not know what had been said in that proceeding. I was counting on that secrecy and had been working with Gary Engels and Jon Krakauer to alert the various arms of law enforcement that an indictment and an arrest warrant might be coming down. Now the law would really be looking for Jeffs; it would no longer be a figment of his imagination.

The grand jury had met on Wednesday, June 8, the indictments were handed down on Thursday, June 9, and the results were leaked almost immediately. By Friday, June 10, I was swamped by media calls. I couldn't believe it. I asked Gary what had happened. At that point, he was pretty cavalier about it, saying that prosecutor Matt Smith had decided to go ahead and break the news. "That was a huge mistake," I told my old friend. Our goal of keeping the police informed and ready in case Warren started to move collapsed.

I hung up and tried to contact Candi. Her phone went straight to voice mail, as if it was shut off or she was out of range. I spent the next day contacting her friends in the refugee subculture, but no one had heard from her. She was gone. It had only taken the FLDS a matter of hours to connect the dots and figure out who had testified against the prophet. Gary and I spent the next week trying to locate her but were unable to find a thing. Our star witness was in the wind and I was worried sick.

Gary Engels was so devastated by her disappearance that he considered resigning. I was sweating bullets, because that was the last thing I wanted. A veteran cop, Gary was a fine investigator and a good friend, and without him, we would never have had Candi testifying in the first place. We had been through way too much together to let something like this leak get in the way of our friendship, and besides, it wasn't his fault. So we did what we had always done and got back to work.

A couple weeks later, as I was leaving my office to go home, fumbling for my car keys, my cell phone rang. It was Candi, and she sounded like a changed woman. I listened to her with deep disappointment. The church had gotten to her. She explained that she had gone away on a camping trip with her father, Bill Shapley. Out there in the wilderness, Bill had helped her "understand" what was happening, and why Uncle Warren was forced to do the things that he was doing—because the government was wrongfully accusing him of crimes and wanted to lock him up and maybe even kill him. She would not testify against him in a trial. She had changed her mind about Randy, too, because he had a wife and kids, and she did not want to hurt them. As the familiar robotic words came out of her mouth, it was all I could do to keep from snapping, "Candi, have you lost your mind?" But that would have gotten us nowhere. She also felt betrayed by Gary and Matt.

I had to keep the thin line of communication open, to try to reestablish the trust, because she was too important to lose. Any diatribe on my part would just push her away, so I held my temper and we spoke for a while about other topics to settle the waters.

I did ask her to consider the fact that her father previously had been kicked out of the church by Warren but had suddenly been readmitted, and his family reinstated, after she came forward as a witness. She knew how rare that was. She brushed it off; her father was a good and humble man who had successfully completed the repentance process. I didn't buy that for a minute, but she badly wanted to believe it, and I just had to let it go. After hanging up, I knew that it would be another long tightrope walk to get her back on a witness stand.

I could imagine what she was going through. She was a nineteen-year-old single mom trying to raise twins, one of whom was severely handicapped. She had run from a violent forced marriage, only to have to deal with the harsh realities of the real world. Her parents had abandoned her, but like most abused and neglected kids, she still loved her family. The camping trip was probably her first real communication with her father since he had been ordered not to be a part of her life, and her mother also had suddenly shown up to help care for the children. Although nothing but a ploy on the part of the church, the fact that her family was back in her life was a godsend to Candi in her weak emotional state. It was the closest she had been to them since being ostracized with the scarlet letter of an adulteress.

It came as no surprise to learn that behind the scenes, Warren had made some pretty shrewd counter-moves upon finding out that Candi was cooperating with authorities. He decided that her father, Bill Shapley, had repented enough to return to the FLDS and that four of his wives could be resealed to him. Shapley jumped at the opportunity; Warren had reached Bill, and Bill had now reached Candi.

But the prophet dug his heels in about another wife, Esther, who was Candi's mother. She was out of the family, and would stay out, although she wanted above all things to be back in. She was not allowed to go back to her former husband and was only given a meager "widow's stipend" and allowed to share a trailer with other so-called widows. That desire provided more leverage for Warren to control her, and his fate might depend upon the ability of Bill and Esther Shapley to control their rebellious daughter.

Watching the Arizona situation closely was a potential witness of equal importance in Utah, Elissa Wall. While I had been focusing on Candi, Elissa had established some friendly, but loose, communication with our attorney Roger Hoole. After Candi's name was leaked to the press and the FLDS hit back hard, the pregnant Elissa recoiled. She wanted no part of a similar experience, so Roger simply kept the lines of communication open with Elissa and her boyfriend, Lamont Barlow.

It turned out that the Mohave County prosecutor's office wasn't the only one to leak the news of Jeffs's indictment. On his own, Sheriff David Doran had gone to the YFZ Ranch at 4:45 on the afternoon of June 10 to meet with Merril Jessop. He thought there was a possibility that Warren was there, and he told the bishop about the grand jury's decision, requesting that the prophet surrender peacefully. Merril shrugged and again lied that he had no idea where Warren was—hadn't seen him for months. Jeffs, meanwhile, was lurking nearby behind the walls of R-17, monitoring the situation and waiting for Jessop to finish hustling the sheriff and report back. So Doran had unwittingly beaten Mohave County in leaking the information, and not to the press, but straight to the people we most wanted to stay in the dark.

When Jessop delivered the news of the indictment, the prophet panicked. I have seen this kind of reaction numerous times, when people learn that charges have been filed against them but have no idea of the details. Their thoughts go to their darkest secrets. If Warren followed this pattern, his thoughts would have been about a life of fraud, ritualistic sexual abuse of little girls, using young boys as slave labor, raping children of both sexes, robbing men of their possessions, and reassigning wives.

Who had sold him out? Was it his brother Leroy, whom he had disgraced, misused, and expelled? My clients had told me that Leroy had witnessed Warren's sexual assaults back at the academy but may not have participated. Had Leroy gone to the government as revenge for being thrown out of the church?

Or perhaps "Mother Mary" had finally turned traitor. The sister of Warren's "bitter enemy," apostate Dan Fischer, and a registered nurse, Mary had tended Uncle Rulon, her husband, around the clock during the last months of his life. She had seen the fear in Rulon's eyes as he realized he was about to die. Warren would tell the faithful that "Father's" last words were, "Oh, my God."

Mary knew differently. I interviewed one of the medical staff who was present and another of Rulon's wives, and they both confirmed that in his last moment, Rulon actually had looked into the eyes of his maniacal son and said, "Oh my God—what have I done?" Warren had decided to take Mary, his stepmother, as one of his first brides after the death of the old man. She appeared to be so disoriented by what was unfolding around her that she stood up and proclaimed Warren to be the dead prophet's choice for the job. Still, he did not trust her, because she knew too much. Whenever Warren felt his enemies might be closing in, Mother Mary would be moved to a new secret location to keep her in the shadows.

Leroy and Mother Mary were the goblins he feared most, but the irrational Warren Jeffs had been lashing out in all directions. He was certain that traitors existed even among his closest friends, so everyone was on thin ice. His most stalwart goon, Willie Jessop, was pointedly asked if he was "riding both sides of the fence." Moneyman David Allred was under suspicion for making business deals without the prophet's approval. God warned Warren that some of his wives were falling away, and his own children were told to straighten up or be dispatched to "where the disobedient people are." He was ready to kick out anybody.

For the next three days, the YFZ Ranch was in a frenzy. Instead of building, they were destroying potential evidence. Letters, financial records, family photo albums, and computer disks were trashed. According to the Priesthood Record Warren's brother Lyle provided him with some details of the grand jury episode—his version of the episode, that is. Lyle said that the attorney general of Utah, Mark Shurtleff, had swooped down on Candi Shapley in Salt Lake City, "confronted her, handcuffed her, and carted her off to the airport." Lyle reported that the main question the grand jury asked was, "Did Warren Jeffs perform this marriage ceremony, and she said, Yes."

It was all an ambitious lie, because Lyle had no knowledge of how we had dealt so gently with Candi, nor did he know what was said within the grand jury room. Shurtleff had never seen or spoken with her. Lyle made up the tale to please his brother.

It was up to Warren to explain to the anxious temple workers that danger was knocking at the gates. He had them gather for a circle prayer that was of such significance that even Uncle Fred was invited to participate from beyond the grave. But Warren chickened out at the last minute; before he was to speak, he smiled at Merril Jessop and whispered, "God wants us to leave right now."

With that, the paranoid prophet grabbed Naomi, his first counselor Wendell Nielsen, and his brother and driver Isaac, and they all took off for Austin, Texas, and beyond that, to points unknown. His special hand-chosen temple workers were left in his dust, bewildered and abandoned.

CHAPTER 27

On the Road

With little money and few friends and a circumscribed existence, most fugitives find hiding to be hard work, but Warren Jeffs was not the usual fugitive. He had a network of believers that stretched all the way across America, thousands of people who saw it as an honor and a privilege to give the pedophile prophet shelter, money, literally anything they had, with total loyalty and no questions asked. Many of the numerous places of refuge were not extravagant like R-17 in Texas, but simply modest family homes dotted somewhere on his map of safe havens.

When he had first started traveling incognito around the country, he had been rather modest about his disguises. As he became more adept at hiding in the world of the gentiles, he became almost brazen in his taste for the good life. He was no longer satisfied with just putting on a hat and telling his driver not to exceed the speed limit. Like everything else in his life, the traveling was carried to the extreme, almost as if Warren were an addict chasing the big rush.

Warren and Naomi had dashed from Texas to Oklahoma to Colorado to Washington State, and from Sacramento to Fresno, California, before looping down through Las Vegas and heading east to Florida. Before leaving each place, Warren took time to raise his arm to the square and condemn it to the judgments of God as a curse for the wickedness he had found.

By the end of June 2005, he was in deep cover at the Hilton Garden Inn in Pensacola, Florida, sprawled in the sunshine on a sandy beach. Naomi was at his side, her hair dyed the color of chocolate, with red highlights. Both wore bathing suits as they happily watched the other near-naked bodies around them. Warren reported that he was pleasing the Lord "in this amazing experience of being unclothed, suntanning, dressing like the world with only a swimsuit on."

He had bought a year's worth of new contact lenses, his hair was trimmed, and he was starting a mustache. One of the church-run businesses had just sent him $15,500 for spending money along with a sparkling new Porsche Cayenne. At night, he and Naomi watched television and movies in the hotel room and appeared to be feigning disgust at the pornography as they avidly scrutinized each scene. "They displayed the open corrupt sexual actions one with another," he said. "Men with women, women with women, as though it is the delight and way of life."

During the day, he would sit in the Porsche, turn the air-conditioning on full blast, and phone detailed instructions back to his followers as he checked on the temple work. The Lord had instructed him on landscaping—the types of flowers, grass, and trees to be planted. Nothing escaped divine scrutiny.

He used prepaid, throw-away cell phones routed through complex dock and talk networks as his main means of communication, but bags of mail containing letters of support and plenty of cash for him were waiting at rendezvous points. Warren would often slit open the envelopes to extract the cash and often appeared to have set aside the confessions of repentance unread, at least until he could take sufficient time to savor the transgressions and figure out how best to use the secrets to control the writers.

The man who tried so hard to avoid attention was, however, totally contradictory on that point when it came to cars. He loved hot wheels, and he rolled into the Texas compound one day driving a bright yellow Ford Mustang convertible. Faithful followers obtained flashy vehicles for him, which they would register in their own names, to help Warren roam. He was partial to expensive SUVs and had been known to travel in a Porsche, a BMW, and a Mercedes-Benz; he even for a while had a couple of fiery red Harley-Davidson motorcycles, with fancy biker-dude leathers and accessories, and a picture shows a motorcycle parked with him astride the big machine and Naomi behind him. But looks can be deceiving. The physically weak prophet never mastered the heavy $50,000 Harley and was a failure as a biker. It eventually was stolen, but Warren did not report the theft because the police would have become involved.

The indictment on criminal charges following Candi Shapley's testimony apparently was the prophet's ticket to party as no other FLDS member had ever done; he used it as an excuse to gallivant around the country and live a life that was not possible inside of the FLDS compounds. He had escaped not only from the law, but from the horrendously oppressive rules that he imposed on everyone else. Warren paid a "negro woman" in California $250 to braid Naomi's hair in plaited corn rows. When other wives joined him on the road, they also wore jeans and tops and sweaters and sported new hairstyles.

Tooling along in a new SUV, with pretty young wives made up like gentiles at his side, eluding the cops, keeping the flock scared to death with pronouncements of doom, directing the building of his temple at R-17, and still managing all of the affairs of the church, expelling men and conducting underage marriages, lifted him to the status of a cult hero among the believers. His FLDS acolytes thought the way that the prophet outwitted his enemies was great fun.

The mysterious road trip of Warren Jeffs, fueled by his inner ferocity for secrecy, would continue for many months and take him from "the gentile amusement park called Disneyland" in California, through the heart of Dixie, up to the rocky coast of Maine, across the prairies, and into the mountains. He lived in hotels and motels or secret refuge houses or he might just show up unannounced at the home of a sympathizer. By far, his most preferred stop was the YFZ Ranch in Texas, where he could be smuggled in and out and secrecy and protection were assured.

Eventually, he felt that even the United States might be too small for him, that he might not be able to outrun his mounting troubles. He dyed his own hair and went shopping with Naomi in a Dallas mall to buy expensive clothes "for going among the rich in Europe." He charged his lieutenants with getting false identification papers and passports that would allow him to escape to foreign lands. Obtaining authentic-looking documentation proved to be impossible, and although the negotiators spent freely, they were afraid that the underworld characters with whom they were dealing would double-cross them. They ultimately failed, and Warren eventually called off his plans for Europe, deciding that he would just have to be more careful.

*   *   *

He had good reason to remain paranoid and on the run. Each passing month seemed to bring him more bad news.

Although Winston Blackmore and I disagreed about polygamy and other issues, we had learned to work together and had earned each other's trust. Now that careful maintenance of Blackmore as a source paid a huge dividend when a "what if" brainstorming session between us resulted in a devastating move against the United Effort Plan Trust. Warren Jeffs was still president of the UEP, a position that gave him total control over who could stay on Trust-owned lands and who must go.

Blackmore and I reasoned that if an FLDS follower wished to willingly turn his home over to the church, that should be a personal decision. But nearly all the families in Short Creek had built their home on UEP-owned land, and had lived there for years, and were considered to be only tenants in common—beneficiaries of the UEP Trust—by the church. Then there was an additional group, those who had been expelled by the church but flatly refused to move out. We felt that all of the residents deserved the right to choose whether or not to live in their homes, and not to have the church arbitrarily making that decision. Thousands of people and millions of dollars in assets were involved.

So Winston and I kicked around some ideas during a three-hour telephone conversation. I was parked in Utah, with my cell plugged into the car, and Winston was on a swather in Canada, doing the first cut of spring hay. We wondered if there might be some way to replace Warren, who was on the lam, and the trustees with a new board of directors comprising a fair representation of all beneficiaries of the trust. The reorganization would strip the church of its arbitrary power and allow individuals to make pertinent choices regarding their homes; something stronger than the "life estate" granted to the Chatwins and a few others.

Ironically, it was Warren himself who had opened the possibility of a reorganization through his beloved "answer them nothing" legal strategy. Since he had disappeared, the Trust was being mismanaged and lay at risk of losing all its assets. With Warren not answering the lawsuits, if our clients chose to take a default judgment by the court, they could seize anything of value belonging to the Trust beneficiaries. They could have become rich.

But their intent all along had not been to make a lot of money in a lawsuit; they wanted to deny Warren Jeffs the use of the Trust as leverage to kick their families out of the community by taking their homes and everything they had.

The prophet could not have it both ways; he either had to appear in public and answer the charges in court, or he would remain silent and in hiding and lose. It gave our clients the unique opportunity to pursue home ownership for all of the beneficiaries of the Trust.

I ran our conversation by Roger Hoole, who had taken over from Pat Shea as our Utah counsel, and he consulted with the Utah Attorney General's Office. They concluded that if such a charitable trust was not being managed properly, then the state could step in to protect the rights of the beneficiaries. A special fiduciary could be appointed, and a court could assume control until it was all settled.

On May 27, Third District judge Robert Adkins issued a temporary restraining order that suspended the power and authority of the United Effort Plan Trust.

The prophet went ballistic. His piousness had boomeranged, and by maintaining silence, he was sure to lose the legal challenge, thus surrendering control of the wealth represented by the UEP lands in the United States and Canada.

He concluded that "the devil" was behind the attack because God had absolutely ordered him to tell the courts nothing. He instructed his UEP board members to ignore the courts until forced to give up. Then, he predicted, the faithful could expect to be driven from their homes, perhaps even killed, and if they survived, they would be scattered across the nation to live in rented homes among the gentiles. It was still another test from God, he said. When all else failed, Warren could always place the blame with God as a test of faith.

When Ross Chatwin's brother Andrew learned that the UEP Trust was no longer under the control of the prophet, he decided to come home again.

As a boy, he had attended the sadistic Alta Academy, where he had gotten Warren Jeffs in trouble by tattling about being whipped badly by the sadistic schoolmaster. Uncle Rulon was still alive at the time and allowed Andrew to go unpunished. When Andrew turned eighteen, he was given a piece of UEP land on which to build a home so he could start a family. Not being one to forgive and forget, Warren exacted revenge when he became the prophet's mouthpiece: He ran Andrew out of town.

Now Andrew was diabetic, having trouble continuing to work in the construction trades; money was tight, and his kids were getting ready for school. Since the house he had built from the ground up in Short Creek stood empty, but was being maintained by his father, he thought he could move back in and live without the burden of any house payments.

The FLDS hierarchy saw it differently. They were not about to allow this apostate, his gentile wife, and their three kids to move in among the chosen ones. Afraid that he would be the brunt of Warren's revenge, Andrew's father had forewarned church authorities that his son would be moving in. When they arrived with their belongings, Andrew found the police blocking the driveway, and the church had suddenly moved another of his brothers, Sam Chatwin, into the house that very day.

Still determined to live in Short Creek, Andrew found an alternative. The Trust manager would allow him to claim another house of equal value, as long as it was empty so he wasn't displacing any other family. Andrew found a potential candidate on a list of properties, and he started moving in, with the help of friends and other castaways. The police soon showed up there, too, and a standoff developed.

The refugees captured everything on video cameras, and the scenes are still disturbing to anyone unfamiliar with FLDS radicalism. I was called on the phone to give what advice I could, and the usual theme played out: The cops were told this was a civil matter, that they had no authority, and that Andrew had obtained legal permission to occupy the dwelling. The cops ignored them.

Throughout the day and into the evening, more police cars rolled up, as did a fleet of automobiles and pickup trucks driven by other FLDS men. The Mohave County sheriff's office was called and within a few hours, an Arizona deputy arrived. He did what any law enforcement agency would normally do: He refused to get involved in a civil dispute because no crime had been committed. The deputy made a report and advised the local police not to meddle in property disputes involving private parties. The local cops pretended to agree, and the crowd drifted away.

As soon as the deputy cleared out for his five-hour drive back to Kingman, the local police and vigilantes returned. About midnight, Chief Marshal Sam Roundy looked out at the gathered throng and turned to his brother Deputy Marshall Jonathan Roundy to ask, "So, are we going to do this?" Jonathan replied, "Let's do it."

There was a burst of movement and from the darkness emerged a throng of about seventy-five men, tramping in military unison with their hands clasped behind their backs. Uncle Rulon had created an organization that he christened the Sons of Helaman, after a figure in distant Mormon history who had fathered valiant offspring. Present-day FLDS boys were trained like soldiers and learned, among other things, how to march. Warren would eventually expand their role to form a network of spies and snitches within the community. The Sons of Helaman reminded me of similar familiar youth groups.

Upon reaching the house, the silent advancing column encircled it within a closed perimeter. Immediately, a herd of work crews with pickup trucks and small bobcat tractors swooped out of nowhere. Colorado City refuse department drivers backed up their trash trucks in the middle of the night. Chief Marshal Sam Roundy threatened Andrew Chatwin with arrest if he did not stand aside, then stalked directly into the house to direct the vigilante raid and actually helped remove the Chatwins' furniture.

FLDS work crews got to work, stacking all of the family's belongings out on the street, then attacked the house and gutted it. Little kids helped haul drywall and build an eight-foot-high fence. Other cops tracked down the former occupant, who had moved across town and into a nicer home to accommodate his growing family two years earlier. Now he was brought back, and he claimed to only have left the place empty temporarily, for some remodeling. The crews worked for four days straight, totally rebuilt the rundown house, and then moved the absentee family back in, all under the watchful eyes of the local police.

Not a shot was fired during this all-out assault by an unfeeling church against a single family trying to find a home. The relentless intimidation, the outright disregard for the law, and the clear threat of violence was more than enough to get the job done. It was unbelievably frustrating for me to watch them repeatedly disobey the law and get away with it. There was just nobody to stop them in the isolated place called Short Creek. It was the FLDS way.

On June 22, 2005, the courts came through. A judge in Utah, the honorable Denise Lindberg, suspended all the known trustees of the United Effort Plan Trust, including Warren, his brother Leroy, and Short Creek bishop William Timpson Jessop. In an accompanying step, Salt Lake City certified public accountant Bruce Wisan was appointed by the court as a special fiduciary to oversee UEP property and protect the Trust assets. That would mean that people living in houses they had built on UEP land could no longer legally be thrown into the street at the whim of the prophet—a significant tear in his armor of invincibility.

Andrew, who had found temporary shelter in the home of an uncle, obtained Wisan's help to get a court order that would allow him back into the home he had built. An eviction notice was posted, and his brother Sam abruptly left. Andrew and his family live there today.

On July 12, a little more than a month after Warren was indicted, Arizona brought charges against eight Short Creek FLDS men on various charges in connection with the practice of forced underage marriages. Among them was Randy Barlow, whose ex-concubine, Candi Shapley, had testified against him before a Mohave County grand jury. Another was Rodney Holm, the decertified former FLDS deputy marshal who had been convicted in Utah for marrying a sixteen-year-old girl and was now facing the same charge in Arizona. The very next day, Arizona and Utah each posted a five-thousand-dollar reward for information leading to Warren Jeffs's arrest. Although I thought the reward was a positive move, the amount was, in my opinion, nowhere near enough to persuade any FLDS loyalist to drop a dime on Warren. To rat out the prophet meant the informer would likely lose everything, including home, job, and family, in addition to being totally shunned by the rest of the hive. As horrible as the Crick might be for them, living there was easier than getting on all alone in a mysterious world they had never learned to comprehend. Any active FLDS member with the guts to come out against Warren would need a lot of resources to start a completely new life, and the ten-thousand-dollar total being offered was nowhere near enough to make that kind of sacrifice. As I expected, no one stepped forward.

In August, Arizona attorney general Terry Goddard moved to force the Colorado City Unified School District into state receivership for gross mismanagement.

About twelve hundred students were enrolled in public schools back in the year 2000, when Warren Jeffs decided to remove all of the FLDS kids from the district because the curriculum allegedly was an abomination to God. In reality, the move was just another money-making scheme to profit from the gentiles.

The FLDS kids would be home-schooled instead, leaving only a sampling of students who were mostly from nearby Centennial Park, the community that had broken away from the FLDS and no longer followed Jeffs. This reduced the student body to about four hundred children, but there was no accompanying slash in the payroll for the more than one hundred employees and eighteen administrators. Nearly all of the teachers, administrators, groundskeepers, and maintenance personnel were FLDS members and kept their jobs, drawing salaries from the taxpayers. The resulting out-of-whack ratio of about three students to every teacher in the system continued to funnel public funds into the FLDS community.

Steadfast Warrenite Alvin Barlow was the longest-tenured public school superintendent on record in Arizona and had been amply rewarded for his tenure. While bouncing teacher payroll checks, the district went into debt by almost two million dollars but bought its own airplane for a quarter-million dollars and supplied loyal FLDS administrators with new SUVs and pickups, phones, and computers. It was a bizarre and convoluted scheme that began before I started my investigation, for which I was thankful. I did not need that on my plate, too.

But for Arizona attorney general Terry Goddard to intervene on the old issue of the schools at this particular time gave Warren Jeffs something else to worry about. The various government agencies that had ignored him for so long were awakening.

The prophet, on the run and hiding out, stayed just ahead of the approaching storms. I still did not know where he was. That did not mean that I was idle, though. Far from it. I was staying in touch with Candi in hopes of convincing her how important her testimony in court would be to other young girls who were coming of age on the FLDS bridal farms. But she was no longer the only bullet in the gun. In July, after a quiet meeting in Baltimore with Joanne Suder, the courageous Elissa Wall chose to get involved. "I didn't want to pull any punches in my efforts to get Warren," she would later write in her bestselling autobiography *Stolen Innocence*.

I had been at a conference in Mesquite, Nevada, that summer when Brock Belnap, the Washington County prosecutor located in St. George, Utah, had pulled me aside. He had received a tip that we may have found a solid new witness who might be willing to testify against the FLDS leader, and said, "If there's something criminal involved in this, let me know." Now it was time. Roger Hoole placed a call to Belnap, and he started an investigation, working closely with Elissa and protecting her identity to avoid FLDS obstruction in the case, as they had done with Candi.

Then, another break. At three o'clock in the morning on October 28, 2005, Seth Steed Jeffs, the road-running courier brother of the prophet, was lying on a mattress in the back of a Ford Excursion SUV driven by Nathaniel Allred when police pulled them over in Pueblo County, Colorado, expecting to find a drunk driver. Inside the vehicle, the cops found a cache of unusual material: a laptop, letters addressed to the prophet, church records, $142,000 in cash, some $7,000 in prepaid debit and phone cards, along with a GPS and a glass jar bearing the label "Pennies for the Prophet" and a photo of Warren Jeffs, a gift from the FLDS children. Both Jeffs and Allred were arrested.

The frightened Allred was scared to death, consumed with fear about going to a gentile jail and with guilt for having accompanyied his cousin on the trip. The savvy deputy advised the young man that honesty might buy him a break, but lying would most certainly buy him some jail time. That was all it took. Nate told police that Seth had paid him five thousand dollars to accompany him on the road trip and have sex with him. Jeffs stonewalled police, claiming he did not know the prophet's location, and said, "even if I did know, I wouldn't reveal the information to you." Charges against Allred were dropped in exchange for his cooperation, but prosecutors wanted federal prison time for the prophet's sibling. Seth Jeffs was charged with soliciting prostitution and harboring a fugitive. A plea deal was reached for Seth to plead guilty to harboring a fugitive and the soliciting prostitution charges would be dropped. The final word lay with a naïve federal judge who moralized that he "would not visit the sins of the brother [Warren]" upon Seth Jeffs. Seth got off with a slap-on-the-wrist sentence of three years probation and a $2,500 fine. It seemed straight out of the FLDS playbook.

Seth Jeffs, who had been caught aiding and abetting his fugitive brother, fell on his sword and took a hit for God and the prophet, with no real scars to show for it. He was now a martyr for the cause, and to an FLDS man it doesn't get much better than that. Shortly after his early release from probation, he appeared on *Oprah* from the Texas compound, where he was regarded as a hero. His appearance was scripted by church leaders, and he gave the TV crew the old Red-Cross-in-the-concentration-camp tour of the ranch. He criticized the persecution of his church and showed off seven of his wives and nineteen children. When asked if he thought a young girl should enter into a marriage or spiritual union, Seth opined that it was her choice. "Who really cares?" he asked.

I was frustrated by his bluster, by the apathy displayed by the federal courts, and by the misleading impression left with Oprah's television audience. I was more interested in how Seth had screwed up, made a mistake, and gotten caught out on the roads. Warren, under growing pressure, just might do the same thing.

CHAPTER 28

The Turf War

The Candi Shapley situation became increasingly bizarre after her grand jury testimony. Her emotions were all over the map as she found herself caught between enormous pressure from the church and her family, and her legal obligation to stand by what she had told the grand jury under oath in a court of law.

Out of the blue, her mother, Esther, initiated a cat-and-mouse game with me about a month after Candi had testified. After being kicked out of the church, Bill Shapley was allowed back into the fold for the express purpose of making sure that his errant daughter didn't succeed in giving up the prophet. For Bill, it was a religious calling and his salvation and status in the church was dependent on his success. For his obedience, he was given his wives and family back, all but Esther. Warren wouldn't allow her to be restored as one of the wives of the redeemed Bill Shapley. Over time, she explained to me why Warren had singled her out: She had been raped as a young girl by an older relative who had then piled enough guilt on her to make Esther think the assault was somehow her fault. She had never revealed that secret until Warren came to power, and then in a fit of conscience initiated by Warren's incessant digging into the private lives of members, she had confessed everything to him. Instead of punishing the rapist, Warren considered Esther soiled from the contact, and forbade her from rejoining Bill as a wife when he was allowed back in the church. Besides, she was past her childbearing years and had become a liability instead of an asset to the family. Instead, she was given a small widow's stipend and permission to visit with her other two daughters, who remained in Bill's custody, while she went to live in seclusion with a group of other such "widows." Even those "privileges" would be at risk if she was disobedient, and Lyle Jeffs, Warren's brother, was her watchdog.

Consequently, Esther also was conflicted about whether to defend and do what was best for her daughter Candi or please the FLDS authorities. A short time after our first meeting in a little park near Coral Canyon, the FLDS punished Esther by whisking away her daughters Annay, thirteen, and Billie, sixteen. The girls went willingly, but it was a clear message to Esther that Big Brother was watching and her youngest children could and would disappear at any time if she didn't do as she was commanded, and "keep sweet" about it. She was scared that she wouldn't see her children again, and she had written down the tag numbers of the Chevy Suburbans that had taken the girls away. She then quietly passed the plate numbers to me. I in turn passed those along to the FBI, who started to consider their options of how to deal with the situation. The FBI agents felt they needed to locate the two missing girls and place the entire crew of Esther, Candi, and the two younger sisters into the federal Witness Protection Program. I was hoping Esther would be strong enough to take a leap of faith and leave the only life she had ever known. She agreed, and was about to take the plunge and go into the program, but just before the FBI was about to make the final arrangements, Esther backed down. She just didn't have the strength to turn her back on the cultural and religious ties that bound her to the only home she had ever known. This on-again, off-again contact went on for several months before Esther called me urgently one evening in December 2005. She had a key to her ex-husband's insurance office and sometimes would sneak in there after business hours to call me without being overheard. One evening she called from there, worried that the FLDS was monitoring her movements. About fifteen minutes into the call, she became nervous because there were people milling around outside, and they seemed to be checking out the building. Soon they were banging on the doors and windows of the office. "They're here! They're going to be coming in!" she cried.

I worked out a quick code: Use the word "notebook" in a sentence if it was the police, and not just some God Squad enforcer, who entered the room. Almost immediately, I heard a lot of noise, and then she said,

"Okay, I'll have to check my notebook and get back to you." The crooked cops had her. An hour later, she called again, as calm as a summer pond, her words cryptic and machine-like. "Hello. I'm not going to be talking to you anymore. I'm okay and there's nothing to worry about. I am happy. Please don't bother me or try to call me." I asked if anyone was listening to the call, to which she responded, "Yes, I have to go," and the phone went dead.

Three days later, the distraught Esther called yet again, asking if she could come by my office. Once inside, she told me that Lyle Jeffs, the prophet's strong-arm brother, had threatened to take away her widow's stipend, and had warned that he was awaiting word on whether she would even be allowed back on FLDS Priesthood property. That would have marked the end of her shelter and any means of support; she feared being left homeless and destitute. While we spoke, Lyle called on her cell phone. Esther went stone-faced, using her best "keep sweet" voice to repeat "yes, sir" three times, then she said "thank you" and hung up. Lyle had just delivered the death blow that she would never be permitted to see her children again, and would not be welcome back in the Crick. Esther broke down and sobbed, talking of suicide and how to make it appear accidental. I offered help, but she just turned it away. All I could do was spend time with her and try to convince her that there was more to life than living under the rule of tyrants. She was inconsolable—a plyg woman who was almost sixty, on her own with no home and no means of support, who now didn't even have her children to love her. Once again, there had been no due process of law, and no mercy.

Lyle was not yet finished; he was waiting the next morning as Esther approached her car after leaving the motel room where she ended up spending the night after leaving my office. He had been following her. This time he dangled an attractive carrot under her nose: The prophet might be magnanimous enough to reinstate her in the church on probationary status, and allow her to keep her stipend, as long as she would obey the priesthood in all things. What else could she do? Esther accepted Lyle's offer and became a tool to help control her traitorous daughter.

I gained valuable insights in how ruthless the FLDS can be in response to a challenge, and the tactics they would use and great lengths they would go to to threaten a witness. I wasn't sure that Candi would ever make it to a courtroom, but I hoped that, sooner or later, a stronger witness would somehow emerge.

That moment was approaching faster than anyone expected. Elissa Wall trusted us, but she had remained apprehensive of the process. She had been observing Candi's experiences, using them as a roadmap for what lay ahead. She wanted some protection against what we all feared, inevitable FLDS retaliation. Roger Hoole, representing Elissa, and Washington County prosecutor Brock Belnap drafted a confidentiality agreement that would not only protect her identity, but would also allow her the freedom to withdraw from the action if the pressure became unbearable.

As part of the camouflage, the prosecutor put off charging Elissa's ex-husband, Allen Steed, with anything at all until after Warren Jeffs was arrested and tried. To name Steed prematurely would tip off the FLDS that Elissa was involved. Elissa's safety was more important than Steed. Under those conditions, she agreed to go forward.

A civil suit accusing Warren Jeffs of placing an unidentified child in an illegal and incestuous underage marriage was filed under the pseudonym of "M. J." on December 13, 2005. Not only were the initials fictitious, but the filing was made far away from Short Creek, in Cedar City, Utah. The plaintiff sought damages from not only the prophet but also from the FLDS church and the UEP Trust. The lawsuit kept Elissa so far in the background that there was little for the FLDS to track.

Two weeks later, on New Year's Day 2006, Elissa Wall did one of the hardest things a victim of abuse can do: During long interviews with detectives and attorneys from Washington County, Utah—basically, a bunch of strangers—she relived her experiences in an outpouring that left her tearful and exhausted. Step by step, Elissa grew more determined, and at the end, the authorities were convinced she was going to be a strong witness. On April 5, 2006, Elissa Wall completed two more exhaustive interviews with the police and prosecutors, and Brock Belnap felt that he had heard enough. He hit Warren Jeffs with two felony charges of rape as an accomplice.

The identity protection went to a higher level when the prosecutor identified the plaintiff in this case as Jane Doe IV. Only a handful of people knew that Elissa, M. J., and Jane Doe IV were the same person.

The biggest dog in the hunt for Warren Jeffs was the FBI. The Bureau had been there all along, but they kept their support very quiet. Now, because Warren had crossed so many state lines so often, he was wanted as a federal fugitive in addition to being sought on the various state and civil charges. As 2006 dawned, the Bureau got into the game for real, bringing to bear their immense resources.

A lot of these guys were friends of mine. We had a history of working together on other cases long before the FLDS investigation came along: I had helped them break up a ring of gem thieves; and I had assisted in a sting operation to catch a pedophile who had been preying on a thirteen-year-old girl, as well as several other cases. Over the years, I had learned to trust them and also had learned how to obtain their help and resources. When I approached them with an idea on how to put even more pressure on the prophet, they were receptive.

On June 27, 2005, the FBI issued what we call a UFAP (Unlawful Flight to Avoid Prosecution) warrant for the arrest of Warren Jeffs, backed up with a reward of $50,000.

Over the next year, Gary and I lobbied for even more federal help, and on May 6, 2006, the FBI bumped him up to the Ten Most Wanted list and doubled the reward to $100,000. Finally, the prophet's words had been proven right: He was now among the elite of the international criminals being hunted by the FBI, right up there with Osama bin Laden.

My popularity among the FLDS members had sunk to new lows in Short Creek over the past few months. When I walked into the Colorado City Mercantile Cooperative (the general store), I was always treated to an impressive display of mobile communication devices as cell phones were whipped out to report that the demon gentile private investigator was back in the Crick. Soon, a plyg-rig convoy of trucks would show up on the streets, not just one, but six or eight. It was annoying.

Then the goons went too far. They decided to harass me at my home, something I would not tolerate. That spring, my wife mentioned that she had seen some pickup trucks with tinted windows pull into our driveway a couple of times and just sit there until our dogs barked at them. Then they would slowly back out and speed away. Since my house is situated on twenty acres at the end of a dead-end road that is two and a half miles long, there was no reason for anybody to just happen to be coming out to our place unannounced.

A few days after she told me about the trucks, she called me to the front porch; they were back. A pickup truck towing a trailer was idling in our driveway. Four people were in it, and when they spotted me, they took off. I jumped into my white SUV and we raced down the dirt road and then onto the highway, where I pulled up beside them and motioned for them to pull over. Instead, they tore along for another eight miles until they swerved onto another dirt road, stopping only when it dead-ended at the DeMille Turf Farm. I boxed them in.

Not knowing who they were, their intentions, or whether they were armed, I was reluctant to approach the truck, but they were just sitting there, so I stalked over and rapped on the driver's window until he rolled it down. Inside sat three buttoned-up men and one woman, who wore a typical fundamentalist prairie dress. It was the FLDS.

"Hey! Do you know who I am?" I shouted in the driver's face. All four looked down and refused to answer. I was furious, they had crossed the line by coming to my home and it would not be tolerated. My face was now within inches of the man behind the wheel as I screamed again, "Do you know who I am!" The driver, staring down at the floor, shook his head that he did not. Then I asked the others, who did the same, so I cleared up the mystery for them.

"I'm Sam Brower! Why were you at my house?"

"Oh, we were just lost," the driver mumbled.

I was seeing red. These thugs were invading my family home and needed a lesson, fast. "Listen," I told him. "You come to my house again and trespass on my property, I'm going to splatter you all over my driveway. You understand? Go back and tell the people who sent you . . . you come to my house again, I *will* splatter you. Do you understand?"

They sat there not saying a word, and I wanted to make sure there was no misunderstanding. I reached in and knocked the baseball cap off the driver's head. It flew into the face of the guy in the back. "You understand me?" The guy quickly nodded his head and said he did.

"So, if you were lost, why are you here?" I demanded.

"Uh, we came here to buy some turf."

The farm had just been mowed and there were no rolls or strips of turf left except for little chunks. "Okay. Get out and get your turf." While they started dutifully loading little scrap clods of soil into their trailer, I called a detective friend and told him what was going on. He said, "Sam, get out of there before you do something stupid."

I agreed. My goal was not to hurt anyone, just to humiliate them enough to make certain they had gotten the message. The church goons did not return.

I had not seen Candi Shapley for some time when she contacted me in April 2006 and asked me to explain the latest legal wrinkle concerning her upcoming appearance in Kingman, Arizona, for the trial of her ex-"husband," Randy Barlow. The Arizona subpoena for her appearance as a witness first had to be cleared through a Utah court hearing, which also required her to appear. I explained that it was just a formality to make the Arizona subpoena executable in Utah and explained the consequences of not appearing. But Candi was a no-show at the hearing, and the judge issued a warrant for her arrest on a charge of failure to appear. Once again, our star witness was gone, and this time she was a fugitive. Every cop in the nation had her name.

Gary and I watched her home for more than a week and finally spotted Esther driving up with someone else in the car. I trailed them for a while, but lost her when they turned into a fast-food drive-through. Esther Shapley wouldn't have gone to Candi's home just for the heck of it. Candi had to be nearby.

Early the following morning, Washington County deputy Matt Fischer, a savvy cop who had been on assignment in Short Creek for a year, decided to stop by Candi's apartment. She got there at nearly the same time, and she was arrested.

Candi called her mother, Esther, from the jail to ask for help, without success. She then reached out to Gary and me. Engels was hamstrung because his jurisdiction was in Arizona, and Candi was in Utah. I agreed to help, but I demanded that she first tell me what had been going on—the truth. As I spoke to her in the Washington County Jail, a story of the FLDS luring her away from her home spilled forth.

According to Candi, shortly after she had called me for advice about the Utah court date, her mother had summoned her. Esther had been baby-sitting one of the twins and they made arrangements for Candi to pick up the child at R&W Excavation in Short Creek. That immediately sent up red flags for me because R&W was owned by church enforcer Willie Jessop.

Candi saw nothing unusual about that. Her uncle and aunt both worked there, as her mother also did on occasion, so she willingly went on over. She was surprised to find her father there, too, since Esther and Bill were still officially apart. And they were both wearing gentile clothes, which was totally out of character. Then Willie Jessop pulled into the parking lot in a new, blue GMC Denali and handed the keys over to Bill Shapley. It was all very strange.

Bill and Esther urged Candi to climb into the truck with the twins so they could all go and visit some people in Phoenix. On the way there, Candi began asking questions and they explained that the FLDS could not take the chance of her testifying against Randy, because that information could also be used against the prophet. The FLDS leaders needed for Candi to disappear and had tasked her mother and father with the ugly job of kidnapping their own daughter and grandchildren.

"Eventually things will get back to normal and the prophet will find a good priesthood man for you," Esther reassured her.

"I don't *want* a good priesthood man," Candi retorted. "I've already had one of those."

They ended up at a condo that Candi said belonged to another FLDS loyalist by the name of Paul Holm, where she was supposed to remain in hiding. But after a few weeks in Phoenix, her handicapped baby took a turn for the worse and once again needed urgent medical attention. Candi feared that if her little girl didn't receive specialized care back at Primary Children's Hospital in Salt Lake City, the baby probably wouldn't make it. The FLDS phobia against using unfamiliar hospitals was ingrained in her. The new doctors would demand information. So a rendezvous was set up with another of Candi's sisters in Mesquite, Nevada, with the understanding that the sister would transport the child on to Salt Lake and Candi would sneak back into hiding.

Once in Mesquite, Candi threw a public fit within sight of gentiles. Her parents decided to avoid a scene by letting Candi go on to Salt Lake, too. Deputy Fischer found her the following morning.

Now in jail, she was furious at her parents and the church for luring her and her babies away.

As the father of two daughters and a son who I love dearly, I often struggle to understand how an FLDS mother and father can set aside normal parental instincts and knowingly place their underage daughter into a sexually abusive relationship with a man who might be decades older than the child. My youngest daughter was only fourteen when I started working these cases, and the thought of such an event taking place involving one of my girls left me nauseated.

I felt sorry for the things Candi had gone through. My heart went out to her, and every time I see one of those little girls in a prairie dress at the Crick, I think about Candi's plight and that of many other young girls there and ponder the simple truth that they just don't stand a chance.

They will never become a concert violinist, or even play guitar with friends in their garage. They won't be physicists or chemists, or help their own children with their geometry homework, because they will never learn geometry themselves. Ambitions, goals, and achieving one's potential are limited to what a maniacal religious zealot lays out for them. The only thing on their horizon is bringing as many children as they can into the world, to replenish the insatiable requirement for ever more wives and ever more children. I try not to dwell on that bleak future when I see the kids working in the summer gardens of Short Creek, but it's a hard image to flush from my mind.

I suppose those feelings came to the surface when I called Esther and bluntly told her to get hold of Bill Shapley and get their daughter out of jail. It was their duty to help her out of this mess. Neither of them was aware at the time that I knew that their ruse had gone awry. Esther told me that she didn't have the money, and I snapped back that Bill certainly did. Esther promised to see if he would help. After a couple of hours, I called back. She claimed that Bill was unavailable. I was furious. A few years later, in December 2010, I came across a photograph in *National Geographic* of a kindly Bill Shapley watching some of his fully-clothed daughters swimming in a mountain pond. Where the photo seemed to portray a family having fun, all I saw was a devious father.

I couldn't bear to watch Candi sit in jail, although the FLDS just might lure her away again or find some other way of keeping her quiet if she got out. The bail was five thousand dollars, meaning that if she went through a bondsman, it would cost about five hundred dollars, and a friend or family member would have to co-sign on the bond. None would, so I personally took care of it, carrying the liability if she didn't appear in court at the appointed time. That was never fully reimbursed.

I told Candi that the time had come for her to do the right thing. As part of our deal, she had to let me know where she was in the future as the trial neared. The good part was that she was now extremely angry with her family and the church hierarchy. She told friends about how she had been lured away and held hostage. She told Gary and me the same thing. If she could keep that state of mind, and keep focused on the truth, then I felt we had a chance.

A short time later Candi informed me that she had hired an attorney, something that few victims ever do. Since I had been the one who had bailed her out, I knew Candi had little money. I therefore suspected that the FLDS may have supplied her with a lawyer. Her new attorney promised that henceforth Candi would show up and testify.

CHAPTER 29

Arrest

On her wedding day, July 27, 2006, Merrianne Jessop was only twelve years and twenty-four days old. She had a blazing mane of bright red hair and a smile that reached across her freckled face from ear to ear. In the outside world, she would have been a sixth grader.

When she was only nine, Warren Jeffs commanded her father, his loyal lieutenant Merril Jessop, to fetch the girl to R-17 in Texas, where she could mature and begin receiving "trainings" on becoming a "heavenly comfort wife" for the prophet. Now the time had come, and Merrianne was summoned by her mother, Barbara. She was told to hurry and clean up, because something important was about to happen.

After a shower, she put on a fresh set of the long underwear required by her religion and slid into baggy sweat-suit pants before adding stockings up to her knees. Her best dress, a simple garment with a pretty crocheted collar that buttoned modestly around her neck, came next. Her mother brushed the girl's long hair and fixed her plyg-do. Now, clean and dressed and with her hair appropriately styled, Merrianne was escorted to a place she had never seen before: the inside of the temple of the YFZ compound, where she would be "spiritually placed" with fifty-year-old Warren Jeffs as another child concubine.

One minute the child had been out with the other kids and an hour later she was being sealed in marriage "for time and all eternity" to a fugitive who was on the FBI's Ten Most Wanted list.

The event was more than just another instance of Warren Jeffs grabbing up another preteen girl as a wife. It was a three-bride ceremony that gathered the FLDS elite into a power-sharing tribal ritual in which they intentionally bound themselves together in a criminal act with the exchange of underage girls who were called "Daughters of Zion," one of whom was not yet a teenager. Slathered with a veneer of religious-sounding hocus-pocus to make it seem that it was all God's doing, the triple wedding was a sham, and each one was illegal.

It was also a perfect example of the "I'll scratch your back if you scratch mine" arrangement among the like-minded villains of the three-member First Presidency that ruled the FLDS: President Warren Jeffs, First Counselor Wendell Nielsen, and Second Counselor Merril Jessop. The prophet knew he was pushing the envelope with the preteen Merrianne, but he was a genius at getting others to share in the culpability of his crimes. The fathers, and the mothers, would all get their hands dirty right along with him. None could accuse another without implicating themselves.

Bishop Merril Jessop had contributed his twelve-year-old daughter Merrianne to marry the prophet. Warren Jeffs contributed one of his own daughters, Teresa, who had turned fifteen the previous day, to marry thirty-six-year-old Raymond Merril Jessop, one of the bishop's sons, who was already a polygamist. Wendell Nielsen chipped in his own fifteen-year-old stepdaughter, LeAnn, to be a bride of Merril Leroy Jessop, age thirty-three, another of the bishop's sons. Family, fortunes, and fate were being knitted together in a huge criminal conspiracy.

None of the girls had to be dragged to the altar. The children were filled with the belief that these marriages were good and pure, and they understood the prestige that would come from being placed with such important men.

Wendell Nielsen said the opening prayer, then Warren took over as presiding "mouth"—the authorized speaker—and performed the first two ceremonies. The prophet would happily report in his journal that he then made Merril Jessop "mouth," temporarily granting him authority, and assumed his place beside his petite bride-to-be for his own grotesque ceremony. The top of the diminutive Merrianne's head came up to about the middle of the torso of her lanky husband, who stood six feet four.

The marriage delighted him, and he exuberantly admitted one of his most heinous crimes to his scribe for the Priesthood Record: "There was sealed Merrianne Jessop to Warren Steed Jeffs. That's me!"

Merrianne was given to the care of Warren's favorite concubines, Naomi and Millie, for further training, and two weeks later, the child was led to the ceremonial temple bed that had been designed to the prophet's specifications. There, she was sexually assaulted by the panting, praying Warren, assisted by Naomi and at least one other wife, in a mockery of a loving marital union.

The event was recorded on audio tape and later transcribed.

"That feels good. Now repeat the words from your mouth . . . How do you feel, Merrianne?" Warren prompted as he violated the little girl. A timid child's voice replied, "Feels good." Ever obedient and keeping sweet.

There is the sound of rhythmic, heavy breathing from the prophet, who then says, "Everyone else let go of me. Back away a little."

More hurried breathing and then some chanting gibberish is heard, and five minutes into the "ceremony," he tells Merrianne to prepare "for the greater light, the revelations of God on your behalf." He has the women tie his hand to Merrianne's, and then his gasping continues until a silence is noted and the ritualistic rape of a child is completed. The girl has hardly uttered a sound. Warren then issues long, tangled prayers for all involved, and asks his little bride to come up and give him a hug.

The child's innocence was gone forever, but we had not seen the last of little Merrianne Jessop.

A month later, on the night of August 28, 2006, I left my home in Utah and struck out on I-15 for the five-hour drive down to Kingman, Arizona, to witness the trial of Randy Barlow, who was charged with raping young Candi Shapley. The breathtaking route cuts across Las Vegas and passes Hoover Dam and the Grand Canyon before bending back toward Kingman, but my mind was too preoccupied to enjoy the views.

I could think only about how our mercurial witness would do the next day on the stand. Gary Engels had called to confirm that she was indeed going to show up, which was one problem solved, but what might happen next was up in the air. I checked into a small motel in Kingman about 9:30 P.M., had a bite to eat at a nearby restaurant, then climbed into bed and fell almost instantly asleep.

It seemed that I had just closed my eyes when my cell phone rattled to life on the night stand. I blinked awake. The amber numbers on the bedside clock showed that it was about midnight. I groped for the phone and answered, recognizing the excited voice of an FBI special agent from the Utah field office. I had worked closely with him over the years. He gave me the news: "They got him!"

"Got who?" I stammered, still fuzzy with sleep.

"Warren!"

I sat bolt upright in bed. "You're shitting me," I blurted.

"I wouldn't be calling you at midnight to shit you," he responded.

It was a strange, surreally joyous moment. After all of the months and years and work, the demented prophet had finally been caught. Now it would not matter if he chose not to speak; the evidence and the witnesses would do the talking.

Warren Jeffs's long ramble around America ended with a blind-luck capture on I-15 outside the town of Apex, Nevada, nineteen miles northeast of Las Vegas. Nevada highway patrolman Eddie Dutchover pulled up behind a new red Cadillac Escalade about nine o'clock that night and could not make out the temporary license plate, which was obscured by a plastic cover. Warren had worried a long time about how overlooking some small detail could potentially trip him up, and it appeared that perhaps one of his revelations had actually come true.

There were two men and a woman in the vehicle. The driver got out and handed over a Utah driver's license bearing the name of Isaac Jeffs, which sparked something in the officer's mind. It also stated that Jeffs had a concealed carry permit for a weapon, which earned a second, harder look at the driver, who was finding it hard to stand still.

Dutchover approached the SUV again and spoke with the woman inside, who presented a license in the name of Naomi Jessop. Because nobody in the FLDS has the authority to perform legal marriages, Naomi still carried the surname of her father, Merril Jessop.

The trooper turned to question the second passenger, a lanky man sitting on the right side of the back seat, staring straight ahead and eating a salad. The man studiously avoided looking at the policeman, and when asked for an ID, said his name was John Findley. Asked if he had any written ID, such as a driver's license, the man produced a receipt from a Florida business for the purchase of contact lenses. Dutchover noticed that the big jugular vein in the long neck was pulsing wildly. "You're so nervous it's making me nervous," the trooper said. "Is everything okay?" He asked the uneasy passenger to also get out, and made the two men stand apart while he continued to investigate. Their stories did not match. The driver, Isaac Jeffs, said they were headed for Utah, while the passenger, John Findley, said Denver was the destination.

Another red flag popped up when it was discovered that the big SUV was registered in the name of still someone else, a John Wayman out of Hildale, Utah, and the two men differed on who Wayman was and why they were using his Cadillac. Dutchover was at a critical point, alert to the possibility that he was dealing with more than just a few tourists passing through the state. He was alone with three suspicious people at the side of a darkened interstate freeway, and one of them was licensed to carry a concealed firearm. Something was very wrong; these guys were acting like drug runners, but so far, he had nothing substantial against them except the unreadable temporary license plate.

To further complicate matters, the computer had crashed at the highway patrol dispatch center, and the trooper had been unable to promptly run the registration. Had he been able to do so, and had it come back clean, he may have been forced to let the three people go on their way. But his training kicked in and he kept them talking, even getting a signed waiver to search the vehicle, thereby maintaining control of the scene while waiting for backup and for the computer to recover.

Dutchover remembered the photo of Warren Jeffs on the FBI's posters at the Highway Patrol headquarters, and the next trooper on the scene confirmed the likeness, but the tall guy kept insisting he was not Warren Jeffs. Another call got the FBI out there, and a lot more cops were on the way.

When the troopers began searching the Cadillac SUV, and found it filled with computers and other material that would certainly lead to the discovery of Jeffs's true identity, further denial became futile. An FBI agent asked once again for his real name, and the pale, nervous man finally gave in. "Warren Steed Jeffs," came the answer, with a sigh of resignation.

The Federal Bureau of Investigation was not going to tolerate a mistake on this one. Earlier that very day, the authorities in Boulder, Colorado, had announced they would not file charges against an itinerant oddball named John Mark Karr, who had been arrested in Thailand and hauled to the States after making a false confession that he had murdered little beauty queen JonBenét Ramsey in 1996. The FBI had not been responsible for the Karr case, but the bungling of the Boulder district attorney's office had left a cloud hanging over law enforcement nationwide. Nobody wanted another mistake. The FBI was going to be sure of what they were doing.

I spent a half hour on the telephone with the FBI as they tried to pin down Jeffs's identity with certainty. They had him on "the List," but neither they nor the Nevada State Police had day-by-day involvement with the case. By contrast, my life had been dominated by Jeffs and his cohorts for years. My office overflowed with documents, transcripts of old court cases, boxes of tapes, files and folders, and thousands of hours of recordings of Jeffs's droning lectures. My brain was just as full. I probably knew more about the FLDS than most members of the religion did. Without a doubt, this was the prophet.

During the two and a half hours they spent alongside that interstate highway, the authorities pulled an astonishing array of material from the cavernous SUV, everything a man on the run would need for survival: a police scanner, a radar detector, a couple of GPS navigational devices, a bunch of laptop computers, three iPods, better than a dozen cell phones and walkie-talkies; wigs, knives, and sunglasses; twenty-seven bricks of $100 bills, each worth $2,500; about $10,000 worth of prepaid credit cards; a duffel bag jammed with envelopes that contained even more money; the keys to no fewer than ten new luxury SUVs standing by to be exchanged as fresh vehicles whenever the old ones became too hot; a *Book of Mormon* and a Bible; and finally, a photograph of Warren with his late father, Rulon. The captured computers eventually would yield a trove of evidentiary material, including the audio tape of Warren having sex with Merrianne Jessop.

The police took a picture of a blank, emotionless Uncle Warren after he surrendered on the roadside. He was wearing baggy Bermuda shorts and a T-shirt, with short black socks and dress shoes. A loyal woman member of the FLDS would tell me later that the moment she saw that police photograph of him standing by the road, showing his flesh in shorts, she decided to bolt from the cult. "It was the straw that broke the camel's back," she said. "It's not so much that he was dressed in clothes that he has kicked others out of their homes for wearing, but that he was wearing them and he had a tan!"

Warren Steed Jeffs was taken to the FBI office in Las Vegas, and at 5:07 A.M. he was photographed, fingerprinted, and booked into the Clark County Detention Facility. The self-appointed prophet was now behind bars, but for some mysterious and frustrating reason, his traveling companions, Isaac and Naomi, had been questioned and released. That decision caught me off guard.

Isaac and Naomi were apprehended in the same vehicle as one of the most wanted criminals in America, and for many months had been facilitating his continued freedom. I couldn't understand why they had not been charged with aiding and abetting a fugitive, obstruction of justice, and—I am sure that, with a little head-scratching, there could have been a few more charges. They would most likely have been easy convictions and would have left both Naomi and Isaac facing serious prison time. Perhaps Isaac, the brother, would have stayed silent rather than help prosecutors, but Naomi was different. A shrewd manipulator and Warren's closest confidante, she may well have turned on him to save her own skin, in my opinion. The information she had would have been valuable beyond measure.

While there was no way of knowing her role at the time, if she had been detained long enough to process some of the evidence found in the car, they would have discovered Naomi's importance. Instead, they let her go. It was a lost opportunity.

A lot of potential evidence walked out the door when Naomi and Isaac were set free. To this day, I don't have an answer for why the Feds did not seize that opportunity. An FBI agent who I asked about it later was as disgusted as I, hinting only that they had gotten orders "from upstairs." It wasn't the first time, nor would it be the last time, that law enforcement agencies would make perplexing decisions in this investigation and never explain why.

I was ecstatic that Warren had been caught, but it meant an almost sleepless night of phone calls and e-mails in my motel room in Kingman. I wasn't the only one awake. The news instantaneously swept through not only the FLDS and the refugee community but the national media as well. By the time I walked through the grove of tall trees flanking the main entrance of the columned Mohave County Courthouse on the morning of August 29, I was exhausted.

Candi looked a lot better. She had long before rejected the FLDS dress code, and it seems that as soon as a woman leaves the cult and tastes that newfound sense of freedom, one of the first things she does is get a new hairdo and update the stale wardrobe. In her appearance before Superior Court judge Steven Conn, Candi was a stylish twenty-year-old young woman whose wavy red hair complimented the black pants, tailored vest, and black heels.

Her mother, Esther, wore a drab brown ankle-length prairie dress and sat on the defense side of the courtroom, right next to the mother of the perpetrator on trial, Randy Barlow, in a silent show of solidarity. Barlow, whose bail had been posted by Willie Jessop, was facing two Class 6 felonies for sexual conduct with a minor, as well as the more serious charge of rape, because Candi had told the grand jury that he had raped her twice after she was forced to marry him when she was only sixteen. Barlow sauntered into court wearing jeans and a gray shirt, seemingly unconcerned for a man who could be sent away for several years in prison if convicted. I wondered if he knew something we didn't.

Barlow was actually the second of eight FLDS men who would be tried in Arizona's crackdown on underage marriages. The first, Kelly Fischer, had been convicted and got forty-five days in jail and three years of probation, a disappointing sentence. Judge Steven Conn's rationale for such a light sentence was that it was normal for a first conviction for statutory rape. The judge apparently didn't take into consideration the fact that Fischer was a loyal FLDS member and might well reoffend if called upon by his church leaders to do so. Five of the eight men indicted were eventually convicted.

Soon after Candi took the stand, I had the sinking feeling that this trial was over before it even started. Only a few minutes into the general background opening questions from Mohave County prosecutor Matt Smith, I saw Esther rise. She moved all the way across the courtroom and took a new position, directly in Candi's line of sight, as if the witness was not already painfully aware of her complex family situation. The church hierarchy was using Esther to play on that weakness. It reminded me of something out of the *Godfather* movies.

Smith asked Candi how she had learned she was being placed with Barlow. She remained cool, and after a long pause looked right at him. I was stunned to hear the words that followed from her mouth. "I have nothing else to say," she told the prosecutor. I cringed, almost able to hear Warren Jeffs's "answer them nothing" mantra rolling around in her head.

Smith had not expected such explicit opposition. Everything he had was flying right out the window as the prime witness and victim deliberately defied the court. He pressed forward, and she became adamant and her stare hardened. "I have nothing else to say."

Judge Conn instructed her to respond or face the possibility of contempt of court. Candi remained firm: "I am not willing to answer any more questions."

She crashed and burned before our eyes. Following the courtroom disaster, the state tried to salvage something from the wreckage.

There was a little more legal wrangling, but it was over. After Candi balked, the man who she claimed under oath had savagely raped her walked out of court a free man. It was unbelievable. She was ruled in contempt of court and sent to a shelter for abused women on a thirty-day sentence. It was later shortened to two weeks when Matt Smith felt there was no need to continue victimizing the victim.

Having gotten to know Esther, I was not surprised by her strange actions. The church leadership had backed her into a corner, and I didn't expect her to have the courage to defy them. But I was highly disappointed with Candi. At least she didn't lie; she just refused to answer. The charges against Warren in Arizona remained in place, but if Candi would not even testify against Barlow, there was no chance that she would take the stand against the prophet.

Of the other three Arizona men who ended up not being convicted of the charges against them, Rodney Holm, the former deputy marshall, remains a convicted felon and registered sex offender in the state of Utah. His Arizona charges were dismissed. The indictment against Terry Barlow was dismissed and Donald Barlow was acquitted.

I wouldn't allow Candi's and Esther's performances in court that day to alter my relationship with either of them. I never burn my sources, no matter how frustrating. Who knows what the future might hold?

CHAPTER 30

Guilty

Warren Jeffs, wearing a dark blue prison uniform that drooped over his skinny frame, had his initial appearance in court before Las Vegas Justice of the Peace James Bixler on Monday, August 31. Arizona and Utah had agreed that Utah would try him first, because it had the stronger case and the charges there were more serious: two first-degree felony counts of rape as an accomplice. Warren was not represented by a lawyer at that initial hearing, and when Bixler asked if he would fight extradition, the prisoner answered in a soft voice that he would not.

The following day, he was transported by a Utah Department of Public Safety helicopter over the 150 miles to the Purgatory Correctional Facility in Hurricane, Utah, and within twenty-four hours he was on a closed-circuit television loop for a six-minute hearing before Judge James L. Shumate, who set a hearing for September 19. By the time of that preliminary hearing, Jeffs had legal representation, a Salt Lake lawyer named Walter Bugden, and the identity of the plaintiff, the fictitious Jane Doe IV, was legally revealed to him: It was Elissa Wall.

A number of Warren's FLDS followers were in the courtroom. He occasionally stole a glance at them, pleaded not guilty to the charges, and was ordered held in Purgatory Correctional Facility without bail. After being on the FBI's Ten Most Wanted list for more than a year, he was thought to be a considerable flight risk.

While Bugden would be the local counsel in Utah, celebrated Las Vegas defense attorney Richard A. Wright was hired to be the overall honcho for what we called "the beauty show" of Jeffs's well-tailored and well-coiffed lawyers. FLDS legal costs had been huge before Jeffs was arrested, and now the price tag had to be skyrocketing.

In our country, every defendant is entitled to a fair trial and a lawyer, and some attorneys specialize in the high-profile defense arena, where the money is good and the spotlight is bright. Wright was described in the *Las Vegas Sun* newspaper as having "been involved in some of the biggest legal cases in recent Las Vegas history—gamblers, a boxer, murderers and a grandmother—all with low-key aplomb." He was so good that he managed to win a sentence of life in prison instead of the death penalty for a man who raped and murdered a nine-year-old girl whose body was found in a casino bathroom, with the entire crime caught on security video. Wright also did some work in 2008 for Antoin "Tony" Rezko, a Chicago political hack known to associate with the mob who ran up hundreds of thousands of dollars in markers and debt to several of the best casinos in Vegas, while also being entangled in political corruption and influencing peddling charges back in Illinois. The Nevada Attorneys for Criminal Justice had named Wright the "Defender of the Decade" in the year 2000.

While awaiting his preliminary hearing after arriving at Purgatory, Warren Jeffs was escorted from his cell to see a visitor just as another prisoner was brought out. They recognized each other instantly, and Warren called out, "Is that you, Doyle Dockstader?"

Dockstader, a tough survivor of the prison system who was then charged with assault and other crimes, became unhinged at the sight of his former Alta Academy headmaster. "I haven't forgotten you," Uncle Warren said as they passed in the jail hallway, both under guard.

"I can't describe it," the shaken prisoner told me later. "All the things he had done to me just started coming back." Two nights later, Dockstader climbed a fence of the prison exercise yard and escaped, shredding his skin and clothing on the sharp concertina wire in his determination to flee. After a couple weeks on the run, he was captured in Las Vegas following a chase in which he rammed a police car while trying to get away.

The shock felt by Dockstader concerned me. Almost from the start, there had been side trails in my investigation that reeked of insidiousness and mystery. Individually, they might be dismissed as foggy memories, old wives' tales, or simple overreaction, but combined, they formed a frightening picture. While the stories might never rise to the standard of proof required in a court of law, it would be imprudent to ignore them.

Here was a man who had an actual army made up of thousands of people who were blindly obedient to him. I had heard one bluntly state, "I would cut my wives' throats if the prophet called upon me to do so."

Warren's belief that the church should practice "blood atonement" was only the tip of the problem. I had been told by several former students at the Alta Academy of how the headmaster had required what he called survival classes to help prepare them for the day when "the streets of Salt Lake City would run with the blood of the wicked." Those classes were taught with the help of the feared Dee Jessop, who would personally demonstrate how to cut the throats of an assortment of animals and butcher them in front of the schoolchildren. Stories were commonplace of senior girls at the academy being required to slit the throat of a sheep in order to graduate.

Nobody ever forgot the great slaughter of the dogs in Short Creek. There were hidden caches of guns and explosives around FLDS enclaves. Selected men underwent specialized military-style firearms training at a paramilitary camp in Nevada.

Warren had constantly carped about God's imminent judgments wiping the gentiles from the face of the earth, and had toured the entire country praying for the destruction of whole cities. The religion itself was founded on the principle that its members were above the laws of the land. It was never much of a leap to believe that despite their protestations to the contrary, the FLDS had the means and the will to do something horrible.

The question of whether the prophet's grip on the faithful would remain strong while he languished in jail actually was easy to answer. The people had already been conditioned to the prophet running their world from the back seats of luxury cars prowling the highways of the United States.

Doyle Dockstader knew exactly what Warren Jeffs was capable of and may have been the only prisoner to fear the gangly misfit. Other inmates regarded him as just another child molester who had gained notoriety by talking a lot of religious mumbo-jumbo and had a group of brainwashed followers. The jail's land sharks showed no mercy; child molesters are at the bottom of the prison food chain. Although confined to his own cell, and out of the reach of other inmates, he was ridiculed and taunted from a distance. The nonstop noise and foul language, and the aggressive nature of the prisoners, was completely foreign to the delicate sensibilities of the soft, clumsy man.

Jeffs's mental state began deteriorating from the moment the steel doors had slammed shut behind him for the first time. He had been thrust out of his element, and the shock of not being in control of every aspect of his life and the lives of those around him soon gave way to the rude awakening that he was no longer an extraordinary being. In prison, he was just another convict.

In Utah, there is no insanity defense. If found mentally incompetent to stand trial, those charged are detained in the criminal section of the state mental hospital until deemed capable of understanding the charges and participating in their own defense. Psychologists were hired to evaluate Jeffs, but he answered very few of their questions and would not participate in their diagnostic tests. The official prognosis was that although he was mentally ill and depressed, he was competent to participate in the proceedings. He could stand trial.

The preliminary hearing in Utah was an on-again, off-again affair that got under way on November 22 and ended on December 14, 2006. Then his attorney deluged the court with appeals, fighting hard even in this most routine of legal steps. All the while, his client remained locked up in his little cell. He was having a tough time in there.

As the days turned to weeks, and then months passed, Warren's condition continued to slide. He summoned all the rituals he could concoct to make sure that his six-by-ten cell was spiritually clean and pure, so that God could come and visit and provide revelations. He awoke several times each night to rededicate the tiny chamber all over again. He prayed so long that his knees became herniated and bled. Some of the jail staff made bets on how long he could stay kneeling before toppling over.

Unable to control his compulsions, and despite knowing that he was being viewed through the video cameras, the prophet masturbated so frequently that the guards continually reprimanded him. He ignored them, as he teetered on the brink of fantasy and reality. Any doubt that he was out of control vanished the day he stood at one end of his cell and ran full-tilt and headfirst into the wall at the other end, repeatedly. He would later attempt to hang himself with his pajamas, which resulted in trips to both the hospital emergency room and the psych ward.

The judge was unable to clear away the blizzard of defense motions and make his final ruling until five months later, on May 28, 2007. By then, Warren was a physical and emotional mess. Although he wore a neat dark suit, white shirt, and white tie, he was so gaunt that the shirt collar hung loose around his scarecrow neck. During the proceedings, he would sometimes nod off, drooling to the point that his shirt grew wet.

His condition had been a problem for the prosecution. They wanted to make sure Jeffs was capable of participating in his own defense. To maintain his delicate mental balance, the jailers had pampered him.

He was allowed nearly unlimited telephone access and a constant stream of visitors. He participated in long-distance worship services, led teachings from a pay phone, and wrote new revelations and letters to be passed along to his followers. He assigned code numbers to specific individuals in the church hierarchy because he knew his conversations were being monitored and recorded while in custody. He was still building Zion from his jail cell and was still able to keep a tight rein on his followers. They firmly clung to the idea that the government was persecuting the prophet and church only because of their "unpopular religious beliefs." In this, they were immovable.

Warren was still captain of their ship, steering them all to salvation in the hereafter. Jeffs made every effort to conduct business as usual, and he almost succeeded—almost, but not quite. He was out of his element and missed the comforts and pampering he enjoyed as the FLDS monarch.

The jail's medical staff made a point of dropping by just to talk to him, and he was allowed a special diet to help to stave off his weight loss. A regimen of medication was prescribed to treat his depression and stabilize him, but he usually would not take it, saying the government was trying to poison him.

He had some disturbing revelations during the Lord's visits at night. Among his dreams was the sad prediction that his Naomi, who he referred to by the code name 91, was about to die. Warren dispatched orders to prepare her funeral arrangements, designated who would speak, and indicated where she should be buried. He spent hours in his cell communing with the Heavens concerning Naomi's mission in the hereafter. It would have been a stunning illustration of his prophetic powers, except that it was all just another manifestation of his psychosis. Warren spent a long week mourning his loss before learning that Naomi remained alive and well.

At the conclusion of the hearing, after finally binding the prophet over for trial, Judge Shumate was taking care of a few housekeeping legal matters and getting ready to recess. Suddenly, Warren stood at the defense table and said, "May I approach the bench, Your Honor? I just need to take care of one matter." Awkwardly scrawling on a white tablet, he stood to speak and was fumbling to tear off a piece of paper to present to the court.

The judge glanced up, surprised, and immediately denied the request, instructing Jeffs to take up whatever it was with his lawyers. To allow the prisoner to start talking directly to the court and not through his attorneys risked jeopardizing the entire process. Shumate scowled at the defense lawyers, who closed in around their client to see what he was talking about.

"I just have this one matter, it will only take a minute, Your Honor," Warren sputtered, gesturing with the sheet of paper. "This will just take a minute." At that instant, a news photographer snapped his shutter.

Shumate barked, "Court is recessed!" and almost bolted from his own courtroom while the lawyers scrambled to take away the paper and keep their client under control.

The picture was distributed to the media, but it gave no clue as to what Warren wanted to talk about. Photography is an important part of my work and I wondered if there might be some way to digitally discover what was on the other side of that paper. I obtained a good copy and got busy with my computer, enhancing and enlarging. Whatever Warren had written became faintly visible on the back of the sheet. Of course, the writing appeared backward in the snapshot, so I made a mirror image, then zoomed in. As I sharpened it and filled in the pixels, some of the words became clear.

He had written, in part, "I have not been a prophet and am not the prophet." He had intended to announce to the court that he was not the prophet of the FLDS after all.

Ben Winslow, a reporter with the *Deseret News* in Salt Lake City, had called while I was working on the image and I gave him the information. Ben jumped on it, enlisting the help of a photography lab and a handwriting expert. Winslow's story, headlined I AM NOT THE PROPHET, spread to the national media.

Judge Shumate had not allowed Jeffs to make his statement in court, but outside the courtroom no one could shut Warren up, and he was intent on delivering the message, even revealing it to the deputies who were escorting him out of the courthouse. He would make the same confession to several FLDS leaders and family members, recorded on the jail's pay phone, admitting that he had never been God's messenger and he knew that because, of course, God had told him so. While his followers believed everything else he said, this was more than they could bear to accept. The entire episode became comical as Warren tried to convince his people that he was a fraud and a liar, saying, "the truth is not in me." Even after confessing to his mother and several church leaders that he had "immoral relations with a sister and a daughter," nobody would listen. He had conditioned them so completely that not even he could reverse the brainwashing.

One regular visitor to the jail was Warren's brother Nephi, and the scene of Warren admitting to him once again that he was not, and never had been, the prophet was caught on the jail's surveillance tape. Nephi disagreed, insisting just as strongly that Warren *was* the prophet and this was only another of the Lord's tests. "Just a minute," Warren replied, as a blank stare settled over his countenance. He momentarily looked away from his brother, apparently receiving a strong and clear voice that no one else could hear. "This is a message from God," he insisted, still listening to the communication from on high. "THIS-IS-NOT-A-TEST!"

As sad as it was, I broke out laughing while watching the pitiful scene on video. When the jailer took Warren from the visiting room, the shocked Nephi remained motionless for several minutes, his hands over his face, weeping.

Despite being locked up, Warren was still able to manage the affairs of the church. According to his records he was able to smuggle out documents and communications which skirted jail security including a detailed schematic of Warren's jail cell, and its location inside the Purgatory facility. There also were detailed instructions to his counselors, directions to kick some FLDS members out of their homes, move some others to places of refuge, and assign routine household chores to various wives. Warren, at least for a little while, was back in form.

I got the chance to see the prophet in person when I accompanied attorneys Roger and Greg Hoole to a deposition in May 2007, at Purgatory. It involved a new client named Wendell Musser, who Warren had kicked out and was determined to prevent from visiting his own infant son.

Musser had been ordered by Warren to be the caretaker for several of the prophet's wives at a hideout near Florence, Colorado, while the prophet was on the run. When Musser was arrested for driving under the influence on his way back to the safe house one evening, Warren was furious. The incident might have tipped off the police to the refuge location where his wives were hidden. Wendell was told to go away and repent from a distance, which he did. After a couple weeks the separation from his family became unbearable and he tried to return to see his wife and son, only to find the house had been abandoned and his wife and child gone. Warren had assigned them to another man. Wendell was beside himself, broke with the prophet, and started legal proceedings to at least get legal visitation rights with his son. Musser turned out to be a world of information on the inner workings of some of the FLDS hierarchy.

The day of our visit, the prophet was extremely gaunt and the green-and-white striped jail uniform hung on him. Beneath the short-sleeved pullover, he wore thermal long johns with long sleeves, despite the fact that it was midsummer. He had made a point of showing his followers that he was sticking to the religious mandate of covering his flesh. The shorts and T-shirt in which he was photographed when arrested were explained away as having been a necessary evil to blend into the gentile world.

He knew exactly who I was, and he gave a polite "How are you?" when we were introduced. I was pleased that he was looking better than the last time I had seen him in the courtroom. Richard Wright, Warren's Nevada attorney, was present and on the advice of counsel Warren exercised his right not to answer Roger and Greg's questions for fear he might incriminate himself. He refused to answer even the most benign and elementary of questions.

After about thirty minutes of listening to Warren plead the fifth, we decided to leave. As I stood up, Warren unexpectedly thrust his hand out to me, and without thinking, I automatically took it. I immediately felt that I had made a terrible mistake. I had no desire to shake hands with someone that I knew to be the perpetrator of such heinous crimes against children. I had lost sleep over the brutality that Warren had inflicted on children and on his own people, and felt that the custom might intimate some sort of tolerance for his atrocities. I would rather have kept things on a strictly formal basis, minus the handshake. At least I did not get the treatment that my buddy Gary Engels got when he first met Warren. The prophet had surprised Gary, too, by telling Engels that he forgave Gary for persecuting him. Jeffs didn't lay a surprise blessing on me, but as I left the jail, I felt the overwhelming need to wash my hands.

The prophet was aware that we intended to report his noncooperation to the judge and that we would seek a contempt of court order, but that wasn't much motivation for someone who was already in jail to answer our questions.

But I had an idea for another way to apply pressure. I dug around and found out that Warren's commissary account was kept filled with the maximum amount of money allowed by jail regulations. So we devised a motion for the court to seize that money, and any other assets we could find, for as long as Warren refused to speak to us, and earmark those funds to cover my investigative fees for locating Wendell's family.

Minutes before the commissary account was to be seized, our client's wife and son suddenly showed up at his front door, and Wendell Musser was able to obtain a legal order providing for visitation with the boy. The prophet gave in rather than surrender his ability to buy his jail goodies. The small victories were adding up, and it seemed to make up for the handshake.

CHAPTER 31

Elissa

A long year passed between the preliminary hearing and the trial of Warren Jeffs in Utah for the two felony charges of rape as an accomplice, but much was happening. The FLDS and its prophet had never before been taken to the mat as they had been over the past few years, and part of my job was to continue staying a jump ahead of them.

During that stretch, we finished our work on the Lost Boys and the Brent Jeffs civil suits. They were won by default because the prophet refused to appear in court. We may have won, but our clients did not want to be put in the position of collecting monetary damages from their own families. They chose instead to make a public statement that their goal was to effect change within the community by bringing to light the rampant child abuse hidden in the shadows. Each client received a token piece of property in Short Creek. A trust fund to help other displaced children remains a future possibility.

One unexpected result of our lawsuits against Warren and the FLDS church led to a parting of the ways between Jeffs and his longtime Salt Lake City attorney Rodney R. Parker. The sandy-haired lawyer tried to convince Jeffs that he could lose everything if he didn't step up and defend it. Warren fired him, answered them nothing, and lost.

*　*　*

Jury selection for the Jeffs trial began on September 7, 2007, and part of my job was to keep Elissa Wall beyond the reach of the FLDS and the media, getting her safely to and from the courtroom. That proved to be a logistical nightmare because the media was stacked up everywhere and I believed the FLDS loyalists hated her enough to endanger her safety.

Chief enforcer Willie Jessop or his buddies would park right in the open directly in front of the glass-fronted entranceway to the building in which Brock Belnap, the Washington County prosecutor, had his office, and just sit there peering in. The silent message: *We are watching.*

So we made careful arrangements with the court, its staff, the bailiff, and the police to maneuver the witness from the secret location where she was staying to the courthouse, which was in the middle of a cordoned-off two-square-block area. Timing had to be precise, for Warren Jeffs also would be moved through the building, and the court wanted no chance encounters. For help, I once again enlisted Jon Krakauer, who had become a good friend that I could trust to move quickly and wisely if things got tight.

The trial began a week later, on September 13, and after Jon and I navigated Elissa through the media madhouse, she took her place in the second row between Roger Hoole and her husband, Lamont. I went to my assigned aisle seat two rows behind her. Reporters filled most of the other seats, but a group of FLDS loyalists sat nearby to support their prophet, glaring at Elissa.

The opening statements were crucial, and Belnap focused the scope of the trial for the jury; it had nothing to do with religion, nor with polygamy. He said the state would prove that the defendant, Warren Jeffs, was an accomplice in the incestuous rape of a fourteen-year-old minor child. The trial was about that, and only that.

Making the defense argument was another member of the FLDS legal team, the impeccably coiffed and dressed Tara Isaacson. She insinuated that "no rape [had] occurred" at all, that any sex that took place had been consensual, and that Elissa had initiated contact. I have been through many trials involving sexual abuse, and the defense almost always launches a rabid attack upon the victim. That strategy would be followed precisely in this trial.

One reason the defense chose Isaacson is that they clearly wanted another female to grill Elissa about intimate details. Isaacson's entire presentation had been carefully built into a computerized PowerPoint presentation that would lead the jury through the events, but when the computer malfunctioned, Isaacson was left stumbling for words without the video guide. She bored in as coldly as possible but did not do a very good job at presenting her argument off the cuff.

Elissa had been nervous on the drive into court that morning, fussing with her long hair, but once she took the witness stand, she settled in quickly as Craig Barlow from the Utah attorney general's office led her through her testimony. I watched the jurors carefully as they were introduced to the grim life of a girl inside the FLDS. They sat stone-faced as she described the total lack of sex education, the way girls and boys were taught to treat the opposite gender as they would treat snakes, and how a girl would be assigned by the prophet to an older man she might not even know.

As we drove home that evening, she wanted to know if she had done all right, how I thought the jury was reacting, and she worried about the upcoming defense cross-examination. She was expressing normal insecurities, and I gave her comforting words, but I had been unable to read anything into the day. I had learned over the years that the best policy was to be positive, but noncommittal.

That night, we parked Krakauer's car, with a bicycle lashed to the top, inside the sally port at the courthouse and left it there. Then we made sure that everyone saw Elissa arrive for the second day of trial in the pickup truck.

Willie Jessop was up to his old antics, treating the court process as some kind of game and attempting to intimidate our witness. He tried to rearrange the assigned seating in the courtroom so that he could sit directly in Elissa's line of sight during her testimony, and behind her in the courtroom. It was the same intimidation tactic the FLDS had pulled in Arizona during the Candi Shapley testimony. This time, a savvy bailiff picked up on what was happening and gave Willie a warning, which he ignored. The bailiff informed the judge, and two deputies removed Jessop from the courthouse. He was barred for the remainder of the trial.

Elissa testified that day about the impossibility of her leaving Short Creek rather than obey the prophet. She was only fourteen at the time, was not old enough to drive, had no money, and lived in an FLDS community, completely dependent upon the family to which her mother had been reassigned after her father had been kicked out of the church and banished. "I had no options," she declared. I believed her, and I thought the jury did, too.

Her description of the sham marriage ritual performed by Warren Jeffs at the Caliente motel in Nevada and the eventual rape by Allen Steed was harrowing. In a tearful voice, she told the spellbound court that when Allen, her nineteen-year-old cousin, began to undress her, she begged, "I can't do this, please don't. I was sobbing. My whole entire body was shaking I was so scared. He didn't stop. He just laid me onto the bed and had sex."

The defense took its turn after the lunch break in court, and Tara Isaacson spent the afternoon lashing Elissa with sharp questions designed to make the witness look like a vengeful adult woman at the time of her wedding instead of a brainwashed underage child who was forced into an illegal sexual arrangement, and into having sex against her will. Elissa had plenty of options, Isaacson declared, but chose not to use them. I thought that was a ridiculous argument, since a fourteen-year-old cannot legally consent to sex in any situation. Left unsaid was that Elissa's entire life up until that point had been one of those "keep sweet" journeys that had intentionally limited her choices.

When it was time to leave at the end of the day, we had a woman member of our team slip into the pickup truck that we had used to come to court in the morning to serve as a decoy for the media and the FLDS. Right behind the pickup, Jon and Elissa calmly drove off in the opposite direction in Jon's waiting car with the bike attached, totally ignored. I was right on their bumper to make sure we were not followed.

The next day, Elissa's sister Theresa Wall Blackmore testified, recalling how the "sad, hopeless, depressed" Elissa had telephoned her the day after her wedding, crying throughout the conversation. "She hated to be near him," Theresa said of Elissa's feelings for Allen. The defense did not question her.

Becky Wall, another sister, followed and underlined Elissa's testimony. She also attempted to define the treacherous "keep sweet" policy within the FLDS: "Even when it hurts, you were to act happy . . . That was how you conquered the evil inside of you."

I blanched at that and flashed back to a conversation with one of my sources. The man had been summoned to the Jeffs compound to meet the prophet himself and had found Warren in a posh office, seated in what was described as a "tricked out" massage lounger with built-in speakers. Reclined in comfort, Jeffs delivered a "training" about the man having a dark heart and how he was no longer worthy to hold priesthood and be in the church. On the bottom of Warren's fancy left boot was written the word KEEP, and on the right one was SWEET. He then cast the man out of the church and community, broke up his family and devastated his life from the comfort of his fancy recliner.

The final witness for the state was almost an afterthought: Jane Blackmore, a veteran midwife in Canada and first wife of Winston Blackmore before leaving the faith and her husband. She had delivered hundreds of babies and had treated scores of FLDS girls below the age of eighteen for pregnancies that were terminated due to complications. Among those unfortunate girls was Elissa Wall, who had suffered a miscarriage while visiting family members in Canada during the time she was pregnant with Allen Steed's baby.

The defense put on a case that had little meat to it. Warren Jeffs did not testify in his own behalf, so Walter Bugden and Tara Isaacson were relying on Allen Steed, who spoke so softly that he was admonished by the judge several times to speak up. Out of frustration, Steed ended up standing in the witness box to deliver his testimony so he could be better heard, but really only succeeded in looking foolish. The prosecution had delayed filing charges against Steed until after Warren's case had been decided, to prevent the FLDS and the press from discovering Elissa's identity. Now that secrecy was no longer a factor, Steed realized that he was trapped. He knew that it was illegal in the state of Utah to have sex with a fourteen-year-old girl, no matter what the circumstances, so to admit to sex with Elissa in any fashion would be tantamount to admitting to a crime. It was obvious that a rape charge would soon be heading his way, so he lawyered up with a little-known Salt Lake City defense attorney by the name of Jim Bradshaw. Bradshaw seemed to be out to make a name for himself in a very high-profile case.

It did neither of them much good. Any competent defense attorney would urge that his client not say anything that may be incriminating, a constitutional right guaranteed by the Fifth Amendment. But Steed either got bad advice or didn't listen to his lawyer; he repeatedly admitted under oath to having had sex with the girl.

Both sides rested their cases on Friday and the jury began deliberations, but was granted a weekend break after a few hours. For Elissa and the prosecution team, that meant holding our breaths in anticipation. Nobody had been able to read the faces or body language of the stoic jurors. I had no idea which way they would go, and things wrapped up so quickly that it had seemed surreal.

On Tuesday, September 25, 2007, the trial ended with total vindication for Elissa Wall. Warren Jeffs was found guilty on both counts of being an accomplice to the rape of a minor. Allen Steed was charged with rape the day after the Jeffs verdict.

In November, after two months of a presentencing investigation, Judge Shumate gave Jeffs the maximum penalty under Utah law. Each count carried a five-years-to-life prison sentence, to be served back-to-back. In addition, there was a cumulative fine of $37,000.

I stood in the parking lot of the Washington County attorney's office after the sentencing and watched a helicopter take off to ferry the prophet straight from the courthouse to the Utah State Prison at Point of the Mountain, some twenty miles south of Salt Lake City. There, Warren Jeffs, in shackles, hobbled into his new world. It was a good day.

The once powerful religious fanatic had become a very small fish in a very large pool of sharks, subject to regular prison protocol. All of the special privileges were stripped away as he went into lockdown, shattered by the sudden realization that the heavens had once again failed to intervene on his behalf. Despite the money, the influence, the high-powered lawyers, and the devotion of his flock, Warren had lost everything because of his crimes. An attorney tried to take his deposition in prison and reported that Warren was so mentally out of it that he had been chained to a wall for his own safety. His only communication with the outside world was through his attorneys.

A few months later, in February 2008, he was extradited from Utah to the jail in Kingman, Arizona, to await trial on four counts of sexual

misconduct with a minor, four counts of incest, and one count of conspiracy to commit sexual conduct with a minor.

Warren Steed Jeffs received two life sentences for his crimes in Utah, had
been extradited to Arizona to face additional charges there, and had a
federal fugitive charge waiting in the wings after the state charges were
completed to seal his fate. It began to appear as if Warren may finally
have been taken to task. But five months later, an emotionally disturbed
young woman picked up her telephone and dialed the New Bridge Family Shelter in San Angelo, Texas, claiming to be an abused teenage bride
named Sarah who was being held prisoner at the YFZ Ranch.

CHAPTER 32

Sarah

On March 29, 2008, Alisa Thomas at the New Bridge Family Shelter in San Angelo, Texas, listened carefully to a sobbing, breaking young voice on the crisis hotline, hoping to establish some sort of personal bond that would persuade the troubled caller to trust her. This one seemed a little different; perhaps the caller was a little more desperate, but it was a challenge getting the details from her. Information emerged only in bits and pieces, and the hotline veteran was convinced the caller was a terrified victim of child abuse. After forty-two minutes, including several long pauses, the conversation finally came to a tenuous close. The girl promised to call again. Thomas was dubious. She had heard that same promise many times before from other girls looking for help, and that second call seldom came.

This one did. In fact, over the next two days, the same girl telephoned frequently and would stay on the line anywhere from a few moments to more than an hour. Jessica Carroll, another experienced hotline volunteer, pitched in to field some of the calls. Working around the caller's bouts of uncontrollable weeping, the women pieced together a shocking but disturbingly familiar tale.

Victims of child sexual abuse are smothered by fear, guilt, embarrassment, and shame. As a general rule, the perpetrators of the crime are skilled at keeping their victim quiet by keeping them too terrified to reveal their dark secrets. Hotline workers are trained to break that stranglehold and convince the anonymous callers to take a giant leap of faith and believe they will be safe in exposing the harm that has befallen them. In this new case, enough details seeped out during the meandering conversations for the workers to begin a preliminary profile of the victim. The caller said her name was Sarah. She claimed to be sixteen years old and said she had been placed in a polygamous marriage when she was only fifteen. She already had one baby, was pregnant again, and her husband, who was forty-nine, beat her.

When coaxed to give her location, Sarah said that she was confined to one of the buildings at the fortress-like religious compound called the Yearning for Zion Ranch outside of Eldorado, Texas. The caller insisted that the prophet Warren Jeffs himself had chosen and "sealed" her to her husband, who already had several other wives. She had been at the ranch for three years. Her parents did not live there.

The mention of Warren Jeffs and his YFZ Ranch rang loud alarm bells with the hotline workers. Everybody in the area knew about the polygamous YFZ compound and knew that Jeffs and his cult believed their eternal salvation depended upon the practice of plural marriage, including placing little girls with much older men.

Even though six months earlier the prophet had been convicted in Utah of being an accomplice to rape, and now was in jail in Arizona awaiting trial on additional charges, Sarah nevertheless was still clearly terrified.

Carroll and Thomas finally had heard enough. They pressed a speed dial button that connected their phones directly to the Texas Department of Public Safety—the Texas Rangers.

A few days later, on April 1, 2008, my own telephone rang at my office in Cedar City. "Sam, I need your opinion on something." It was Flora Jessop, and if Flora was calling, I could be sure that the subject would have something to do with the FLDS.

Over the past four years while I had been chasing Jeffs and working on legal actions involving the FLDS and the United Effort Plan Trust, I had stayed in contact with Flora, whose activism against the church that had misused her as a child was unrelenting. She always had her ear to the ground. Jeffs was in prison, but the church remained strong, isolated, as suspicious of outsiders as ever, and extremely secretive. I had believed for some time that things were approaching some kind of tipping point, and whatever it was probably was going to involve that fortress temple down in Texas.

"Hey," I said. "What's up?"

"A young girl is calling me. She says her name is Sarah, and she claims that she is being kept against her will by the FLDS. She sounds like she wants to get out, but I'm not completely sure." It is not uncommon for a scared FLDS girl to call Flora for help, but most of them vacillate at the moment of truth and change their minds, unable to let go of the demented life that has been thrust upon them.

"So what can I do for you?" Flora knew the drill as well as anyone: Get the facts, call the authorities. She asked if I would listen in on the next call and help assess the situation: Was this really a little girl in trouble, or was something else going on? The Short Creek police had threatened to arrest Flora for helping other girls escape from the FLDS, and she needed to be sure this wasn't some sort of setup.

Before long, the mysterious Sarah made contact again, and Flora brought me on the line to let me eavesdrop, a perfectly legal action in thirty-eight states, including Arizona and Utah, with the consent of only one party to the call. To keep from spooking the caller, I muted my phone and listened over the speaker, turning on a tape recorder to capture the conversation. I heard a shaky voice relating still another sad and disturbing story from inside the church; and I listened with an investigator's neutral, professional ear, because I had heard similar stories, this bad and worse, from many other girls.

After only a few minutes, my impressions began to take shape. This kid used FLDS terminology, a certain style of speech unique to Short Creek, like calling the pizza place "Craigo's" or the grocery store the CMC. She knew Mormon religious terms, used FLDS idioms that an outsider would not know, and provided accurate information about Short Creek, from the medical clinic to the local store. My conclusion after that first call was, "Dang, she's got a lot of information." However, it would be imprudent to listen in on a call that came in out of the blue, from someone I don't know and can't interview, and just take it at face value. As an investigator, and as I accumulate more information, I am in the habit of not only evaluating, but constantly reevaluating every story and piece of evidence that I come across. Until I am able to actually see and personally assess the person on the other end of the line, I will always have a certain degree of doubt concerning the veracity of the caller.

My impression was that she was probably a member of the FLDS or at least somehow involved. If the call to Flora was a setup, hoax, or just some sort of practical joke, the person on the other end of the line was damn good at it, and she had done her homework. The jolting centerpiece of her story was the assertion that she was only sixteen years old and had been abused by her own father, had been made pregnant by him and had a miscarriage. An FLDS doctor had been summoned to the home but had refused to take her to the medical clinic for treatment. That was a match, because the FLDS uses public hospitals only as a last resort and she knew the name of the doctor, Lloyd Barlow. She said she had been forced to clean up the mess herself.

Sarah avoided saying where she was; she seemed afraid and unwilling to commit to have someone go and help her. That reaction was also totally consistent with the situation, since all FLDS children are taught to distrust the outside world. I was privy to several calls over the next few days, as Sarah fleshed out her ever more riveting narrative. It was becoming impossible not to lend credence to the precise details. Everything might not be exactly accurate, but something was going on with her. She was, without a doubt, terrified. Neither Flora nor I had ever set eyes on this mystery caller. We made the decision to turn our information over to a trusted law enforcement agency to carry the information farther through the system.

The following day, Wednesday, April 2, Leslie Brooks Long, a sergeant in Company E of the Texas Rangers, drove over to see the volunteers at the New Bridge Family Shelter. Long had worn the famed little silver badge with the circled star since 1997, and his turf covered a great deal of West Texas. He had received specialized training on sexual assault against children.

He interviewed Carroll and Thomas independently and listened to the tapes of the soft voice on the recorded hotline. The caller had finally identified herself as Sarah Jessop, with a date of birth of January 13, 1992. She said she was the mother of a baby who was eight months old. Ranger

Long did the math: if that birthday was correct, then Sarah was sixteen. And if the baby was eight months, Sarah could not have been more than fifteen when the child was conceived. Now she was pregnant again.

Sarah had told the hotline volunteers that she had lived at the YFZ Ranch since she was thirteen, and that Jessop was her maiden name. She had been placed with an FLDS man whom she identified as Dale Barlow, who she said hit and hurt her, both physically and sexually. The ranger knew that a fifteen-year-old girl could not legally consent to sex in the state of Texas. According to the law, Sarah also was too young to be the legal spouse of Dale Barlow or anyone else.

Sarah's dark story had spun out through more calls to the hotline, and she had been asked about the possibility of escaping her captors. Sarah was terrified at the consequences of getting caught if she tried to escape the only life she had ever known. There was a manned guard tower at the main entrance to the YFZ Ranch, as well as mounds of slag and debris piled high in strategic locations that provided sentries with a view of the entire compound and beyond the fences that enclosed it. With guards always around, she was even torn in her decision to seek help. She wavered, changed her mind, switched from promising the hot-line workers that she would try to escape to asking them to forget that she had ever called.

Momentum was building, though. A child in distress draws a strong and immediate response from law enforcement. If the girl was in danger, the ranger realized that time was of the essence. He ran a check on Barlow through law enforcement databases and found that an FLDS member named Dale Evans Barlow had been convicted in Arizona of unlawful sexual conduct with a minor and as part of his sentence had been given three years of probation, beginning in August 2005. That probation was still in effect, a fact that added validity to Sarah's claim.

Long decided that there was probable cause to obtain a warrant to search the YFZ Ranch, and a major investigation began to take shape as he prepared the legal steps needed to search the compound for the distressed teenager identified as Sarah Jessop and to arrest Dale Evans Barlow on the charge of sexual assault of a child in violation of Texas Penal Code Section 22.011. Since a child was involved, he conferred with the Texas Department of Family and Protective Services to have some of their specialists involved in the investigation.

On Thursday, April 3, Judge Barbara Walther of the Fifty-first District Court signed a search warrant.

I had learned over my years as a P.I. that things are not always as they seem, and my caution lights continued to blink as I listened to more calls from Sarah to Flora. Until enough evidence is available to say for certain that something is a fact, I will not take a position one way or the other. Although the girl was persuasive with her general story, discrepancies would occasionally pop up, including the way she had begun to sometimes shift from using the name of "Sarah" to calling herself "Laura," and saying that Sarah was her twin sister down in the Texas compound. Scared, mixed-up kids often stumble through their stories and this one was fairly accurate given the circumstances. I would have liked to have seen some more evidence, but if Sarah or Laura or whatever her name was needed help, time was critical.

The circumstances had grown compelling enough for me to alert my comrade-in-arms Gary Engels, who could push the information to the authorities in Mohave County, Arizona. I explained to him the saga of Sarah and played some of my tapes of her emotional calls. We brainstormed it for a while, and both of us concluded that some legal wheels needed to be set in motion to investigate the possibility that the girl was being held captive by her father in Short Creek.

Independently, and without knowledge of each other, authorities, in several western states, including Gary and me, had begun responding to the disturbing calls from a child crying for help. The Texans got to the starting line first.

CHAPTER 33
Standoff

By late afternoon on Thursday, April 3, a short string of dusty government sedans was driving north on U.S. 277 just outside of Eldorado, population 1,951, the only town in Schleicher County, Texas. After less than a mile, they peeled onto a chip seal track called County Road 300. The cars were carrying Brooks Long and three other Texas Rangers, County Sheriff David Doran and two of his deputies, and nearly a dozen specialists from the Child Protective Services Division of the Texas Department of Family and Protective Services. They were headed for the YFZ Ranch.

Everyone was on edge. The plan was to negotiate a soft entry into the compound, keeping things as low-key and friendly as possible. Nobody on the search team wanted this to blow into a repeat of Waco, the infamous 1993 violent standoff between the federal government and the Branch Davidian religious cult led by another maniacal prophet, David Koresh. Brooks Long, who had been at the Waco siege, remembered all too well that before it was over some fifty-four adults and twenty-one children had died. Waco was only a two-hour drive to the east, and it was very much on the minds of the investigators approaching the YFZ Ranch.

This time, Long made certain that advance security precautions had been taken, a prudent measure because of the ranch residents' unpredictable nature. The police and CPS professionals had managed to keep such a tight lid on things that even the families and close friends of the officers involved were unaware of what was about to happen. An unmanned aerial surveillance drone from a federal agency did a fly-by and took photographs providing an up-to-date, accurate layout of the compound. Things appeared normal.

Even with the recon flight, the exact number of people at the ranch remained uncertain. Sheriff Doran, relying upon church leaders and personal visits, estimated the FLDS population to be between one hundred and one hundred fifty. I have a lot of respect for the sheriff, but he and I were in sharp disagreement about those numbers. I knew the FLDS inhabitants routinely hid when any outsiders came around, and there was always a transient population of FLDS workers being brought in for specific construction projects.

It would be futile to simply ask any church member, "How many people are here?" FLDS members could be expected either to stay quiet or to lie with smooth and practiced ease. My own guess was that there were at least five hundred people at the ranch.

Even a group the size of the sheriff's low estimate would be much too large for a handful of deputies and rangers if something went wrong, so several dozen officers from various agencies had been put on alert. If immediate backup was needed, a Quick Reaction Force was stationed just out of sight at an abandoned federal anti-missile facility that once had been part of the "Star Wars" missile defense program. It was now the command post for the police operation at the FLDS compound.

Sheriff Doran had established a civil relationship with the people at the ranch and their on-site leader, Bishop Merril Jessop, over the past months. Both Doran and Long had been allowed on the ranch property without incident to deal with minor matters ranging from environmental issues to home schooling inspections to a vehicle accident involving the death of a child. Those earlier meetings had been touchy, but cordial.

If anyone stood a chance of getting past the front gate without igniting an incident, it would be them. In fact, they had considered just this sort of scenario for years as part of their normal "what-if" planning; the sheriff's office was too small to handle a major confrontation, so the ranger had accompanied the sheriff on previous visits, hoping to get the lay of the land in the event state assistance might someday be needed.

This trip was of a much more serious nature than anything they had undertaken before at the ranch. Their plan was just to talk to Bishop Jessop and try to win his permission to peacefully let them do their jobs. The search team would be looking for sixteen-year-old Sarah Jessop

Barlow, her child, and Dale Evans Barlow, the man purported to be her abusive husband. The search warrant allowed them to go into every building on the 1,691 acres of the YFZ Ranch, because the people they sought might be anywhere.

Significantly, the warrant would allow them into the huge temple that was the centerpiece of the entire property. Church leaders were certain to consider that to be a major encroachment onto sacred ground by gentiles, and could be expected to oppose having the law paw through the building that was the heart of their secretive society. But the Texas lawmen were professionals who were used to having their way in matters of public safety. One way or another, they were determined to carry out their duties.

The sedans slowed and stopped at a metal gate off County Road 300 that was secured by a chain and padlock. Beyond this cattle gate, a dirt road stretched for another mile to the primary entrance of the main compound, where an interior guard station with tinted windows squatted ominously, its roof bristling with communications antennae, satellite dishes, and spotlights. Sheriff Doran called Bishop Jessop and asked him to come out for a meeting.

The gate barring the entrance into the ranch lands had been dented by a propane delivery truck and hung somewhat askew. It remained firmly locked, even after Jessop emerged to speak with Doran and Long. He listened politely, then entered into a time-consuming stall that went nowhere, telling them that he needed to make some calls to gather more information, and then contriving excuses as to why access was impossible. He told the officers that only about two hundred fifty men, women, and children were on the ranch—a lie.

The authorities tolerated the charade in hopes of keeping things calm. One reason for the secrecy of their arrival was to avoid the media. It was hard enough keeping everyone safe and negotiations on an even keel without having to attend to the press as well. They wanted to wrap things up before the reporters found out what was going on and descended on the scene.

The stall was frustrating. At one point, Sheriff Doran found himself talking on the phone to a man who identified himself as Dale Barlow, the specific target of the warrant. Barlow was adamant that he was not even at the Texas compound, but in Arizona, and insisted that the officials should just take his word as the truth and go away. They refused. Even if this caller was indeed named Dale Barlow, how could they know it was the right one? There were at least two other men with the same name up in Short Creek. Even if this was the correct Dale Barlow, that did not get them any closer to finding Sarah, who was their more urgent priority. Had she been at the ranch with him and then been taken elsewhere before they arrived with the warrant? All the Barlow call did was eat more minutes off the clock on a time-sensitive warrant.

Throughout those fruitless hours, the lawmen and child protection specialists watched the situation behind the gate become more dangerous for them. Pickup trucks had filtered from the ranch compound onto the entrance road, with several FLDS men in each, until nearly the entire mile-long track from the far gate to the security shack was clogged with randomly parked trucks. More than fifty men loitered in and around the approximately twenty vehicles, posing a visible, defiant threat to the safety of the search team. This was a serious development. When the authorities realized their small party was outnumbered by a possibly hostile force, they called back to the Star Wars command center for reinforcements. Tactical teams were dispatched and an armored personnel carrier on loan from neighboring Midland County drove up to the gate. The formidable armored vehicle had SHERIFF written in large black letters on each side and was loaded with heavily armed officers, their bubble-like black helmets sticking out of the hatches. It was there as a show of muscle and for protection, not really to do battle. The hope was to dissuade the FLDS men from making any aggressive moves.

Normally, when Texas Rangers serve a search warrant, they give little more warning than a hard knock on a door, followed by a loud announcement of who they are and what their business is, and then they make entry. Anyone or anything in the way will be moved aside, one way or another. The police at the ranch had a legal search warrant to execute and had been patient long enough. Merril Jessop was given a final warning to get out of the way or be arrested for obstruction of justice and failure to obey the lawful command of a peace officer. If necessary, the police could simply crush right through the blockade. There were no guns mounted on the bulky armored personnel carrier, but it was a combat-style vehicle that could roll right over the pickup trucks. In the face of that ultimatum, the bishop grudgingly stood aside, and the trucks moved out of the way while the authorities drove past the cattle gate and down the long road. It had taken almost three hours to travel that single mile, but they were at last on FLDS property.

The search for Sarah could finally begin.

About ten o'clock that night, my friend Randy Mankin, editor of the weekly *Eldorado Success*, called me, sounding like he was wound pretty tight. "They're out there at the Ranch right now serving warrants," he said. That got my attention.

I grilled him for more information, but although he was a close friend of Sheriff Doran, he was empty beyond that one tidbit. Over the years, Randy had learned not to allow his obligations as a reporter to interfere with his friendship with the sheriff. They each had a job to do. But the intrepid Mankins had teamed with the owner of the local radio station and rigged a connection to the station's 100-foot-tall antenna, and that allowed them to pick up fragments of police radio conversations originating from the FLDS compound. Anything broadcast in the open was considered fair game. By using secure frequencies for the current operation, the police had kept things silent on the news for longer than anyone thought possible within such a close-knit community. Even the best reporters around had been excluded.

Whatever might be happening at the ranch down in Texas sounded to me like a positive development. At last, the authorities were doing something and there was some hope of holding the outlaw church accountable for its crimes. But at the time I had no idea that the momentous development in Texas had anything to do with the lengthy, disturbing calls to which I had been listening from Flora's source.

After Randy's call, I was up most of the night working my sources, and by dawn, my telephone was ringing off the hook as news media outlets from around the country pounded me for information. I had by then appeared on numerous shows speaking about the FLDS, and good producers never throw away a telephone number. They were under pressure to find someone who knew something, anything, about what was happening in Texas. That I was in Utah did not matter as the media frenzy built. I could not complete one conversation or interview that morning without five more stacking up.

In my view, the Texas authorities actually were doing much more than just refusing to tolerate child abuse. I thought the surprise raid might be the very thing to prevent what everyone most feared—another Waco, or even a Jonestown. In that 1978 massacre, a similar enigmatic prophet, Jim Jones, had created a "People's Temple" in Guyana, murdered a congressman and a reporter, and led 912 followers to their doom by drinking poison. I believe that past behavior is the best predictor of future behavior when it comes to religious fanaticism.

Given the right conditions, I felt most FLDS members were fully capable of "drinking the Kool-Aid." They followed Warren Jeffs's orders without question. I feared the worst.

CHAPTER 34

Search

Once the authorities were inside the FLDS compound, they discovered that the inhabitants had been busy while the roadside negotiations were dragging on. The faithful had used the time to come up with plans designed to foil the efforts of the law officers, and confusion reigned.

It was obvious from the start that the number of residents at the ranch had been grossly underestimated. Hundreds of the FLDS faithful were there, and none would cooperate. The sterility of the place, as evidenced by the total absence of ordinary kids' possessions like bicycles or dolls, surprised the outsiders. When the police gave some of the more curious children rides in the big armored personnel carrier, FLDS adults reprimanded the youngsters and ordered them away.

As the law enforcement team continued talks with Jessop and other leaders, the Child Protective Services workers set about trying to find Sarah, the girl who had made the calls. At first, they requested that all of the girls at the compound be brought to a central location, which was identified as a school. The FLDS responded by selecting only girls who were well briefed and unlikely to give up any secrets. The stymied interviewers then decided to fan out into other buildings and homes to search for the rest of the girls. The CPS workers were escorted by police officers, but also by FLDS "guides" who were the eyes and ears for the church and served to intimidate anyone who was questioned.

CPS worker Tina Martinez interviewed LeAnn Nielsen Jessop, who appeared to be about sixteen. When Martinez asked her age, LeAnn did not answer, but looked up at her husband, Leroy Jessop, who was present during the entire interview. "You are eighteen," Leroy coached. The girl then quickly attempted to convince Tina that she was indeed eighteen, that her birthday was March 23, 1991. She had a ten-month-old baby and was Leroy's fourth wife. As the investigators went about their business, young girls in their long dresses began investigating them right back. A friendly kid who looked about thirteen approached a ranger.

"Hello," she smiled, and shyly asked, "What's your name?"

The ranger looked down from beneath the brim of his big cowboy hat at the typically well-groomed FLDS girl who was carrying a journal. "My name's John," he replied, pleased at her cordial manner.

The girl scurried off some distance and scribbled in her little book, then came back. "What's your last name, John?"

"Smith," the ranger answered, hoping to strike up a conversation.

The kid ran off again and wrote some more. Then she spun around so fast that her skirt flared in a circle, and all traces of politeness disappeared. She thrust an accusing finger at the Texas Ranger and shouted, "John Smith, in one year, you will wither!"

"What?" he blurted, dumbfounded. The charming child had turned into a soothsaying harridan in the blink of an eye.

"In one year, *you will wither!*" the stern little voice repeated. Then she ran away and disappeared into the meandering flock of other neat little girls in long dresses. The ranger told me later that the kid had really creeped him out.

The CPS interviews were proving to be equally disturbing and distorted. A girl might give one name, saying she was sixteen, and confirm that she was married, only to deny it all later. The teenager might then give an entirely different name, vow that she was not married, give a different age, and daintily disclaim any knowledge of a photograph on a nearby table that showed her with an older man and a baby. All of the girls stuck to the church script and insisted that no age was too young for them to be married.

While the interviews were going on, fifteen-passenger vans belonging to the church shuttled children from place to place. Girls who had not been interviewed were whisked from homes that had not yet been entered by authorities and taken to places that had already been searched and cleared. Children would lie, claiming that they had already been interviewed, when they had not. Tension was growing.

Compounding the identification problem was how few surnames there were within the group. Jessop and Barlow are even more common within the FLDS than Smith and Jones are in a telephone book in Seattle or Atlanta. The different combinations of FLDS first, middle, and last names, with no records to prove which are correct, defy logic. It is not unusual to find children who are named after the prophet, Warren Steed Jeffs, or have various reworks such as Warren Jeffs Steed or Steed Warren Jeffs, although they may be related only distantly to the prophet, or not at all. With females, the names change through marriages and when they are reassigned to new husbands, at which time their children's original names also change, no matter how old they are. Generations pass, but the same names echo over and over again. It makes things exceedingly frustrating for any outsider trying to make sense of the Byzantine FLDS genealogy.

As the hours went by, there was still no sign of the Sarah who was the object of the search. There were some Sarah Barlows and Sarah Jessops, but not the Sarah Jessop Barlow they sought. Nor did they find any sign of the alleged abuser, Dale Evans Barlow. But as the night dragged into the early morning hours, everyone understood the investigation was no longer about helping just one girl; it was clear that multiple children had been abused and forced into polygamous sexual unions.

Despite the deception and misinformation, within the first six hours authorities found eighteen girls between the estimated ages of twelve and sixteen who were in various stages of pregnancy or had given birth. The law enforcement people could not ignore such an abundance of evidence that crimes had been committed.

While the search continued in Texas, I plunged into working my contacts involved in the various investigations of the FLDS and found the entire network of church members was on edge as the police probed around the nooks and crannies of the Texas compound and interviewed its residents. The search at the YFZ Ranch was regarded as an existential threat of the highest order.

Sooner or later, the searchers would be faced with breaching the sacred white limestone temple that dominated the compound, something the FLDS leadership had no intention of allowing. Law enforcement was trying to be sensitive to the group's religious beliefs, but the authorities had learned that the FLDS could not be trusted. It was made clear to Merril Jessop that the temple had to be searched, and the officers were ready to use whatever force necessary to carry out their lawful duty.

The moment of truth would arrive when the search moved into the temple proper.

Following the developments from my office in Utah, I realized that something was out of whack. I was always dubious about coincidences. I had been drawn into the long dialogue that Flora Jessop was having with a sixteen-year-old abused FLDS girl named Sarah, and now I had learned that the authorities in Texas also had been speaking with a Sarah who also claimed to be sixteen. The alleged abusers in their stories were different—a husband versus a father—as were the locations, a Texas ranch or an Arizona house. The chances that the cases were not somehow related looked pretty slim.

I telephoned Sheriff Doran down in Schleicher County to alert him to the similarities between what he was doing and what was happening at my end. By the time I was able to get through to him at the ranch, the sheriff, who had been without sleep since the raid began, was clearly frazzled. He knew that I would not be calling in the middle of that mess if I did not think it was important, so he listened for a few minutes before his attention was abruptly snatched away. "Yeah, e-mail me those recordings," he said, his voice quickening. "I gotta go, man. They're starting to take kids out of here."

After talking with the sheriff, I remained at my computer keyboard to monitor the developments in Texas when my "no-coincidences" rule took another sharp jolt. I had received an e-mail from still another FLDS girl asking for help: "I can't call the cops it would only make it worse . . . (It involves missing persons.)"

Unlike the anonymous caller, I knew this contact extremely well. The message had been sent by none other than Candi Shapley, the one-time child bride whose grand jury testimony had once rocked the entire FLDS and precipitated Warren Jeffs's run as a fugitive. I had worked hard to help prepare Candi emotionally to actually take the witness stand against the prophet and against her abusive former husband, but at the critical moment, she had backed down, apparently coerced by the church and her parents into keeping silent. Nevertheless, I had stayed in touch, because I try never to burn my sources. When I read her comment about "missing persons" in the e-mail, I immediately thought about her twins and considered the possibility that the FLDS was once again using her children as hostages to make sure that Candi remained muzzled.

I wrote back that if she wanted my help, I was on her side. The answer came back immediately:

OK so what if I was to tell you my girl is missing and I don't know where she is? I'm not saying she is . . . What would I do? Where would I start?

I wrote, "If my daughter was missing, I would kick over every rock and look behind every bush until I found her, and if that did not work, I would get mad-dog mean. But everyone's circumstances are not the same. If you really, really want to find her, trust me and let me help you find her."

She e-mailed back that she was undecided about what to do. We both had been through this before. I understood the pressure on her. Candi knew that if she summoned the courage to "make a stand," that there would be a price to pay. She stated that "all hell will break loose. My Family will 4ever despise me, and threaten me in some way." She knew it was now or never. "Their so called teachings and training (known as brainwashing) really mess with ones mind."

Candi signed off, leaving me alone with my thoughts. Why was she contacting me right now, at this particularly anxious time, after months of silence? I also thought it curious that the urgent e-mails from someone as plugged into the FLDS as Candi Shapley had not mentioned a word about what was happening at the YFZ Ranch, which was by now international news. The timing seemed more than accidental. Was she somehow involved with the Texas situation?

Sheriff David Doran was watching part of his own personal nightmare come true. The authorities had found much more than they had anticipated, and while the situation remained peaceful, it had not gone well and was not yet over. State resources were being stretched to the brink.

The authorities had been exceedingly careful, knowing that it is a traumatic experience for everyone involved when victims of abuse must be removed from their homes. None of the cops or the experienced social workers had ever imagined having to deal with such intense trauma on the vast scale that confronted them as Friday drew to a close.

It was time for the Child Protective Services specialists to make some crucial decisions. Having been met with such confusion and lying, the CPS workers needed to get all of the children together if there was to be any hope of sorting out who was really who. That would be impossible while everybody remained at the ranch. Transportation was arranged and by the end of the day, 162 FLDS children were moved away, many to a temporary shelter at the Eldorado civic center, where cots and beds were set up. They were later taken to the old restored Fort Concho in San Angelo, to be housed until arrangements could be made for temporary foster care or group homes.

Another decision was a shocker for me. Swayed by emotion for the distraught kids, the CPS allowed mothers to accompany their children to serve as buffers because the fearful kids had never lived in the outside world. Allowing possible abusers to stay with their victims was unprecedented. The FLDS leaders seized the opportunity and let only some of the mothers go—those capable of keeping the kids from spilling their guts about what actually went on at the ranch. The chosen moms brought along cell phones and cameras and stayed in constant touch with the FLDS leadership.

No less alarming to me was learning about the press access that was being allowed by the FLDS. The entire religion loathed outside attention, but now the church instructed those mothers to go against their lifetime of training and actually be nice to the reporters and photographers of the gentile media.

When I heard about the decisions, I could predict with near certainty what would happen next because it had happened before. If the FLDS women were giving interviews and providing pictures of weeping, frightened kids, the Texas operation was at risk of being a replay of the infamous '53 Raid in Arizona. The FLDS propaganda machine had swung into operation with a public relations gambit that would prove to yield immense benefits for the church. Opening their secret lives to the hungry media was extremely rare, and the reporters jumped at the chance for exclusive information.

Rod Parker, the longtime lawyer for the FLDS who had been fired by Warren, was back on the job, this time to help frame the church message. Although he is not a Mormon, Parker was likely very aware of the importance to the FLDS of the old 1953 Arizona raid, and how that story could be spun to match what was currently happening in Texas. Once again, the child abuse of the organization was about to be buried beneath an avalanche of media coverage, orchestrated by the claims of a twisted church and its spin doctors claiming governmental abuse.

The attention of much of the country was riveted on the pictures of mothers and children. Most of the media played the story straight, but some had bought the FLDS lies: Heartless cops and government workers were snatching babies from their loving, polite, clean, and God-fearing families in defiance of the First Amendment of the U.S. Constitution, which guarantees freedom of religion. In the age of the Internet, people from all over the globe joined the conversation.

That the Constitution does not give anyone permission to engage in criminal activities under the guise of "religion" was mostly ignored. Worshipping God is much different than raping children and breaking families apart.

CHAPTER 35

Seizure

Bishop Merril Jessop was out of his league. After decades of intense internal power struggles, the FLDS had abandoned any pretense of shared leadership in favor of "one-man rule." Warren Jeffs made almost every decision, but in this time of ultimate crisis, he was sitting in an Arizona jail cell, and the bishop could not reach him. The police were on the doorstep of the sacred temple and Uncle Warren was unable to call the shots. Jessop, the on-site ranch manager, was now forced to make decisions on his own, a situation that carried serious repercussions should the prophet later believe Jessop had made the wrong choices.

Jessop had to do something, because despite all of the dodges and lies, the police were connecting the dots as children and young wives were taken away for further questioning.

Meanwhile, Ranger Brooks Long was putting together an expanded search warrant to supplement the original one, a section of which vividly described why things were so complicated. Long told how a CPS worker interviewed a girl named Arta Jessop Barlow, who was pregnant and had a two-year-old child and claimed she did not know her own age. The worker then interviewed another girl, eight-year-old Viola Barlow, who contradicted that story. Viola said that Arta had four children and was not even sixteen! According to Viola, Arta was "spiritually united" to Richard Jessop Barlow, who happened to be Viola's own father. The mother of Viola was Richard's first wife, Susan Black Barlow. Arta was the second wife, and both were still married to Richard. That was only one of the many convoluted stories being uncovered—tales that were strange to begin with and were further complicated by determined FLDS efforts to deceive.

Ranger Long also was able to cite having personally seen a document that showed one man being married to more than twenty wives. CPS workers had interviewed a number of underage girls who were married to much older men, and some of those girls were already mothers themselves. Veda Keate had been married to Warren Jeffs at the age of thirteen and had conceived her child at fourteen. Veda was now nineteen, and her daughter was four. Around each corner, the investigators seemed to uncover a new piece of evidence that would alarm them even more, including the very notable disparity in number between males and females at the ranch: There were twice as many girls as boys.

With most of what they were finding, a new warrant would not have been required because the new evidence fell under what is known as the "open fields doctrine." If a peace officer observes a syringe and a spoon in the back seat of a car during a routine traffic stop for a broken tail light, he is justified in conducting a more thorough search of the vehicle to look for other evidence of a crime unrelated to the original reason for stopping the vehicle. At the YFZ Ranch, police had crossed that legal threshold almost immediately upon entering the grounds.

After three days of searching and uncovering fresh evidence, their probable cause was building, and with the church leaders proving untrustworthy and deceitful, it was clear that the ranch was a hotbed of criminal activity. The police were now prepared to go after the temple itself and a smaller adjoining annex, and specifically any records and data that were stored inside. Long wanted the contents of locked safes, locked desk drawers, locked vaults, computers, and computer peripherals that may contain information verifying child abuse. There was overwhelming evidence that multiple incidents of child abuse had taken place on the ranch and a new warrant was prepared and signed by Judge Walther. This time the FBI also showed up with a warrant of its own.

Merril Jessop was still operating under an oath to "keep sacred things secret." As bishop he probably knew what was inside the temple, and he understood that if law officers breached the inner sanctum, many of the church's most sensitive secrets would be at risk. But the doors were still locked, and while the kids and many of the women were gone by the night of April 5, the men were still there—loyal, dedicated, ferociously faithful men who would do whatever they were told. They would resist if called upon to do so.

But there was a counter-balancing force at work on Merril Jessop, an unusual woman I will call Lorraine to respect her privacy. Lorraine had been a wife of the late prophet Rulon Jeffs. After his death she was hounded by Warren to become another one of his wives, but she refused and left the church. She still maintained close ties to many of the people within the religion, people she had known her whole life and was anxious to help if she could. She had been invited to go to Texas to stand by as a sort of cultural translator and help shed light on some of the religious practices and family histories. When things began to heat up at the temple site, Lorraine remembered that she still had the bishop's number in her phone. As tensions escalated, she made the decision to try to contact and reason with the only man that had the authority to avert violence.

To her surprise, Merril Jessop answered the call. He did not want to talk to her, but Lorraine was persistent, and he was so desperate for guidance that he reluctantly listened. Lorraine became a calming voice as the crisis unfolded, urging Merril to carefully think through this potentially dangerous situation and not do anything rash. Don't let it turn ugly, she said. Since Uncle Warren was not around, Merril felt reasonably safe talking to Lorraine, and her warning carried some weight, whether he wanted to admit it or not.

As the cops prepared to enter the temple, the behavior of the FLDS men took on a more menacing tone. They spread out until one of them was positioned every sixteen feet or so along the perimeter of the wall that surrounded the five-acre temple property. They would periodically hold their arm to the square and pray loudly for God to bring down "whirlwind judgments" upon the heads of the police, the defilers, and strike them dead. Dozens of harmonized deep voices were begging for the Lord to intervene and punish the unbelievers.

The police cleared a path through the chanting men, who stood their ground and simply would not get out of the way. The cops wrestled a huge battering ram into position at the temple's massive oak front door, and the FLDS prayers for death turned into hymns, with a defiant, all-male chorus singing old Mormon songs of faith. The chant of the hymn "The Spirit of God" rang out as the battering ram smashed against the big door with a booming, cannon-like thunder. The ram was so heavy that officers had to take turns handling it, and the doors were so thick and sturdy that it took police more than an hour to break through. All the while, the FLDS men sang out and prayed, chanting for the destruction of the officers, their voices rising like a demented choir. Even some longtime policemen and Texas Rangers were shaken by the unrelenting calls for divine intervention. "Really weird," observed one. When the door eventually cracked, the watchers moaned in shock and dismay.

The battering continued, and soon a second crack appeared, which increased the calls for God to rain down the ultimate punishment on the intruders. When the ram made a third large split, the twelve-foot doors flew apart with an echoing *boom* and the entrance to the cavernous temple was finally breached.

All around the wall, the men of the church collapsed like marionettes whose strings had been cut. Some dropped to their knees in disbelief, others fell prone and scrabbled in the dirt, and still others stood sobbing like children with their faces buried in their hands.

Loud, agonized cries ripped the air, the sound of shattered faith. Through a life of conditioning, the men immediately accepted their own blame; it was their own unworthy thoughts and actions that had precluded God's direct intervention from saving their temple. In response to other failures, such as when predictions for the end of the world had failed to materialize, the prophet had always preached they were at fault, being unfit for the Lord's use. Now, once again, the prophet himself, already in prison, would have to magnanimously shoulder the blame and suffer and atone even more for the sins of his slothful followers.

Most of the police felt sorry for the wailers, but there was no time to waste. They fanned out into teams for the temple search.

The search was long and tedious and each room, from the basement to the Holy of Holies on the top floor, had to be scoured for forensic evidence. The rangers had received intelligence from former members that secret passageways and hidden rooms were common in FLDS buildings, so the search meticulously plodded along in case something had been overlooked. Finally, one tired ranger went into an office and when he saw nothing unusual, leaned against a large bookshelf. He felt it give a little. He recalled the briefing about hidden rooms in other FLDS compounds and so he began to push and shove, then his fingers felt a latch, and when he freed it, the bookshelf came away from the wall. Behind it was a large door constructed of heavy oak with steel security locks.

The door led into a hidden underground passage with more, still heavier doors blocking the path. Along the way, rangers discovered empty gun safes, and tensions escalated considerably. Trained dogs would later be brought in to sniff around the property, and they located a cargo container buried beneath the home of Isaac Jeffs, the prophet's brother, containing thirty-three weapons stashed inside: pistols, Israeli military industry–made weapons, military-style Bushmaster AR-15s, and even a powerful Barrett .50-caliber sniper rifle with a precision Unertl scope. All were legally registered. A cop who looked at that arsenal gave a low whistle and said, "They could have held us off for a month with this stuff!" Maybe having the cover of an armored personnel carrier as backup had not been a bad idea at all.

Meanwhile, the underground search had turned up some interesting file cabinets and the suspicious gun storage lockers, but no smoking gun. Continuing through the corridor, they moved into the area at which the temple was connected to the smaller temple annex and discovered the final door, a bank-grade Class 1 Hamilton safe door with a thickness of more than eighteen inches of solid steel.

The foundation walls were four feet thick and also were reinforced with steel, and together with the door, they provided a nearly impenetrable barrier. Whatever was behind all of that was well protected. Professional locksmiths were stymied. Workers hacked at the thick concrete beside the door, trying to create a hole, before realizing they would need specialized equipment to break through. Trucks bearing heavy-duty drills of the sort used on oil rigs were summoned, and roughnecks came along to operate them. A drill was set up outside the annex building and the roughnecks began grinding through the foundation at a spot identified on a blueprint.

The crews underground inside, and the crews outside above ground, worked simultaneously, and the outside group finally punched a small hole that they managed to widen enough so that a very small man might make it inside. Ranger Sergeant Jesus Valdez, small to begin with, made himself even smaller by removing most of his clothes, then, armed with a flashlight and his pistol, he wiggled in. The thick foundations had blocked radio contact between the two teams and when the drillers from inside broke through a short time later, they were totally surprised to look in and find Jesus Valdez in the vault looking back at them. Their first thought was that maybe the FLDS had stationed a small, tattooed man with a gun in there. It took a second for it to sink in that both crews had broken through.

Finally, in that sealed vault, the police uncovered the kind of evidence about which I had only fantasized: volumes of documents and marriage records, computer disks and hard drives, audio recordings and flash drives loaded with dictations by Jeffs, in his own voice. It apparently was being kept secure in the underground bunker until the temple vault was completely ready and dedicated. In that cache of documents was the daily "Priesthood Record of the Prophet Warren Steed Jeffs," containing evidence that would almost certainly keep Uncle Warren behind bars for the rest of his life and lead to the incarceration of many of his lieutenants, as well.

Ferreted away behind those thick walls were the detailed day-to-day chronicles of his actions since first proclaiming himself prophet in 2002, including admissions of numerous despicable crimes. Now, those crimes would be revealed to the world.

By the time the searches were complete, a total of 463 children would be removed from the Yearning for Zion Ranch, and a dozen men, including the jailed prophet, would face a wide range of criminal charges. TV news crews descended on Texas, and the small town of Eldorado was overrun with news satellite trucks broadcasting the event around the world. However, the real magnitude of what took place that week would barely be noticed by most of the world. A Waco or Jonestown had been averted. The combined efforts of law enforcement, social workers, and former members who understood the intricacies of the time bomb ticking away within the compound had skillfully avoided disaster.

The patience and professionalism displayed by law enforcement and CPS social workers and investigators; the efforts of a former member to set aside the abuse she experienced at the hands of the FLDS leadership and persuade Merril Jessop to stand down; and a hundred other small details initiated by conscientious professionals on the scene, combined to avert a potential catastrophe on a scale the country had probably never seen before. Considering what the FLDS and its insane prophet are capable of and the violent history of fundamental Mormonism, the real story was how a catastrophe resulting in loss of life was avoided. While the fringe media began to spin a story of government intrusion into the lives of a supposedly eccentric unpopular religion, I breathed a silent sigh of relief that justice had prevailed and not one person had been hurt in the process.

Throughout the raid, Gary and I continued working with Flora Jessop in Utah, listening to our mystery caller named Sarah, who was still insisting that she was in Short Creek. Flora was able to get the caller's phone number from the caller ID feature on her telephone, and I traced it to a Tennessee cell-phone service provider. That did not guarantee finding any address, however. The number had been assigned to an over-the-counter disposable phone that could have been purchased almost anywhere.

Then Sarah dropped a Short Creek address into one conversation, identifying it as a corner house. I knew the place! The following morning, I drove down to the Crick to confirm it. Town records showed that it belonged to an FLDS member named Lorin Fischer. When Sarah called the next time, Flora worked that name into the conversation. "Lorin Fischer is your father, isn't he, sweetheart?" The girl was hushed for a moment, then began to weep. "Am I in trouble?" she asked. "Am I going to be in trouble?"

She again carefully dodged all questions about her exact location, and stymied our attempts to help her. Gary was getting nowhere on the legal side in Arizona because of the lack of evidence. Our attention, and that of the entire nation, turned to Texas. Our stubborn mystery caller, however, was not yet finished with any of us.

CHAPTER 36

Backfire

The Texas rescue attempt at the YFZ compound left everybody unsteady. CPS had stumbled onto an enormous case load at a single location. The parents and their children were entitled to mandatory hearings concerning the allegations, and statutory deadlines had to be met. Texas requires that a hearing be held not later than fourteen days after a child is taken into custody. Now it was the court system's turn to be overwhelmed, and Judge Barbara Walther consolidated all 463 children into a single preliminary hearing in San Angelo on April 17, 2008.

I needed to determine if any of our clients might be affected, particularly an FLDS refugee whose wife and children had been reassigned to another man by Warren. Clothing bearing the new father's name was found in the temple at the ranch, along with the wife and one daughter. The other daughter, a thirteen-year-old, was gone, and I feared she had already been given in a fake marriage to the man who had become her new father only a short time earlier. We never found her. She was another of the girls who have simply vanished deep into the FLDS culture.

Back in Texas, I began meeting with many of the people who had been involved in the rescue attempt. Among them was Angie Voss, the Child Protective Services supervisor who had made the actual decision to take the kids away from the compound. Voss asked me to come by the CPS office for a question-and-answer session about the FLDS with a few of her co-workers. I was impressed by Voss and her ability to make tough calls. She was an experienced veteran who had encountered the most horrible kinds of abuse during her career, and prior to the YFZ raid, she thought that she had seen it all.

When I arrived at the office, Angie introduced me to her colleagues, and we settled in for an informal chat. More people drifted in. Soon, about fifty people were crammed into the room. My impression was that until a couple of weeks earlier, they probably had not known the FLDS from horseshoes. Now they were scrambling to catch up and anxious to get help through the learning curve. They peppered me with questions: *How does this peculiar religion work? Are they really Mormons? What about "celestial" marriages, and being "sealed for time"? Why do the women act like robots?*

While giving them an overview of the world according to Warren Jeffs, I was able to pick up more information about what those beleaguered workers had faced at the ranch.

They had gone out to find one specific child, the girl named Sarah Jessop. Once inside the compound, that original mission mushroomed as evidence was discovered of more child abuse. Underage girls had been placed in arranged connubial relationships with older men, having babies soon thereafter, and even younger girls were in danger of the same fate. One CPS worker told me they had started to think, "Oh, crap, this could turn into a half-dozen kids." Then the number rose to eighteen children who needed further investigation and protection. Eventually, the CPS team reached the astonishing conclusion that it was not just one girl at risk on the ranch, it was every kid there!

I let the CPS workers know that I felt that in removing those 463 children from the ranch, they had made the only choice open to them. Come what may, they had been true to their responsibility to protect children ensnared in a predatory caste system.

I explained to them that kids raised in the FLDS culture just don't stand a chance. That when a boy is born, he has only three options in life: make a mistake and be abandoned by his parents, become frustrated enough to eventually leave the religion and live out his life as a traitor, or grow up to be a perpetrator of abuse. That to be born female promises a future just as dismal. She will either be an underage bride or will later be placed with a man without regard to love. Either way, it is probable that her children will grow up and continue the cycle of abuse, with her as their primary mentor.

It was important for me to let the CPS people know that I had never met nor spoken with any FLDS woman who had not been abused in some form. Not one.

It definitely would have been easier to investigate just a single case at a time, but that had not been possible here because hundreds of children were involved. In my opinion, Angie Voss made the right call. "You should feel fortunate that you have been given this opportunity to make a real difference in the lives of so many children," I told the workers at the San Angelo CPS office.

After the meeting, a few of us adjourned to a smaller venue to continue the discussion. That was when I got my first clue that things might not be shaking out well within the Child Protective Services department. Two senior members of the department had been sent down from Houston, allegedly to help, but by the time our discussion broke up, I had the clear impression that they were really there to plan an exit strategy.

The next day, I attended the hearing. The grounds of the Tom Green County Courthouse were carpeted with FLDS women in pastel prairie dresses and lawyers in suits. Few, if any, FLDS men attended, in order to avoid having to answer questions about their families and marital relationships. District Judge Barbara Walther would hear twenty-one hours of testimony that lasted over several days.

Judge Walther ran a tight ship, but the situation bordered on chaos. One attorney would say something, then another would pop up to object and within moments others would pile on with more objections and opinions. She needed the wisdom of Solomon, combined with a lion tamer's whip and chair. After weighing the evidence, the judge decided there was a significant risk of harm if the kids were returned to the YFZ Ranch, so she ruled to keep all of them in protective custody while foolproof DNA tests were performed to establish parental relationships. All of the children would have to be individually evaluated before any decision could be made about returning them to their parents or placing them in foster care.

I felt optimistic as I flew home. The justice machine had taken over, and it was out of my hands. They were going to have to find a solution, and the DNA testing was a good idea, at least in theory—although I knew the FLDS would fight it.

The FLDS propaganda machine was furiously set in motion, with lawyers, mothers, and spokespeople talking about the impact that the horrible government's action was having on the poor children. The same parents who were performing for the cameras at these staged news conferences had willingly fed those same children into the abusive system of their church, saying nothing when Warren Jeffs chased away their sons and placed their underage daughters with aging men. There was no doubt the children were currently going through a tough time, and naturally they did not want to be separated from their mothers, but the decision could not be left up to them, nor swayed by emotion.

On April 24, there was startling news. A call came from an excited Flora Jessop: "You hear what happened?" Near my elbow, a producer for a major television network was also answering his phone, and his manner changed with each passing second. The police had found a woman by the name of Rozita Swinton in Colorado Springs, and the original calls to the crisis hotline were proving to have been a hoax.

"They took her down and questioned her, and no sooner had she gotten out, and she was calling me again and claiming she was Laura!" Flora was baffled by the caller's nerve: She was either very bold or very sick.

This was a game-changer, not in the legal arena, but in the eyes of the general public. The FLDS was going to have a field day with this.

The story line was carefully manipulated by the former FLDS lawyer Rod Parker, who had been fired during the Lost Boys case but was now brought in to handle the public relations situation at the ranch. He spoon-fed information to a couple of hand-selected FLDS apologist reporters, knowing that all it takes is a few people skilled with pens and television cameras to plant enough doubt to change the tide. FLDS mothers gushed horror stories about how the government was mistreating the crying children, some of whom were suffering from chicken pox and tummy aches. There were pictures galore.

Until then, the media reports had been fairly sympathetic toward law enforcement. But with the new developments, an unlikely mix of radical constitutionalists, bigoted hate groups, and First Amendment defenders loudly protested what they perceived to be government mistreatment of the industrious Christian religious group and its children.

The Texas governor and attorney general began to receive threatening letters and e-mails. I was asked to review some of them to see if I recognized the authors or origins. "What happened to religious freedom?" was the common theme. An e-mail received by the governor's office warned Americans, "It's the Mormons this time, but it could be you next." They seldom mentioned the deviant prophet who had created the mess and was currently in prison for being an accomplice to sexually assaulting a child.

There was also the looming issue of how much money the State of Texas was spending on the hundreds of cases. The financial pressure was growing severe. All of the workers, the emergency housing, the food, the overtime, and the unforeseen extras caused by having to deal with so many children and cases were blowing a hole in the budget. The overall price tag could run into the tens of millions.

Things were simply happening too fast. The state was losing control, it was costing too much, and the PR field had been virtually lost to the FLDS spin doctors after Rozita's hoax was discovered. The case against Dale Barlow, the man who was alleged to have been the abusive husband of the non-existent Sarah and therefore the second target of the raid, was dropped without comment.

Only six weeks after the authorities breached the YFZ stronghold, I received a dismal e-mail from a frustrated source in Austin who had been closely involved with the rescue attempt: "I don't think we can protect these kids much longer." The will to succeed was evaporating in the higher ranks of the bureaucracy. Within a few months, dozens of CPS workers, including those who had been involved in the raid, were fired, forced to retire, or reassigned because they would not agree to keep silent as directed by their superiors.

At the end of May, Judge Walther's custody ruling was overturned by the Texas Third Court of Appeals. That court said there was no evidence of a clear and immediate danger to the children at the ranch and ruled that Walther essentially had mishandled the situation by rolling all of the cases into one. A week later, the Texas Supreme Court allowed the Appeals Court decision to stand. CPS would need to file each case individually in Walther's court and give the specific reasons why each child should be removed and placed in protective custody. Instead of going to that trouble and expense, CPS chose to begin quietly releasing the children, and Judge Walther had to vacate her ruling on custody.

The result was a decisive win for the FLDS, and I watched in power-less fascination as they made the most of it.

Big Willie Jessop, of all people, was now emerging as the chief public spokesman for the FLDS. Knowing his background as Warren Jeffs's tough-guy enforcer, I found it almost impossible to believe. He had not even been deemed saintly enough by Warren to be a temple worker, and had never even been allowed on the temple grounds, but now he was the front man, all over television, playing the religious persecution card.

Willie bragged among his people that he had learned this new skill of leadership at no less an institution than Harvard University. And that part was true. His former assistant explained to me that Willie had paid four thousand dollars for a weeklong seminar at Harvard Law School on how to become a better negotiator. The Ivy League university runs such seminars regularly, but I had to wonder about the standards for being admitted to such a program. By shelling out big money for a five-day course, Willie became a credentialed bullshitter with "Harvard" tacked behind his name.

Willie held a news conference for the gathered national media in June and read a statement that promised the FLDS religion would no longer perform underage marriages in any place where they would be il-legal. While that pledge appeared to acknowledge movement toward change, it was just more FLDS smoke and mirrors. Marrying children was already illegal throughout the country, as was polygamy. Furthermore, no FLDS member has ever had the legal authority to perform a marriage of any kind. I considered anything coming out of Willie's mouth to be suspect.

Few reporters knew much about the religion's background. They did not realize that a vital underpinning of the church was utmost secrecy, and that lying to gentiles was considered normal. After the lie, they would go back to doing whatever they wanted. It had been working in Arizona and Utah for many years, and it was working again in Texas.

The press, however, did have some questions about this new spokes-man. Was Willie the official church representative? Did his words reflect the actual policies of the church or its leadership? He dodged each point. To hear him tell it, he was just some guy handing out a news release. Whatever he said could be denied by the church hierarchy. Willie did not make any decisions without the approval of the prophet, and when asked if Warren had authorized the new policy of no more underage marriages, Willie had no comment.

It was not long after this that I received a telephone call from Winston Blackmore in Canada. A fourteen-year-old girl had shown up unexpectedly at the home of her father, who was a Blackmore follower. The mother was a Warren Jeffs follower who had been reassigned to another man along with the children after the father had been expelled. The girl said she had run away from her mother's new household after being told that she was to be taken down to Short Creek and married to someone she had never seen. The cycle of child abuse continued. The fundamentalists had originally begun to rebel against the "Mother Church" in 1890 because of their refusal to recognize and obey the laws of the land. To cave in to the rule of law now would be to deny the principles upon which their religion was founded.

CHAPTER 37

Sinking Ship

Judge Barbara Walther of the Fifty-first District Court of Texas appeared undeterred by the reversal of the appeals courts, or by the complicated legal docket that she would have to navigate on both the civil and criminal sides of the looming behemoth FLDS situation. As a child in the 1950s, she was a victim of polio, which impaired her ability to walk. She still wears a leg brace. Out of earshot, the merciless FLDS apologists insultingly referred to her as "the gimp." She had been on the bench in West Texas for sixteen years, and there was never any doubt about who was in charge of her courtroom. As the coming months unfolded, Judge Walther would prove more than capable of handling this avalanche of cases.

But Schleicher County had neither the staff nor the resources to undertake such a monumental task of prosecution by itself and asked for state help. Texas attorney general Greg Abbot took charge of investigating the massive amount of evidence surfacing from the YFZ raid. Deputy Attorney General Eric Nichols was appointed lead prosecutor, and at his side would be the highly experienced Angela Goodwin, who was not only a veteran deputy attorney general, but was also a special assistant U.S. attorney.

The difference between the aggressive law enforcement officials and the bureaucrats handling the civil side of the matter was startling. The Texas Department of Public Safety and Attorney General Abbot wanted to put criminals in prison for crimes against children. In contrast, the Texas Department of Family and Protective Services and the

CPS flipflopped and seemed just to want to rid themselves of the untidy mess.

The DNA testing ordered by the judge was a prime example. It was logical to positively identify the parents before handing a kid back. There was no other reliable way to establish family relationships within the insular cult. Both mother and father would have to furnish a DNA sample and prove parentage before being allowed custody. A mobile lab was set up to collect the samples free of charge. Beyond the DNA match, a positive form of identification would be required before a child went back under parental custody.

In retrospect, it is difficult to determine who disliked the idea more, the FLDS church or the state's unenthusiastic Family Services Department and the new CPS team. All of them basically ignored or went around the order.

The church found a loophole. Only a handful of men showed up at the mobile lab to try to reclaim their children, and most of them were among those who had been kicked out of the religion but had remained loyal. Church leaders persuaded some of them that this was an opportunity to prove that they were, perhaps, worthy of being reinstated; just convince the authorities that they were the real fathers with ironclad DNA matches. They would promise the state that they would henceforth provide a good home for the very children they had been ordered to abandon earlier at the command of the prophet. Once given custody, the fathers could simply return their children to the abusers. Nothing would change.

Beyond that, the state agency with the responsibility for protecting children was practically releasing them into the wild. Instead of waiting for the DNA tests, the CPS began handing the children over to almost anyone who showed up with an ID and signed for them—mother, father, brother, neighbor, total stranger, or group of strangers.

The CPS's own release manifest would reveal that nearly twenty percent of the children taken in the rescue attempt were released to people other than their parents. More than a dozen names were in a column entitled "Not Listed," which meant the agency did not know to whom the children had been given.

At least two children were released to Seth Jeffs, the prophet's trusted brother, a courier who trafficked young brides for the prophet and who had also been arrested for soliciting prostitution with another man while on a road trip to deliver money to Warren. Seth Jeffs tried a tactic commonly used by FLDS members to confuse gentiles by giving his middle name, Steed, in place of his true surname of Jeffs, but he was caught in the act. He was a convicted felon on federal probation and had lied to the CPS about his real name, and he got the kids anyway. It was incomprehensible.

The real reason behind the bizarre CPS actions appears to have been costs. The investigation alone had cost thirteen million dollars, and estimates for integrating all of the children into mainstream society had ballooned to somewhere around a billion dollars. Attorneys, expert witnesses, foster-care homes, additional CPS workers, and other required support services would be very expensive and seemed to have no top end.

Texas governor Rick Perry was in France on a week-long European economic junket when word came of the Texas Supreme Court's decision to reverse the Walther ruling. Perry responded with a strong endorsement of the sweep of the YFZ Ranch. "I am substantially less interested in these fine legal lines that we're discussing than I am about these children's welfare." That was great to hear. "I still think that the State of Texas has an obligation to young women who are forced into marriage and underage sex—to protect them. That's my bottom line," the governor stated. He warned the FLDS that he would not tolerate the sexual abuse of children in his state. "If you are going to conduct yourself that way, we are going to prosecute you. If you don't want to be prosecuted for those activities, then maybe Texas is not the place you need to consider calling home."

Governor Perry issued that statement on June 6, after which he flew from France to Sweden. Willie Jessop called the governor's remarks "shocking and outrageous" and added, "Mr. Perry ought to get his facts straight."

Little more was heard from the governor concerning the FLDS.

The Department of Family and Protective Services decided to bring aboard its own version of a special prosecutor and on July 21 hired Charles Childress, whose reputation in Texas as a leading family-law expert was beyond reproach. As a professor and consultant, Charlie had been instrumental in writing many child-protection and family laws. If he could straighten things out, then perhaps the TDFPS and its over-whelmed CPS division could ride his coattails back to respectability.

Charlie was semiretired and lived in Austin, meaning he would have to commute to San Angelo, and he did not really want the job. But old friends pressured him, and Charlie took the assignment because he thought he could do some good. What he found boggled the veteran at-torney's conscience. He later summed it up for journalist Katy Vine of *Texas Monthly* magazine, "Going up to the governor, none of them had any idea what was going on. They had no clue."

In contrast, the attorney general's office knew exactly where it was going, and after sifting through the mountains of materials seized at the ranch, a grand jury was empaneled in Schleicher County in July to hear the findings. For the first time, regular Texans—the citizens of the county and the neighbors of the FLDS—were given the opportunity to see be-hind the false fronts of piety and godliness. After deputy attorneys gen-eral Nichols and Goodwin presented abundant proof of abuse, the grand jury dropped a heavy hammer.

Warren Jeffs and four other FLDS men were indicted with first-degree felony counts for sexual assault of a child. Raymond Merril Jes-sop (age thirty-six), his brother Merril Leroy Jessop (age thirty-three), Michael George Emack (age fifty-seven), and Allen Eugene Keate (age fifty-six), all surrendered and were jailed. Jeffs remained locked up in Arizona. It was a clear message that the Texans were not being taken in by the expensive FLDS lawyers or the public-relations spin doctors.

Within two months, the grand jury handed down indictments on an-other three FLDS men on similar charges: Abram Harker Jeffs (age thirty-seven); Lehi Barlow Jeffs, also known as Lehi Barlow Allred (age twenty-nine); and Keith William Dutson (age twenty-three). That brought the total to eight men indicted on criminal charges so far, based in part upon evidence gathered at the YFZ compound. Ironically, it was the iden-tical number that Arizona grand jurors had handed down in separate cases earlier.

No matter the success of law enforcement in going after the perpetrators of abuse, Texas CPS and its parent agency still wanted out. By the middle of August, they were dumping cases posthaste. In agency terminology, it was called "non-suiting," which was doublespeak for no further investigation required. According to a department official, the non-suits "could be because the children are in a protected environment or are over eighteen. It could be that we found no abuse or neglect."

The standard could not have been set much lower. A parent or guardian and the child had to take a brief parenting and victim awareness course, and then sign a paper promising to keep the children safe. That was it. CPS still had not even determined the true parents through the DNA tests. It was like rescuing a kid from the home of heroin addicts who have been selling their child for sex, then having Mom and Dad attend a seminar and promise not to do it again before sending the boy or girl right back into the dope and sex mill.

The drama of a teenager named Teresa Steed illustrated how out-of-whack the process had become. At fourteen, Teresa had been assigned as an underage plural "wife" to Nathan Carter Jessop, yet another son of the influential Bishop Merril Jessop. She became pregnant at fifteen and was about seven months along when she was taken into protective custody during the YFZ rescue attempt. During that time she had turned sixteen. She gave birth within days of leaving state custody. When CPS started sending children back to their abusers without regard to the potential consequences, Teresa Steed became a stumbling block.

To the Texas Rangers, her situation was an out-and-out criminal act that could not be ignored, swept under the table, or "non-suited." The rangers wanted to interview the girl and obtain the baby's DNA to establish paternity. CPS would not cooperate and refused to reveal Teresa's location. Nathan Jessop, the suspected father, was nowhere to be found.

A summons was issued for Teresa and the baby to appear before Judge Walther. Teresa showed up but did not bring the child, and when Walther asked where the infant was, the girl replied, "I'm not telling you." Walther sternly warned her lawyers to resolve the problem and meet the court's requirements. A peculiar sweetheart deal was brokered between CPS and Willie Jessop, who was not a relative, lawyer, social worker, or officer of the court—and whose involvement was irresponsible at best—in which the baby would be presented at a special private meeting with CPS workers. The Texas Rangers were not invited and were not even permitted to know where the meeting would take place.

The rangers found the secret meeting place anyway and served a warrant to take a DNA sample from the baby that Teresa had brought to the rendezvous. The tests proved conclusively that the infant was not hers. The FLDS had played the inept CPS by swapping babies so as not to implicate the father. The obstinate Teresa Steed, who took part in the charade, then also vanished; as of this writing, a warrant for her arrest is still in force. To the best of my knowledge the perpetrator of the crime, Nathan Carter Jessop, has not been taken to task, due to lack of evidence.

In October, I had begun a three-day drive home from Texas when I received a call from Charlie Childress, who by then was in the thick of the fight. As he went through Warren Jeffs's descriptions and church records, he had been completely undone by the extent of the abuse as a systemic problem.

My name had come up for Childress as he reached out for people who could help bring him up to speed on the complicated FLDS lifestyle. He wanted my views on a proposed budget, and the names of experts he could bring in as cultural translators. Childress believed the only hope for the FLDS children was to take a hard line, just as the lawmen were doing by going after the perpetrators. But his higher-ups wanted an impossible guarantee of victory if any trials were held in years to come. As any good attorney would do, Charlie refused to make such an impossible promise.

I spoke to him again later that night about witness availability and organizing the needed budget, and I headed out again the next morning for Utah, somewhat upbeat that perhaps the game was not over after all. Childress had the sound of a man who wanted to take it all the way. By the time I turned into my driveway the following day, I received another call. Charlie Childress had submitted his plan to the bosses, handed them the budget, outlined his plan, and had been rebuffed. They had pulled the rug out from under him. Within a week, he submitted his resignation, retired again, and was gone. We never spoke again.

Childress was replaced by his deputy, Jeff Schmidt, another excellent attorney, who replowed the same barren fields that Charlie had just tilled, and with the same result. I talked with Jeff frequently and gave him the same information; he talked to the same victims and witnesses, read the same reports and records, and came to the same conclusions. CPS again applied pressure. Schmidt also refused to budge.

"Sam, when I took the job I made a commitment to the CPS mission to protect children from abuse, neglect, and exploitation," he told me. "I just can't do what they are now asking me to do. I just can't do it."

The Texas bureaucracy, not just the FLDS, had now become a foe, and there was only so much that any of us could do. Schmidt continued to disagree with his supervisors. He said a disk containing vital evidence came up missing from his desk. Schmidt also said a formal complaint to his superiors about his treatment was dismissed as quickly as it was filed. He was left with two stark options: do as he was told, or get out. He transferred to the section dealing with elder affairs.

Apparently, the people in charge of CPS had lost focus on the stated purpose of their agency: to protect children. Instead, it seemed that they were trying to save their own reputations and careers, and a lot of money. Some Texas legislators were now openly complaining that the price was too high.

A final line of defense was the Court Appointed Special Advocates, known as CASAs, trained volunteers who are assigned to work with attorneys and protect any child caught up in the system. CASAs act as third-party advocates to monitor a situation until the children are completely safe. They don't care about politics or the media; they protect their charges fiercely, and heaven help anyone who gets in their way.

Debra Brown, the executive director of the Tom Green County Child Advocacy Center, wrote a carefully crafted letter of concern to Governor Perry on October 23, 2008, to put everyone on notice that the ship was sinking. She gave me a copy.

> Dear Governor Perry:
>
> CASA or Court Appointed Special Advocates, whose mission is to speak for the best interests of children, has staff and volunteers that have been involved with the FLDS situation in Eldorado since the attempted rescue of the children in April 2008. We have met the families, worked with the children in care as well as in their homes and are appalled at the extent of the abuse to these children emotionally as well as sexually.

It is far more widespread than we could have ever imagined, yet Child Protective Services seems determined to sweep this case under the rug and call it quits. CPS recently nonsuited most of the families and now has only ten cases involving thirty-seven children remaining. The original case total was 468 children.

Please intercede on behalf of the children and help Child Protective Services validate their mission of protecting children.

I visited the Yearning for Zion ranch in Eldorado last Thursday and was amazed to see three new large buildings under construction. This indicates to me that the sect is staying at the ranch and must feel that it is safe to carry on business as usual.

There are literally dozens of young men from Utah and Arizona called the "Lost Boys" that have been forced to leave their homes within the FLDS community and turned out into the streets with no money, little education and no knowledge of the real world simply for watching a movie or asking the wrong questions.

We have many teenage girls aged twelve to sixteen that are married or "sealed" to older men. Many of these girls have babies.

We have met and visited with several men that were forced from the community for questioning the Prophet. For this action their wives and children have been reassigned to other men like property.

Children have told us that they were taken from their mothers, given new mothers and have not been allowed to see their biological mothers at all.

The FLDS has claimed to have a wonderful home school program, but many of the children are testing below grade level by several years.

We have a goldmine of information corroborating abuse of children and need to act upon it now, as we will never have this opportunity again. This situation is only going to get worse. By refusing to pursue these cases, Child Protective Services gives the impression to the public that no crimes or violations were discovered. This is absolutely incorrect. If we abandon these children, because of fear of lawsuits or costs to our state, we are no better than the men who systematically sexually assault the young girls in the name of religion . . .

This behavior has been unfettered in Utah because fifty years ago the state abdicated their authority and has been fearful ever since of taking on the FLDS. As Texans, we have historically supported the right cause no matter the pain or consequences. I think we can do no less in this cause for these children.

Time is of the essence. Please do what is in the best interest of these children and intervene on their behalf. Don't let this problem become insurmountable on your watch as the leader of this great State.

Instead of receiving help, Brown and her CASA volunteers were criticized by CPS officials. Brown later bitterly told reporter Paul Anthony of the *San Angelo Standard-Times*, "What the media says and what the public thinks is a zero in the equation. It should be what is in the best interests of the child. Who cares what Willie [Jessop] says? Who cares what Nancy Grace says? Who cares what anyone says?"

The CPS spin was that their actual goal had been accomplished because the FLDS had learned the hard way that, by darn, you don't mess with Texas. From now on, those people at the ranch knew the state would be watching, and Willie Jessop had promised that the FLDS would stop underage marriages. It was a naïve and self-serving position. The FLDS had not changed, and had no intention of doing so. All that CPS had accomplished was to teach the FLDS how to fine-tune their crimes in order to better escape detection in the future.

CHAPTER 38

Stalker

As dispirited as I was over the inability of the Texas DFPS to protect the children from future abuse within the FLDS, I was heartened by the justice being meted out to some of the perpetrators. The grand jury was changing the complexion of the overall case.

I was particularly pleased when November brought four more indictments, this time including two of the biggest names in the breakaway religious cult: sixty-eight-year-old Wendell Loy Nielsen, the first counselor of the prophet, and Frederick Merril Jessop, seventy-two, the second counselor and the bishop at the YFZ Ranch. With Warren Jeffs already in jail, that meant that the entire ruling First Presidency was now under indictment, thus emasculating the FLDS leadership. Their trials are pending.

Child Protective Services continued non-suiting the victims until all of the children but one were back with their FLDS parents, mostly at the ranch. It seemed fittingly symbolic that the last child standing was Merrianne Jessop Jeffs, the red-haired girl whom Warren had "married" only a few weeks before he was arrested two years earlier, when she was a mere twelve years old. She had been part of the three-bride ritual on Thursday, July 27, 2006, at the ranch in Texas, when the leadership had locked their fates together.

All of the men involved in that extraordinary triple ceremony had been swept up by the law. Of the three grooms, Warren Jeffs was already doing his prison stretch on the Utah charges and was facing more charges in Arizona and Texas as well as federal fugitive charges. Raymond Merril Jessop and Merril Leroy Jessop were later tried and convicted of sexual assault of a child and received ten years and seventy-five years, respectively, in the Texas State Prison. The remaining two men involved, fathers of a pair of the brides, were Wendell Nielsen and Merril Jessop, both of whom had been named in the latest grand jury bills. All were charged with serious felonies.

Merrianne was a different story. When she was taken during the raid, evidence was discovered that suggested she may have already become a mother herself, at the age of twelve. She would spend several months in a state-monitored foster home, but she was still within the control of the FLDS. In her pocket was a cell phone with which her mother, the ferocious Barbara Jessop, secretly text-messaged advice about how to obstruct the questioners and frustrate her foster parents. "Please stay angry," read one, while another instructed, "We need you to keep crying, pout, sleep in. Crying will get you what you want."

When the state's workers tried to interview her and determine a course of action for her future, they found the girl had been transformed from a milkmaid waif into a spitfire defender of the faith. "She was a real little brat," one told me.

Merrianne plopped herself in a big overstuffed chair while being evaluated, was flippant and rude, and played the familiar "answer them nothing" card of her jailed "husband," Warren, to the hilt. There was no doubt that she had been well coached on how to take control of an interview.

Then one of the workers handed her a photograph showing a red-haired baby that looked just like her, and asked whose child it was. Merrianne grasped the picture and stared at it hard. She got up, walked unsteadily around the large chair, curled into a fetal position on the floor behind it, and began to weep uncontrollably, rocking back and forth as if she were having a nervous breakdown. She went from being a smart-mouthed child bride to being a sobbing mess in a heartbeat. This time, it wasn't an act; it was eerily reminiscent of the pain of a mother unable to turn off her love for her child. Such was the legacy that Warren Jeffs bestowed on the children he chose as concubines.

The CPS finally gave up on Merrianne, too. Once again they brokered a deal with Willie Jessop and assigned her to a foster home—one within the FLDS, and with the usual sort of history that goes along with those beliefs.

A twenty-one-page report titled "Eldorado Investigation" reviewing the eventful year of 2008 was released soon thereafter by the Texas Department of Family and Protective Services. It stated that a total of 439 children had been removed from the YFZ Ranch, and that 274 of them, from 91 families, had been the subjects of abuse and neglect. One in four prepubescent girls was involved in an underage marriage. That CPS had not done more was shameful in every way imaginable and will exact a toll on hundreds of children in the years to come.

Appeals and affidavits, supplements and responses, orders and objections, motions and memorandums. The work load was as heavy as ever with ongoing case preparations against the FLDS: tracking down a lead on another place of refuge, digging up information on a newly discovered FLDS shell corporation, or talking to sources down in Short Creek. It never ended.

I began the day on May 12, 2009, in Short Creek, meeting with some potential witnesses on a case, and had to race to catch my plane to Texas for a hearing the next day on the motion to suppress evidence seized during the law enforcement intervention at the YFZ Ranch. The FLDS defense lawyers were fighting the search warrants with everything they had.

I flew into San Angelo at ten o'clock that night, so beat that I had to check my hotel reservations on my BlackBerry to find where I would be staying.

A cheery and efficient young woman checked me in at the front desk, assigned me to Room 233, and handed over the key. Her next words snapped me wide awake. The clerk said my room was right next door to that of my friend. What friend? Nobody knew where I was staying, a habit I had developed long ago because of the sensitive nature of my work. Hell, I hadn't known where I was staying until I had gotten off the plane thirty minutes earlier.

I asked which friend it was, and she scrolled through her computer, then replied, "His last name is Jessop. First name is Dee." The clerk gave an accurate physical description, because he had checked in using his driver's license and a credit card just a couple of hours earlier. The FLDS enforcer was stalking me. Instead of going to my room, I called my contact with the San Angelo field office of the FBI.

While I waited in the lobby, my mind raced to recall the miserable story of Dee Jessop. He was the brother of Willie Jessop, but by another mother, and was only half the size of Big Willie. He was currently facing charges (later dismissed) for harassing people whom the FLDS perceived as enemies of the church but who were living in Short Creek. And now the sick son of a bitch had tracked me down and rented the room next door? I was getting madder by the second, wondering what that depraved little creep was planning. If anyone was crazy enough to take on the assignment of some sort of attack, it would be Dee.

The FBI agents showed up along with some local officers. My room was undisturbed, and Dee was nowhere to be found. I suspected as much, because guys who carry out special assignments for the church always have access to electronic equipment, including police radio scanners. When the local police were called to the scene, I figured Dee would have heard the dispatcher, and would have bolted.

The desk clerk told us that she had received several calls throughout the day from a man claiming to be Sam Brower, who said that she should expect some friends to also arrive at the hotel, and they all wanted to stay in nearby rooms. She told the caller that Mr. Brower would be given Room 233. When Dee Jessop showed up, he asked for Room 232, but when he learned it was already booked, he instead took Room 234.

It was enough of a threat for the FBI to book me into another hotel under an assumed name and keep a lookout for Dee during my stay in San Angelo. It was frustrating that no crime of any substance had been committed, because he identified himself properly to the desk clerk, and the other "Sam Brower" was an anonymous caller. I had a stalker, I knew his name, and I would take appropriate precautions in the future.

During the court hearing the following day, the FLDS attorneys became annoyed at my presence and decided to rustle up an impromptu subpoena to try to compel me to return to Texas in a few months for a deposition. To do so would give Dee Jessop or some other FLDS nut case another chance at me. In my opinion, it was pure harassment. It would have been foolish to play their game, so I filed an affidavit back in Utah saying that it would be unsafe for me to travel to Texas if the FLDS had advance knowledge of my presence. The court dismissed the subpoena. From then on, it was imperative for me to take special precautions to keep my whereabouts secret while traveling. I never discovered for sure how they had known about my trip in advance.

Ever since I had first begun searching for Warren Jeffs and investigating his cult, the FBI had been helpful—not always in the public eye, but always seeming to be around at the right time, such as when they served their own search warrants during the YFZ raid, elevated Warren to their Ten Most Wanted list, and showed up when the prophet was arrested. They had the resources, manpower, and technology to do things that no one else could.

So I was happy to help out in May when a joint task force of federal agencies prepared to conduct massive simultaneous raids on scores of church-affiliated businesses and safe houses. I went down to Short Creek to help agents locate and identify the homes and companies in which they were interested. A few weeks later, more than two hundred agents were fully briefed, had their gear prepared, and were primed to carry out what would be one of the largest federal criminal operations in recent history. Dozens of arrests of FLDS leaders were anticipated.

We were all waiting in anticipation for the storm to break. Then, only days before the operation was to launch, an e-mail was received from a higher-up that said, in an abbreviated version:

> I'm not sure how best to phrase this, but the bottom line is that . . . Washington, D.C., has essentially quashed the FLDS case and will not allow us to seek search warrants for the businesses and individuals that we submitted to you. Accordingly, please withdraw all search warrants and apologize to your magistrate judges . . . I apologize for your wasted efforts.

We were stunned. The guys in the field believed they had a strong case that would be complicated but also a slam dunk, but the guys behind the desks in the nation's capital couldn't get past their fears of stirring up public opinion by going after members of a controversial religion.

Some members of the task force left work early that day, so distraught at the stand-down order that it made them sick. I felt the same way, but I was far outside of the federal loop, and they didn't owe me any explanations. All too often I had seen similar events primed and poised to go, then called off without any plausible explanation. I wanted the battle to go on, and I worried that Washington had lost its nerve.

The criminal trials in Texas began at the very end of October 2009, and the first man up was Raymond Jessop, accused of one count of sexual abuse of a fifteen-year-old girl. He had been one of the grooms in the three-ring-circus marriages. When Willie Jessop saw me enter the courtroom, he became visibly upset and complained to the lead FLDS attorney, who apparently explained there was no law preventing Sam Brower from attending the trial. At a recess, Willie darted over to a state trooper who was the court bailiff and protested that he had a restraining order against me. The trooper asked where the order had been issued, so he could check to see if it existed. Willie stammered, "In Utah, and he isn't supposed to be within 500 feet of where I am." I had gotten to know the trooper, who was aware there was no such order. Willie insisted that I be taken not only out of the courtroom, but tossed out of Schleicher County, too.

The trooper replied with a deadpan expression and a slow drawl, "Well sir, we're not in Utah. This is Texas, so we are not going to be able to help you, unless he scares you, sir. Is that it? Does he scare you? If so, we can escort *you* safely out of the courtroom . . . sir." Willie's moon face turned bright red as he returned to his seat.

It was an amusing moment, but the best part of the trial came when the jury returned a verdict of guilty. After that, additional evidence was presented about Raymond's other child brides and his lack of remorse for being a serial pedophile. The jury decided to send Raymond Merril Jessop to prison for ten years. In Texas, child molesters complete an average of eighty-five percent of their time before being paroled. In the case of a zealous church member who will in all likelihood return to the exact same lifestyle he lived before being sent to prison, chances are very good that Jessop will be required to complete all ten years.

The next man up was fifty-seven-year-old polygamist Allen Keate, who was tried in December and ran into a buzz saw. The DNA testing positively proved that he was the father of many of the children taken at the ranch, including one from an underage "spiritual wife" he had taken when she was only fifteen.

Keate was in deeper water, too. He also was the father of Veda Keate, whom he had given to Warren Jeffs as a bride when she was just a fourteen-year-old child. During the trial, a Texas Ranger testified that in exchange for Veda being placed with Warren, Keate was later given two young brides, one of whom had previously been married to Warren's brother Leroy and at the age of fifteen was reassigned to Keate after Leroy had been booted out of the church. Allen Keate was now on trial for that sweetheart deal. The clear connection of an FLDS barter system in underage brides drew an audible intake of breath from the Texas jurors. Keate was found guilty and sentenced to a prison term of thirty-three years.

After that, the march of the self-proclaimed martyrs went like clock-work and averaged a trial every two months. Even those who made nego-tiated plea agreements drew lengthy prison terms as the jurors looked through the smoke-screen arguments of religious persecution and saw flagrant child abuse.

The mystery of Rozita Swinton had bothered me for a long time. She had not only ignited the entire Texas saga, but she had jarred us in Utah and Arizona with her calls to Flora Jessop, which I had overheard. Then came the simultaneous, unexpected exchange of e-mails with Candi Shapley.

With so many other developments in the case since the raid, I had put those events aside, but I had never lost interest in whether there had been some link between the two women. Since Candi seemed to have drifted back under the influence of the FLDS after collapsing as our wit-ness in Arizona, my only hope of answering that question was to find Rozita and try to piece the puzzle together with her help.

About a year and a half after her original calls, I made an effort to locate her. It had to be done carefully to be sure that I would not be in-terfering with any ongoing police investigation. She had also made a 911 call for help to the police in Denver, claiming to be an abused little girl who had been able to get her hands on a cell phone. The whole city of Denver had been looking for that nonexistent child. Rozita had been charged with filing false reports in Colorado before the Texas raid and had voluntarily spent some time in a mental hospital, but now she was free.

I arranged to meet her at a public place in Colorado Springs, Colorado, and we spent a few hours getting to know each other. I found Rozita to be an intelligent and fascinating young woman who had managed to make it through a childhood that was a living hell. She was surprisingly open and recounted what she could recall about how she had gathered information on the FLDS. She seemed deeply remorseful for any trouble that she may have caused as a result of the Texas raid.

It did not take long to understand that Rozita was almost incapable of telling an outright lie, and equally incapable of telling the whole truth. By her own count, she is beset by at least fifteen different personalities.

Her mind had started forming new personalities to cope with the abuse her father, a convicted murderer who has denied accusations of abuse, had inflicted on her starting when she was only two years old. Rozita's other personalities are repressed most of the time, but when one of them is released by some unknown trigger, she is usually unaware of any actions that follow. The real Rozita is repressed somewhere within the inner reaches of her mind, and memories of events involving other personalities are marginal at best.

But was there a link between Candi and Rozita? It is a fact that there was a photograph of Candi Shapley on Rozita's computer. She also had done so much research on the FLDS, it was safe to assume she had read of Candi's saga.

But I felt there was something stronger in the mix. Warren Jeffs kept several places of refuge and safe houses in Colorado Springs, and Candi had personally told me how she had been lured to Colorado Springs during the ugly episode in which the FLDS sought to prevent her from testifying against the prophet in Arizona. I concluded that it was quite possible that during that time, the two women may have shared neighbors or acquaintances, and perhaps had been drawn to each other with their similar stories of abuse.

For example, both claimed they had been held captive by their abusers. Candi had told me that after her unsuccessful attempt to run away from Randy Barlow, he had confined her to a room that she was not allowed to leave unattended. Rozita claimed to have had similar experiences that were woven into her story when she became the fictitious

Sarah Barlow in the telephone calls to Texas and Laura during the calls she made to Flora Jessop.

So, in my view, perhaps it was the FLDS leadership's compulsion to protect their prophet from prosecution in Arizona that brought the two young women into proximity in Colorado, and that may have culminated in the law enforcement intervention in Texas.

Such a possibility seems just as plausible as the lottery-winning-size chance that the two victims of such similar abuse just happened to be at the same place at the same time, both of them entwined with the FLDS, and that they would not have touched each other's lives in some way. The arrival of Candi's e-mails asking for my advice about her children came at the same time Rozita was reaching out by telephone with her story of abuse in Texas. I do not think it was a coincidence.

Since Candi Shapley's e-mails during the intervention at the YFZ Ranch, I have not heard from her. She probably is trying to get on with her life, but I think that sooner or later she will surface again. Candi knows way too much, and I don't feel that she is yet finished being a victim of the FLDS.

That there was no badly abused girl named Sarah Barlow identified at the YFZ Ranch was a good thing. That the compound was entered by the authorities and hundreds of abused children were discovered as a result of Rozita's hoax telephone calls also must be viewed as a positive development, although it was totally unexpected. The hope is that the strange actions of a mentally disturbed young woman will have beneficial consequences for potential victims of abuse for generations to come.

CHAPTER 39

Town Without Pity

In the corkscrewed view of the FLDS, Warren Jeffs's incarceration is a badge of honor for him; he is seen as a martyr and the defender of the faith by his followers, who are reminded of their prophet's plight every time they set foot inside the huge LeRoy S. Johnson Meeting House. Only the faithful are allowed to enter the building, and as they do, they must walk through grim replicas of Jeffs's former Arizona jail cell that have been erected just inside the two entryways. The mockups are a somber reminder that it was their lack of faith that put Jeffs in such a horrible place—that God is requiring his noble prophet to suffer and atone so the rest of them can attain salvation. It is a guilt trip that keeps the flock obedient and the money rolling in.

But fueled by recent events, they are firm in their belief that Warren will eventually prevail. They point to the fact that the prophet was never even tried in Arizona, though he was faced there with multiple charges of sexual misconduct with a minor. When he was extradited from Utah to the Mohave County Jail in Kingman, Arizona, in February 2008, he found that he preferred the Arizona accommodations over the tougher Utah State Prison. His attorneys dragged out the pretrial proceedings, relentlessly badgering the witnesses and victims.

More than two years later, Mohave County judge Steven Conn pointed out that Jeffs had spent twenty-eight months incarcerated in Arizona, waiting for trial. That meant that even if he was now convicted, he had already served more than the maximum amount of time for the offenses charged. The court would allow credit for the time already served, and Arizona would have no further claim on him. The victims agreed to allow Warren to return to the Utah State Prison in the hope that he would soon be extradited to Texas to face much more serious charges.

I did not consider the Arizona decision to be crucial, since the Utah conviction, based on the Elissa Wall trial, remained strong and the Arizona charges were comparatively minor. It was a wise move on the part of the prosecutors and victims to get Warren to Texas where he could do some serious time. But in Short Creek, the believers felt that their faith was being vindicated, just as it had been when Texas gave back the kids. The town became meaner and more openly aggressive.

The inevitable result of generations of intermarriage within such a small community that intentionally excludes outsiders has been incest and near-incest.

Rulon and Warren Jeffs's obsessive desire to create a pure Priesthood People has resulted in a closed, corrupted gene pool, and Short Creek today is a reflection of its own decades of inbreeding.

Down in the Crick, the offspring of cousins, half-siblings, and other family members are now paying the price, with the border FLDS community carrying the world's largest population of verifiable cases of the genetic disease known as Fumarase Deficiency.

The recessive gene for that particular disease traces directly back to one of the founders of Short Creek, the late Joseph Smith Jessop, and his first wife, Martha Moore Yeates. One of their daughters married John Yeates Barlow, a relative, and their family bloodlines have been preserved over the decades. Joseph Smith Jessop left behind 112 grandchildren, and the surnames of Jessop and Barlow are among the most common within the FLDS. Nearly every Short Creek family today, no matter what their surname, can be traced back to those two families. Given that there are only about a dozen or so family last names, it doesn't take long to see the frightening possible impact of inbreeding.

In the small religion-inspired petri dish of Short Creek, Fumarase Deficiency erupted and grew. The closed loop of relationships increased the chances that both parents would carry a single copy of the mutated gene, and therefore show no sign of the disease. But when they had a child, they could pass the gene along and the baby would have the abnormality.

Fumarase Deficiency results in an interruption of the Krebs cycle, a metabolic function that enables the body to process food at the cellular level. An infant with the mutated gene may be born with an abnormal brain inside a small head, or be unable to grow at a normal rate as his or her nervous system is attacked. Development is stunted, physical deformities are frequent, some organs do not function properly, and seizures can sometimes be so powerful that the child may be bent backward like a pretzel. Most victims do not survive beyond a few months. Any stricken babies who do grow will be dogged by illness, unable to care for themselves, and mental retardation will usually limit them to just a few words.

It is currently estimated that more than half of the children in the entire world who suffer from Fumarase Deficiency live in Short Creek. There is no cure. Of course, the church members rationalize that when such a child is born, perhaps with a large part of its brain missing, it is only another of God's tests. In my opinion, it is another intolerable example of child abuse, propagated through a misguided reliance on faith. Church members have been approached by medical professionals trying to convince them to be tested for the offending gene before marriage, but church leaders will not have the gentile world interfering with the will of God when it comes to marriage and procreation. So the disease continues to spread.

A troubled Short Creek resident named Ruth Cook had a daughter who was among the stricken children. When the little girl was about two years old, Ruth took her twisted, agonized child, whose spine was breaking from the backward convulsions, to the FLDS staff at the Hildale medical clinic. Hospitalization was out of the question, because gentile doctors would ask questions. The clinic staff did nothing, deciding the baby was "too pure a spirit to be on earth anymore." The baby eventually died.

That was one more incident contributing to Ruth's mental instability in a town where every tragic event seems to lead to another. Her father, a brute named Jack Cook, had molested all of his daughters. The Washington County authorities prosecuted him and he spent five years in the Utah State Prison. In a television interview upon his release, Cook was asked about the molestations. With a smarmy look he wisecracked, "I was just doing what a dad does. Don't they all do that?" He is now dead, but his daughter Ruth lives on, a damaged girl who became a damaged adult with damaged children.

There is no place in Short Creek for people like Ruth Cook; the townspeople don't want her around. She had married one of the Barlows, only to be sent to a mental hospital for complaining about the FLDS priesthood and about various church members molesting one of her daughters. When released, she was homeless and broke and returned to Short Creek, where she survived in an old pickup truck and was openly despised.

Still, she wanted to do the right thing because she remained a believer, and the FLDS was the only life she had ever known. I frequently see Ruth trying to clean up the town by gathering trash, or riding around on a bicycle, a woman in her forties, singing "I'm a Child of God" and announcing that she wants to marry Uncle Warren.

After a late meeting in town one night, I got into my car and Ruth, who was sweeping up at the gas station, came over for a chat. She was standing about six feet from where I sat behind the wheel when a man named Samuel Bateman drove past in his big diesel pickup truck, then stopped and backed up so that the rear end pointed at her. Bateman hit the gas and the big tires dug into the road, spraying Ruth with rocks and dirt, as if she were being peppered by a shotgun.

Ruth refused to leave her hometown. A February 2010 report to the Mohave County Sheriff's Office states that she was arrested by officer Hyrum Roundy and clapped in handcuffs while picking up trash around the meeting house. Claiming that court was already closed for the day, he drove her several miles outside of town, let her out, and told her not to return because she was not wanted in Short Creek. She walked back anyway, only to be picked up again, taken back out, and dumped off with a warning that she had better never come back. "We don't need your kind," the cop said.

Ruth again trudged back toward the lights. This time, she told the police that the same Dale Barlow who had been a target of the Texas raid and was a convicted sex offender showed up with one of his buddies and beat the hell out of her. Mohave County police took a report. The problem with pursuing the matter was that Ruth would be an unreliable witness in court. About a month later, an unknown assailant shot her in the head with a high-powered air rifle. The slug penetrated her skull and landed her in the hospital, unconscious. She could not identify the attacker, because in typical cowardly Short Creek style, the assailant had shot from behind. Nobody will be held accountable.

The cocky confidence that they can get away with anything, and that the prophet is being martyred by the evil government, was rewarded again during the summer of 2010 in a stunning court decree. The full Utah Supreme Court had considered the appeal of Warren's conviction in the Elissa Wall case, and Justice Jill N. Parrish decided the lower trial court had made a mistake by giving an erroneous instruction to the jury. Therefore, the judge ruled, Jeffs was entitled to a new trial.

This decision rocked everyone involved. Such a narrow point of law was at the root of the decision that even many lawyers could not understand her reasoning. CNN's senior legal analyst Jeffrey Toobin commented on television that he had had to read the decision twice before he could understand it, and he called the court's decision shameful. The "answer them nothing" prophet had gamed the system once again.

Warren had been sent back to the Utah State Prison from Arizona before ever facing trial there, and now his Utah conviction—of two consecutive sentences of five years to life for being an accomplice to rape—had been overturned. As of that moment, Warren Jeffs no longer stood convicted of a single thing.

CHAPTER 40

The Telephone

I had no sympathy at all for the frail Warren Jeffs on the morning of November 30, 2010, when a pair of Texas Rangers shuffled him across the tarmac in Utah, wearing handcuffs and leg chains and shivering in the cold, and put him on the plane for Texas. The mousy-looking man in the thick glasses did not look like much of a threat, but I knew differently.

During his time spent in prison, Jeffs had just about fallen apart. After getting up off his cot in the morning, and pulling a thin prison bathrobe around himself, he would spend most of the day just sitting on the toilet, hour after hour, staring at the walls. At times, a feeding tube was stuck in his nose and left in place for an extended period because he refused to eat and had to be force-fed. His knees were ulcerated from kneeling on the cement floor. He was uncooperative, unresponsive, drooled like a baby, and required constant attention and care. It appeared that he was failing fast, both physically and emotionally.

It would be good to finally get him down into the stern criminal justice system of Texas, and within the jurisdiction of the efficient Judge Barbara Walther, where he faced charges of sexual assault of a child, aggravated sexual assault of a child under the age of fourteen, and bigamy. The charges were all first-degree felonies that carried maximum life sentences. I was more than satisfied with the crisp way in which Judge Walther had run the previous trials, and with the tenacity of the Texas prosecutors. In Texas, I believed, things would be different—closure might finally be near at hand.

After all, the other Texas trials against FLDS men had proceeded nicely. The perpetrators probably would have received lighter prison sentences had they admitted guilt and remorse, but they would not do that. FLDS defense attorney Randy Wilson summed it up: "These were not predators hanging around a playground. They were instructed by their prophet to do something and they did so." Their inexcusable position was that Warren told them to do it, therefore it was right. Where did it stop?

Leroy Jessop, the remaining groom from the triple marriage ceremony, fared badly when his turn in court had come in May 2010. DNA tests had proven paternity for his child and underage bride, and as he sat in court with a cocky smirk on his face, he was crushed with a harsh sentence of seventy-five years.

It was during the Leroy Jessop trial that my ears had perked up when the FLDS went a step too far and his lawyer filed a motion to declare Leroy indigent, asking that the state pick up the tab to appeal his conviction. Texas refused, and the matter went before the judge for a hearing.

A frequent question throughout the investigation has been, "Where are the Feds?" Now FBI special agent John Broadway, who had participated in serving the YFZ search warrant, appeared on the witness stand and provided a ray of hope that the bureau might be working the case after all.

Broadway produced church ledgers and records that had been seized as evidence, and he testified that the FLDS had a "cash distribution system [that] was set up to evade taxes and to lessen the paper trail." He described the money-laundering scheme, how much the church had paid out in cash, how couriers would arrive regularly at the ranch with stacks of hundred-dollar bills from their far-flung businesses and the constant donations from thousands of members, and how that would be distributed to the hierarchy. With millions of dollars in the pipeline, Leroy Jessop could well afford to pay his own lawyer.

In the days of mobster Al Capone, bootleg whiskey was illegal, and Capone's mob committed crimes such as murder and extortion to support their illegal operation. Capone was tripped up by evading taxes. I think that may very well be the same low-key approach being taken by the Feds as they probe the inner workings of Warren Jeffs's church.

With the FLDS, the Feds are facing one of the largest organized-crime syndicates in the history of this country. Some ten to fifteen thousand members support a religion that participates in child abuse, interstate and international sex trafficking, and other crimes in support of their religious dogma. It is a much bigger gang than Don Corleone ever had in the *Godfather* movies. I have often pondered how the public would react if the same sort of ritualistic crimes that I have investigated within the FLDS had instead centered on a congregation of Satan worshippers. The only difference is that Satan worshippers know without a doubt that they are going to be prosecuted to the full extent of the law if they get caught raping a virgin. If the FLDS crimes had been put in proper perspective, outraged citizens and lawmakers would have demanded action years ago.

The problem is bigger than Utah, bigger than Arizona, and even bigger than Texas, which was blindsided by the enormity of bringing the FLDS to justice. The federal government must remain in this fight, for we cannot tolerate such blatant, massive abuse in this country, and no other entity has the resources to take on thousands of unapologetic fanatics.

As the shift to Texas was made, Warren still remained the uncontested leader of the Fundamentalist Church of Jesus Christ of Latter-Day Saints, but it was a distant leadership, as he became more frail. If he should die, the mantle of prophet would transfer to another man, but the immediate future was murky. Who would lead if he were disabled and ultimately convicted, unable to communicate?

That question was a popular topic of conversation among observers outside of the church. Up for grabs were millions of dollars in church assets, the ability to raise seemingly endless amounts of cash, and control over thousands of lives.

The contest seemed to pit the Old School against the New School. The Old School was led by the tattered First Presidency: First Counselor Wendell Nielsen and Second Counselor Merril Jessop. Warren had resigned when he was sent to prison as president of the church's corporation and he placed Wendell Nielsen in his stead. With Warren's communications limited from the prison, he needed someone to handle the day-to-day affairs of the church. But neither Nielsen nor Merril Jessop was considered a likely long-term candidate. They were getting old, had chronic health problems, and had been under immense pressure from Warren to fund his extravagances and get the Texas YFZ ranch built. In addition, they both were under indictment for committing felonies and faced possible long jail time themselves. Even a few years in prison could have ended up being a life sentence for these aging counselors.

The New School was led by three men. The inside track apparently was held by Warren's brother Lyle Jeffs, who, according to Brent Jeffs, was a close associate of his brother at the Alta Academy. Lyle had become one of Warren's most trusted unofficial lieutenants and was installed in the influential position of bishop of Short Creek. He was not the mysteriously charismatic leader that Warren was, but he possessed the same unrelenting determination and the right pedigree; somebody named Jeffs has been the FLDS prophet since 1987. Over the course of my investigation, I interviewed a couple of computer technicians who had been brought in to work on Lyle's computer. It seemed the problem was Lyle's apparently insatiable addiction to porn. One of the misconceptions held by outsiders is that the FLDS are a very straightlaced, pious people. The fact is, people like Lyle have just become very adept at hiding their behavior.

The second member of this group was Nephi Jeffs, the brother and confidant who had been the liaison between Jeffs in jail and the world outside. He was present when Warren had his "I am not the prophet" meltdown.

The third candidate, and the most startling of all, was Willie Jessop, who forced his way into the top leadership by becoming the public face of the outlaw religion. At an FLDS rally he organized at the courthouse in St. George, Utah, a crowd of several thousand people turned out, and they parted like the Red Sea before Moses when Willie strode through their midst, basking in their applause. The same people who once considered him nothing more than a rude bully now fed his ego, although the prophet still refused to allow him to live within the sacred gates of R-17.

In my opinion, none of the potential candidates would be any better than Warren and any of them could be quite possibly worse.

Upon his arrival in Texas, the prophet was taken to the Reagan County Jail, located sixty-five miles west of San Angelo, where his trial was scheduled to be held. The jail is a holding tank that handles the overflow inmate population from several surrounding counties. Big Lake sheriff

Jeff Garner pledged that Jeffs would receive no special treatment in the ninety-six-bed facility.

What was unmentioned was that the Reagan County Jail is a for-profit facility and provides a telephone in the cell of every prisoner who can pay a service fee and the toll charges. The jail sells calling cards in its commissary and collects a commission on collect calls. The prophet probably could not believe his good fortune.

Starting back in the days he had been on the run, he had conditioned his followers to follow his telephoned instructions, so they were quite used to obeying his disembodied, monotone voice from a distance. In the other prisons and jails where he'd been, he had had to wait in line like any other common inmate to use a wall-mounted public telephone, but now he had been handed a telephone of his own—three dollars for the first minute, and a dollar a minute thereafter. He paid up front for hours and hours of use. The telephone link to his followers reinvigorated the waning prophet.

By the time he appeared before Judge Walther the second time, only a week later, he was already regaining strength and was ready to work the system once again. He hired and fired lawyers, one of whom lasted only a day before Jeffs discharged him. Walther told Jeffs he had no excuse for not having legal representation and gave him a copy of scheduled trial dates and a notice for him to sign verifying that the court had made him aware of his rights. He initially refused to speak or sign his name, but after his third preliminary hearing Warren decided to demand more time from the court to obtain an attorney.

Judge Walther graciously gave him a moment to state his case before the court. Warren began a long discourse about the special considerations he needed in order to put up an appropriate defense in Texas. As the speech progressed, Jeffs would stop midsentence and stare off into the distance for several long seconds as he received revelations on how best to explain his special legal requirements to the court. After about twenty minutes of his tortuous ramblings, Judge Walther had enough and entered a not-guilty plea on his behalf and assigned a court-appointed attorney to represent him. Two weeks later, when Warren's next scheduled hearing came up, attorney Jeff Kearney entered his appearance on Jeffs's behalf.

Kearney had made a name for himself defending one of eleven Branch

Davidians accused of murdering ATF agents in the Waco siege. According to his Web site, Kearney had considered the case a "once-in-a-lifetime" event. His client was acquitted of murder but found guilty of gun charges. Kearney stated: "I did it because it was the right thing to do," adding, "It was a rewarding experience that took my practice to a different level."

With Warren in Texas, the day will surely come when he will be slammed with a mountain of heretofore unheard-of evidence, including the transcription of his sickening sexual assault of Merrianne Jessop, the recording of which was discovered in the Cadillac Escalade he was traveling in when he was finally apprehended. As he traveled, he carried this recording with him, like a trophy to be relived over and over again as the mood would strike him. Judge James Shumate in Utah was privy to a transcription of the recording and immediately sealed it and denied the prosecution's request to present it in trial, stating that it would be too inflammatory to present to the jury, but he said he may reconsider his ruling at some point later in the trial. The tape was never presented in court.

The recordings and documents seized when Warren was arrested were a tiny drop in a very big ocean of evidence compared to what was taken into custody when the temple was breached in Texas. Reliable sources inform me that there is evidence of "temple rituals" that are really nothing more than group sex orgies with preteen victims.

During the next ninety days, Jeffs used his new telephone to rain havoc upon the FLDS people.

He demanded that everyone in the religion provide an accounting of everything they owned from their homes and businesses, down to each piece of silverware and including a list of their wives and children. They were then to pledge all of their possessions to the prophet as a consecration to the church and subsequently be rebaptized and swear allegiance to him. As of this writing, thousands of people have done so, demonstrating the size and continuing loyalty of his following better than any census could.

It is a good thing Warren did not have access to a telephone during the Texas showdown. I believe that had he been in communication with FLDS members at the ranch, it could have turned violent. Among his favorite stories is that of the Zealots of Masada, who held off the Romans for months before finally being overcome. The occupants of the YFZ ranch would have considered it an honor to die at his command. But at that critical moment one of Warren's greatest strengths, his ruthless micromanagement of everyone, turned into a weakness. His henchmen would never make such a major decision without his approving nod. Fortunately, he did not have a telephone then.

But from his cell, he now issued instructions by phone for a huge warehouse to be built at the YFZ Ranch and stocked with heavy earth-moving equipment that he says will be needed to open the roads after the coming Armageddon so the faithful can reach the New Jerusalem in Jackson County, Missouri. He also has written rambling, nearly incoherent threats that the end of the world is (once again) nigh.

On February 17, 2011, Warren Jeffs instructed his henchmen to send out "A Warning to the Nation" and "A Petition to the President of the United States." More than six hundred packets of these documents were sent out from Short Creek not only to President Barack Obama, but to every senator and member of Congress and to various heads of government departments, including Hillary Rodham Clinton, the secretary of state. The petition to the president is presented as a commandment from ". . . your Lord and Savior" to ". . . Let my servant go." Warren supposedly received the revelation in his prison cell while in Draper, Utah.

Another revelation contained in the petition had been allegedly received in Warren's jail cell in Big Lake, Texas, on February 5, 2011. This prophecy is even more stern and says that the president and the "people's [*sic*] of the earth" are going to suffer for not heeding Jeffs's warnings. In it he says that he is going to specifically target President Obama's home state: "Thus shall I cause a great destruction in the land of Illinois, to the loss of life and to your awakening . . ." The petition consists of 956 pages and contains signatures of FLDS members as young as eight years old.

These so-called revelations echo the violent history of fundamentalist Mormonism. While also in prison, in the 1980s, another self-proclaimed polygamous prophet, Ervil LeBaron, wrote similar prophetic revelations, also calling for divine retribution, which resulted in the execution-style deaths of an estimated twenty-five people.

As Warren began to once again savor his intoxicating power over his flock, he enacted another sweeping away of the FLDS leadership, this one even larger in scope than the expulsion of twenty-one men he had "handled" in 2004 when first taking over as prophet and solidifying his authority. Issuing orders from jail, he destroyed almost everyone close to him and expelled more than fifty men from the church by the end of April 2011.

First Counselor Wendell Nielsen was expelled, and he signed over his position as president of the church's corporation back to Warren. That meant Jeffs regained the FLDS treasury for himself. Second Counselor Merril Jessop, who had been the point man during the YFZ Ranch raid, was also thrown out. Warren had previously given him permission to go on the run if the law decided to interrogate him about turning over his twelve-year-old daughter, Merrianne, to the prophet as a child bride. Now that the top men have lost their positions, the question arises of who is going to pay their legal bills to defend the criminal indictments against them. Perhaps it will finally be their turn to hide out, all alone, with no home, no money, and no family support.

Warren also ousted Bill Shapley, the father of Candi Shapley and a frequent yes man, even though Bill had repeatedly proven his loyalty by donating his daughters to the priesthood. Then, surprisingly, Big Willie Jessop was expelled. So were the mayors of both Hildale and Colorado City, along with Jim Oler, the bishop in Canada. It was a major bloodletting. Everyone in the FLDS walked a razor's edge as their irrational leader ranted on. There would be no more guessing about who was calling the shots. Warren was clearly still in control, and he was tightening his grip.

His intransigent little brother Lyle survived the initial cut by becoming Warren's man on the outside, although the prophet has demonstrated that his trust could evaporate in a flash.

I did not care a whit that the prophet was ravaging his own creation, and I shed no tears when men like Big Willie and Merril Jessop were dealt the same painful fate that had befallen so many others. They deserved it, and much more.

But then, far from Jeffs's West Texas jail cell, came still another of those thunderclaps that forever seemed to stalk this long investigation.

On February 23, 2011, U.S. District Court judge Dee Vance Benson in Salt Lake City reversed the decisions of Third District Court judge Denise Lindberg and the Utah Supreme Court, which had wrested control of the United Effort Plan Trust from Warren Jeffs. The UEP was back in his hands. It made no sense at all, and it left me reeling.

The FLDS lawyers, after their initial loss due to Warren's unwillingness to defend the trust himself, had let several years pass before taking steps to regain control of the UEP. The effort was dismissed outright. They later tried again, this time bringing their case to the Utah Supreme Court, and again their motions were denied. Then, in a last-ditch effort to retake the trust, they filed a motion for an injunction to hamstring the attorney general's control of the trust in federal court before Judge Benson. The judge was a "distinguished alumnus" of the 125-year-old Utah law firm of Snow, Christensen and Martineau in Salt Lake—coincidentally, the law firm of FLDS apologist Rod Parker, who was arguing the case before Judge Benson.

The federal judge ruled that the state's control of the FLDS trust was unconstitutional and ventured into "forbidden territory" by intruding on the religious beliefs of trust members. Rather than address the rampant child abuse and other crimes financed by the UEP, Benson said that such excesses by Warren Jeffs and other FLDS men did not justify the State of Utah intervening to reorganize the trust.

The UEP is currently valued at about $110 million, with Warren, as church president, in charge of it all. As always, Warren had a plan and he wasted no time in reasserting his authority. On the same evening that Benson issued his order, a gang of bullies in Short Creek descended on the home of David Jeffs, the prophet's wheelchair-bound brother. David had been among the twenty-one men who had been cast out in January 2004, at the start of my investigation. He eventually had been allowed back in, and then Warren had decided to excommunicate him once again. The mob evicted David and left him in his wheelchair at the home of a relative in St. George.

I considered Benson's ruling to be a misuse of authority which carried with it the implication that any trust set up for any reason, including the organization and funding of criminal activity, can be off-limits to state sanctions as long as it is established under the auspices of religion. For example: If a certain terrorist group decided to establish a trust for

the purpose of funding, planning, training, and carrying out the hijack-
ing of commercial aircraft for the purpose of being flown into skyscrap-
ers, that trust would be off-limits to any government or law-enforcement
intervention as long as it is formed by a group claiming sincere religious
beliefs. The list of possible abuses of such a trust is endless, and under
the Benson ruling the prophet would have even more leverage over the
people if they failed to do as instructed.

But on April 8, state district court judge Denise Lindberg countered
Judge Benson's decision, reprimanding him for intervening in her jurisdiction. For years Judge Lindberg had overseen the affairs of the trust
and experienced blatant FLDS disregard for the law and lack of respect
for the courts. She knew exactly what the church leadership was capable
of and feared that if the trust was given back to Warren Jeffs, even for a
short period of time, the UEP's assets would immediately be plundered
by the outlaw prophet and his henchmen.

Benson lost his temper. In an unprecedented response to Lindberg's
attempt to preserve the trust, he threatened to have the U.S. marshals
drag her before his court to answer charges of contempt for her ruling
countermanding his decision. Along with Judge Lindberg, the attorneys
general of Utah and Arizona as well as our legal team shot off motions
to state and federal appeals courts to block the seemingly irrational actions of Judge Benson. Fortunately the 10th U.S. Circuit Court of Appeals stepped in and reversed Benson's decisions, including his attempt
to charge Judge Lindberg, and put the entire UEP issue back on track to
work its way through the appropriate legal process.

But before the federal appeals court could make their decision, a
great deal of damage had already been done. The FLDS and their leadership were emboldened by Benson's ruling, and just chalked up the appeals court intervention to more gentile persecution. In fact, a few weeks
after Judge Benson's ruling, unknown intruders broke into an old school-
house on UEP property where former FLDS member Stephanie Colgrove
was storing thousands of books in anticipation of opening a new library
in town. Less than a block from the marshal's office, a massive bonfire
twenty feet in diameter was ignited and thousands of books as well as
family artifacts and other personal property were burned. When it was
discovered that it would take days to burn all of the volumes, twelve pal-
let loads of books were distributed to various thrift shops or dumped

throughout southern Utah. There was a precedent for this activity. Years ago, Warren had ordered the only other library in town to be dismantled and its contents destroyed or discarded.

This is only a sampling of the potential for unrest and violence. Lines are being drawn in the red sands of Short Creek as the town and culture begin to fracture. Gangs of young ruffians roam the streets and harass strangers with impunity, and the society has seen an increase in brother-against-brother confrontations.

And there were continuing power struggles too. Big Willie Jessop was scrambling to salvage what he could of his business and the life that had been suddenly jerked out from under him. Ironically, it was the same fate that he had inflicted on so many others, including Winston Blackmore, while acting in the capacity of the prophet's stooge. One day, Willie had been one of the ultimate insiders: a goon for the prophet, the feared enforcer, and the recognized public face for the entire religion, and the next day he was an outcast who had lost everything. All fifty of the workers at his construction company had walked off the job. Willie claims that shortly thereafter, Bishop Lyle Jeffs gave the order for some of his former employees to break into his business and steal all his computers and any other documentation or evidence that could be incriminating to Warren or the church. (Lyle Jeffs has not yet responded to these charges.) Quite unexpectedly, Willie began to sample some of the emotion that had driven one of his own little brothers to hang himself with an electric cord in the closet of his apartment after experiencing a similar banishment from the sect.

Suddenly, Willie had grown a conscience. He recalled that on the day in 2007 when Warren had broken down in jail and announced that he was not really the prophet, he had added the pronouncement that the actual prophet was one "William E. Jessop"—the same William E. (Timpson) Jessop who had been named the bishop of Short Creek upon the disappearance of Uncle Fred. But now, William (Timpson) Jessop had been defrocked as bishop (replaced by Lyle) and had established himself in Colorado. Big Willie found him, and the former bishop soon filed paperwork with the Utah Division of Corporations claiming that he, not Warren Jeffs, was the rightful president of the FLDS. Like so many other FLDS power struggles, this one too seems headed for the courts.

Meanwhile, Big Willie went public, stating that he had been misled and deceived by Warren Jeffs and that he was shocked to learn that Jeffs was involved with child abuse, rape, and other morally and criminally reprehensible acts. Warren was a "mad dog," and Willie was just another unsuspecting victim of the prophet's cruelty. After a lifetime in the midst of the action, few believed him. Nevertheless, William E. (Timpson) Jessop now holds religious services of his own in Short Creek, with Willie as the gatekeeper, and a small splinter group of about 150 people have been attending on a regular basis.

The various power struggles within the FLDS have always been a historical eventuality, but staging a coup against Warren will always be risky business, even if he is in prison. Warren is a master of spreading out the culpability for his crimes among his followers. He has successfully been able to secure the loyalty of many in his flock through their fear that the part they played in his criminal enterprise will be exposed. That fear, on some level, touches every FLDS family and subtly keeps their loyalties directed toward Warren.

As of this writing, investigations involving Mann Act violations and financial crimes are ongoing, but have yet to be charged against the FLDS and its leadership.

Still, after many years of ups and downs, I feel a sense of pride in all of us who have worked so hard to expose FLDS atrocities and abuse.

We did what we set out to do: We exposed the mastermind behind the madness and put him behind bars. Warren Jeffs is now a shell of a man wasting away in a jail cell. His records and dictations, in his own unmistakable droning voice etched in countless recordings, and documents are now available as proof of his unspeakable crimes.

The scores of law enforcement and legal professionals who have been exposed to that evidence are as outraged as I am about the abuse against innocent boys and girls. If even a few children can be spared such treatment in the future, our efforts will have been worthwhile.

In most cases, it is not the troops in the trenches that have to be won over in order to stop child abuse within the FLDS, it is our elected government officials, who sit behind a desk and have yet to be awakened to the kind of systemic abuse that is taking place among their own constituents. They need to pay attention to what has happened and what is happening today within that cloistered organization hidden along a desert patch of ground known as the Arizona Strip and at a temple in West Texas. For every horrible crime I have described, a hundred others equally as ghastly remain untold.

For instance, newly discovered documents report that on September 27, 2004, Warren admitted his plan to put together "a quorum of wives" who would do anything for him, including "assist me against the time of needed blood atonement . . . a sacrifice required for the redemption of Zion to go forward and perhaps given many times." A million words would do no more than scratch the surface in exposing the depravity of Warren Jeffs and his henchmen—and women.

We live in a country in which the practice of illegal, arranged incestuous marriage, the sexual exploitation of women and children as part of religious rituals, the trafficking of children across interstate and international boundaries, and the tyranny of breaking families apart has never been tolerated. There is no question that great strides have been made in this worthwhile cause, and I have faith in the ultimate outcome; but the lasting changes needed to provide for the safety and security of thousands of children have yet to be achieved. Until the FLDS hierarchy, whoever that may eventually be, finds the human decency to stand before the world and accept responsibility for their criminal actions, and sincerely apologize to their many victims with a commitment to never again abuse or neglect another child, it will never truly be over. Until that day, I will remain vigilant.

Acknowledgments

Those in the trenches
Gary Engels, Jeff Lennert, Special Agent Rob Foster, Special Agent Jeff
Goins, Special Agent Scott Schons, Debra Brown, Special Agent Rick Fa-
gan, Special Agent John Broadway, Ranger Captain Brooks Long, Sheriff
David Doran, the Honorable Joe Lodge, Deputy Attorney General Angela
Goodwin, Ranger Nick Hanna, Flora Jessop, Jim Hill, Jeff Schmidt, Joan
Dudley, Joanne Suder, Kirby Lewis, Deputy Matt Fischer, Steve Bailey,
Roger Hoole, Greg Hoole, Charles Childress, Angie Voss, Elaine Tyler,
Lynn McFadden

Special thanks
This book never would have happened without the help of Jon Krakauer;
my agent, Stuart Krichevsky; my editor, Nancy Miller; George Gibson,
Don Davis, Dr. Dan Fischer, Marty Shapiro, Stacey Butler, Michelle
Blankenship, Peter Miller, Ellis Levine.

My guides
Ross Chatwin, Lori Chatwin, Andrew Chatwin, Michelle Chatwin, Isaac
Wyler, Rebecca Wall, Elissa Wall, Deloy Bateman, Brent Jeffs, Brandon
Jeffs, Ward Jeffs, Susan Jeffs, Jethro Barlow, Winston Blackmore, Richard
Holm, Susie Barlow, Jane Blackmore, Candi Shapley, Cookie Hickstein,
Esther Shapley, Rose Swinton, Ezra Draper, Katie Cox, Laura Chapman,
Susie Johnson, Lester Johnson, Marvin Wyler, Charlotte Wyler, Merril

Stubbs, Leroy Stubbs, Patrick Pipkin, Richard Rheem, Don Fischer, Jane Blackmore, Tom Steed, Johnny Jessop, David Jeffs, Robert Richter, Ruth Lane, Shem Fischer, Sterling Harker, John Nielsen, Arthur Blackmore, Arnold Richter, Edith Barlow, Zelpha Chatwin, Leah Barlow, Marsha Chatwin, Don R. Fischer, Walter S. Fischer, Richard Gilbert, Ephraim Barlow, Bruce Barlow, Sam Zitting, Joe Broadbent

Invaluable help and encouragement along the way
Rita Brower, Cassie Meredith, Josh Meredith, Patrick Brower, Amanda Brower, Lee Brower, Brad Brower, Jon Brower, Dawna Woslum, June Beal, Jim Beal, Les Brower, Liz Brower, Brent Hunsaker, Ben Winslow, Bryan Jackson, John Hollenhorst, Willard Bishop, Stephen Este, Carolyn Jessop, Randy Mankin, Kathy Mankin, Kim Edmundson, Ben Bistline, Doyle Dockstader, Beth Karas, Gary Tuchman, Tim Sandler, Shirley Davis, Brock Belnap, Matt Smith, Jerry Jaegar, Chuck Marshall, Deborah Dockstader, Carol McKinley, Dr. Larry Beall, Harry Phillips, Doyle Dockstader, Jennilynn Merten, Tyler Measom, Jon Davis, Kathryn Wallace, Patrice St. Germain, Dr. Richard Cox, Scott Davis, Steve Singular, Dr. Wynn Summers, Jeffrey Shields, Zack Shields, Bruce Wisan, Susie Gentry, Mike Watkiss, Joseph Reeves, Kinzie Ambrose, Marilyn Butler, Senator Harry Reid, Gavin Parke, Dale Smith, Catharine Yrisarri, Oleh Rumak, Dr. Cory Woodbury, Butch Scott, Gene Seleya, Theran Heap, Jennifer Dobner, Special Agent John Walser (Ret.), Dr. Galen Wooley, Dennis Gray, Ryan Shaum

Index

A Note on the Author

Raised in the Mormon Church (the mainstream Church of Jesus Christ of Latter-day Saints, or LDS), private detective **Sam Brower** is the investigator who pushed forward the long and hard legal battles against the radical FLDS and Warren Jeffs. He lives in Cedar City, Utah.